Lecture Notes in Computer Science

T0237779

Commenced Publication in 1973
Founding and Former Series Editors:
Gerhard Goos, Juris Hartmanis, and Jan van Leeuwen

Marlon Dumas   Reiko Heckel (Eds.)

Web Services
and Formal Methods

4th International Workshop, WS-FM 2007
Brisbane, Australia, September 28-29, 2007
Proceedings

 Springer

Volume Editors

Marlon Dumas
University of Tartu, Institute of Computer Science
J Liivi 2, Tartu 50409, Estonia
E-mail: marlon.dumas@ut.ee

Reiko Heckel
University of Leicester, Department of Computer Science
University Road, Leicester, LE1 7RH, UK
E-mail: reiko@mcs.le.ac.uk

Library of Congress Control Number: 2008924625

CR Subject Classification (1998): D.2.4, C.2.4, F.3, D.4, C.4, K.4.4, C.2

LNCS Sublibrary: SL 2 – Programming and Software Engineering

ISSN   0302-9743
ISBN-10   3-540-79229-5 Springer Berlin Heidelberg New York
ISBN-13   978-3-540-79229-1 Springer Berlin Heidelberg New York

Springer is a part of Springer Science+Business Media

springer.com

© Springer-Verlag Berlin Heidelberg 2008
Printed in Germany

Typesetting: Camera-ready by author, data conversion by Scientific Publishing Services, Chennai, India
Printed on acid-free paper   SPIN: 12257416   06/3180   5 4 3 2 1 0

Preface

This volume contains the papers presented at WS-FM 2007, the 4th International Workshop on Web Services and Formal Methods, held on September 28 and 29, 2007 in Brisbane, Australia.

Web service technology aims at empowering providers of services, in the broad sense, with the ability to package and deliver their services by means of software applications available on the Web. Existing infrastructures for Web services already enable providers to describe services in terms of structure, access policy and behaviour, to locate services, to interact with them, and to bundle simpler services into more complex ones. However, innovations are needed to seamlessly extend this technology in order to deal with challenges such as managing interactions with stateful and long-running Web services, managing large numbers of Web services each with multiple interfaces and versions, managing the quality of Web service delivery, etc.

Formal methods have a fundamental role to play in shaping innovations in Web service technology. For instance, formal methods help to define and to understand the semantics of languages and protocols that underpin existing infrastructures for Web services, and to formulate features that are found to be lacking. They also provide a basis for reasoning about Web service behaviour, for example to discover individual services that can fulfil a given goal, or even to compose multiple services that can collectively fulfil a goal. Finally, formal analysis of security properties and performance are relevant in many application areas of Web services such as e-commerce and e-business.

The International Workshop on Web Services and Formal Methods aims to bring together researchers interested in the application of formal methods and reasoning techniques to Web service technology, and in formal theories inspired by developments in the field of Web services. The scope of the workshop is not purely limited to technology aspects. It also covers approaches to analysing and designing systems based on Web service technology, including service-oriented enterprise modelling and business process modelling.

This fourth edition of the WS-FM workshop featured 9 regular papers selected from a pool of 22 submissions after a rigorous review process. Each submission was reviewed by at least three programme committee members, and in many cases four. In addition to regular paper presentations, the workshop's programme also featured two invited talks. In the first invited talk, Jianwen Su gave a survey of research in the area of formal analysis of Web service interactions with an emphasis on the relation between global models capturing all interactions between multiple services at once, versus local models that focus on one service at a time. The second talk by Jörg Desel proposed a formal theory that aims at unifying several notions of soundness and controllability of Web service protocols. After the workshop, the authors of these invited talks kindly agreed to prepare a full invited paper for inclusion in these proceedings.

The workshop was held in conjunction with the 5th International Conference on Business Process Management (BPM). This was the second time that the workshop was co-located with the BPM conference, and this arrangement is expected to continue in the future.

We owe special thanks to all members of the Program Committee of WS-FM 2007 and their sub-referees for their work. We are also very grateful to the numerous people who were involved in the organisation of the BPM conference for lending their support to the workshop organisation.

January 2008   Marlon Dumas
                                                          Reiko Heckel

Conference Organization

Programme Chairs

Marlon Dumas
Reiko Heckel

Programme Committee

Farhad Arbab
Matteo Baldoni
Boualem Benatallah
Karthikeyan Bhargavan
Mario Bravetti
Roberto Bruni
Rocco De Nicola
Schahram Dustdar
José Luiz Fiadeiro
Aditya Ghose
Cosimo Laneve
Mark Little
Shin Nakajima
Manuel Nunez
Wolfgang Reisig
Srinivas Padmanabhuni
Jianwen Su
Karsten Wolf
Yun Yang
Gianluigi Zavattaro
Aoying Zhou
Fabio Casati
Gregor Engels
Rob van Glabbeek
Wil van der Aalst

Local Organization

Marlon Dumas
The BPM Research Group at Queensland University of Technology

External Reviewers

Cristina Baroglio
Marco Bernardo
Laura Bocchi
Dirk Fahland
Alexander Foerster
Baris Güldali
Sarath Indrakanti
George Koliadis
Luis Llana
Olga Marroquin-Alonso
Ismael Rodriguez
Christian Stahl
Emilio Tuosto

Table of Contents

Towards a Theory of Web Service Choreographies

Jianwen Su[1,*], Tevfik Bultan[1], Xiang Fu[2], and Xiangpeng Zhao[1,3]

[1] University of California at Santa Barbara
[2] Georgia Southwestern University
[3] Peking University, China

Abstract. A fundamental promise of service oriented architecture (SOA) lies in the ease of integrating sharable information, processes, and other resources through interactions among the shared components that are modeled as web services. It is expected that not only the participating services are complex and have observable states, but the number of interacting services may be also large. Prior work on choreographies (conversation protocols) all focuses on specifying how the interacting web services should behave globally. Studies have shown that the relationships between global and local specifications of service interactions could be rather intricate. In this paper, we formulate a framework consisting of logical and implementation levels. We survey and discuss the technical problems and known results concerning service design, analysis and verification in this framework.

1 Introduction

A fundamental principle of Service Oriented Architecture (SOA) is to design and model complex software systems as assemblies of bitesize pieces. The pieces can then be managed and re-used. While the paradigm is promising, there is a serious lack of principles to aid the design of complex systems from the existing pieces, and to help the management of systems, small or large. This paper aims at the former problem and attempts to develop a technical framework on which service design principles can be developed. The framework is based on application needs as well as technical results concerning composite service design, analysis and verification developed in the community.

Two characteristics distinguish service design from distributed system design studied in the past. First, working with abstractions is a necessity rather than a preference. There are many reasons a service provider will not reveal the detailed information concerning the internals of a service. Service design must rely on the abstract description of the needed services. Furthermore, it is often required that an abstraction of the composition is fully developed [24,3] which can serve as either a design specification or constraints for verification. This high level abstraction is built from the observable actions of participating services but it is different from system traces. Second, as the SOA popularity grows, the number of available services also increases rapidly. It is necessary to automate (or semi-automate) many steps in service design.

In the services computing community, there have been investigations concerning the design, analysis, and verification of service compositions. Most of the prior work

---

* Supported in part by NSF grants IIS-0415195 and CNS-0613998.

M. Dumas and R. Heckel (Eds.): WS-FM 2007, LNCS 4937, pp. 1–16, 2008.

either focuses on (proposed) standards or concerns sophisticated techniques in various aspects. As an important SOA application domain, business applications embrace SOA on one hand, but on the other hand are struggling with the lack of a framework that can address the complete service design cycle [4].

In this paper, we formulate a technical framework that consists of two levels of abstraction: logical and implementation. At the logical level, specifications focus on how participating services should interact with each other, while the implementation level provides abstractions of services. Among other things, the framework solidifies from a formal perspective the differences between WS-CDL [29] and BPEL [6]. We give a survey on existing technical results over this framework.

This paper is organized as follows. Section 2 gives a general discussion on service design approaches. Section 3 surveys the existing choreography models. Section 4 focuses on the key technical problems concerning service design and analysis. Section 5 concludes the paper.

2   SOA and Service Design

In this section, we give a general discussion on service design under the influence of SOA (service oriented architecture). We argue that service design needs two or more levels of abstraction. On the logical level, specifications will focus on interactions among services; on the implementation level, the goal is to allow service executions to satisfy logical specifications.

A fundamental premise of SOA is to structure complex software systems into "bite-size" pieces, which can then be easily managed and reused. Such a framework is a clear departure from the traditional software development approaches aiming at individual software components due to the changes in many phases of the development process [5]. Among many technical issues is design methodology for constructing new services (software systems) from assembling existing services.

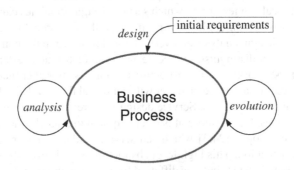

Fig. 1. Life cycle of a business process

To illustrate the issues, consider as an example the life cycle of a business process (to handle, e.g., purchase orders, loan applications, etc.) as shown in Fig. 1. In the design phase, business requirements are used to eventually produce an operational system.

The efforts in this phase could involve designs in multiple layers, from high-level conceptual to eventual coding. Automated or semi-automated *design* and *analysis* tools will provide a significant help in reducing the development time and in improving the quality of design. During the operation phase, business processes, in particular, need to make changes to adapt to the environment better (changes in the market, laws, etc.) and make improvements to achieve business goals. *Evolution* tools could provide support for monitoring the executions, assessing impact of potential changes, and even making the changes.

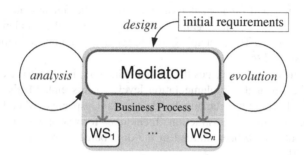

Fig. 2. A mediator process *orchestrates* "component" services

If we focus on the result of the design process from the initial requirements, it is necessary to understand service design methodology. Traditional approaches basically treat the services used as "components" in constructing a new service (or software component). The new service "orchestrates" the component services (Fig. 2). We broadly call such an approach *orchestration*. Typical examples include BPEL [6] and many workflow systems.

There is, however, a new, different methodology called *choreography* that was recently proposed in services computing community [20,21,10,29]. This new approach assumes that the participating services, once "connected", will run on their own with

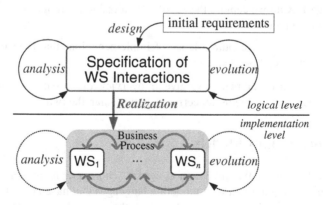

Fig. 3. A *choreography* specifies the interactions between services

no global intervention; the composite service design is then to specify *how* and *when* the participating services should interact with each other. Fig. 3 depicts this scenario.

Comparing the orchestration and choreography approaches, a mediator is an executable program and a part of the implemented business process. Therefore, analysis, monitoring, and updates will need to be performed on the mediator and the used services as a whole. On the contrary, a choreography is merely a logical specification of the observable behaviors by the interacting services at the logical level (Fig. 3). In the ideal case, the choreography completely captures the service behaviors; thus, analysis and updates would only need to be done at the logical level. We believe that a clear separation of logical and implementation levels should be fundamental principle that would allow us to separate and localize concerns and make them independent in developing better systems. The principle is reminiscent of a similar principle in the data management systems [26].

While the logical level describes the global behaviors, it is possible to allow more levels of abstraction in the implementation level. To this end, Mealy services [10] and BPEL4Chor [14] are mathematical and practical (respectively) models in the implementation level with high abstraction. Techniques for reasoning with and verification of such models have been studied in the distributed computing and verification communities [22].

A choreography is "realizable" if there is an implementation of the interacting services whose behavior is identical to the choreography. Often in service design, the choreography language for the logical level and the implementation model are already given. Ideally, each choreography can be realized and every implementation realizes a choreography, i.e., the two levels are "equivalent" in some sense.

However, the current situation is that there are many existing implementation models while new choreography languages are being developed. Instead of being the ideal case, their relationships are not clearly known. Therefore, the ability to clearly separate the logical and implementation levels hinges on understanding the fundamental relationship between choreography specifications and implementations. To this end, we phrase the following two key challenges concerning characterization of choreographies and implementations, respectively.

Challenge 1. Can we capture the set of all realizable choreographies (for a given implementation model)?

Challenge 2. Can we capture the set of implementations that realize choreographies (in a given choreography language)?

In the remainder of the paper, we give an overview of choreography models and then focus on technical problems concerning, in particular, the two challenges.

3 Choreography Models

In this section, we define the key notion of a "choreography model" and give a brief survey of several choreography modeling languages that have been studied. We divide the languages into three categories based on their underlying frameworks: finite state automata, Petri nets, and process algebras. Subsection 3.1 discusses the elements in a choreography model and related notions, and give a summary of the existing choreography modeling languages with respect to these elements. Subsections 3.2 to 3.4 provide more details of the models in each of the three categories.

3.1 Elements of a Choreography Model

As illustrated in Fig. 3, a choreography defines the observable interactions among the participating services. We use the words *global* and *local* to mean the behaviors or activities that are viewed in the *overall composition perspective* and in the *individual service perspective*, respectively. Thus a *choreography model* M typically has two components: a specification C of the *desired global behaviors*, and a representation I of *local services* and their local behaviors which collectively should satisfy the specified global behaviors.

A specification of desired global behaviors is called a **choreography**, and a representation of a service is called a **service implementation**. A *choreography modeling language* provides means to define choreography models, i.e., choreographies, service implementations, and their semantics including a mechanism to compare global behaviors generated by service implementations with a choreography. In this perspective, we informally view a choreography modeling language $\mathcal{L}$ as a collection of choreography models, $\mathcal{L} = \{(C, I) \mid C$ is a choreography and I service implementations $\}$. In the remainder of the paper, we also conveniently view $\mathcal{L}$ as a pair $\mathcal{L} = (\mathcal{C}, \mathcal{I})$, where $\mathcal{C}$ is a collection of choreographies and $\mathcal{I}$ a collection of service implementations.

A choreography can be defined using the following two types of basic elements: (1) a set of *observable actions* that happen at individual services (locally), and (2) a set of *sequencing (global) constraints* of the activities in (1).

Observable local actions are typically of two kinds: *messaging* actions for communicating with other services including sending and receiving messages, and local *activities* that are performed at individual services independent of other services. The use of activities in a choreography is primarily for organizing service operations in order to satisfy the logical requirements of a composition. For example, a "searching for books" (on a catalog) operation should happen before a "checkout" operation.

Sequencing constraints restrict the actions to specified orderings. Although these resemble the control flow constructs in programming, a notable difference is that it may not be obvious how an individual constraint on two activities in a choreography can be enforced when the activities have no connections. As we shall see in Subsection 4.2, some of such cases can be logical consequence of other constraints (that can be enforced), and others simply cannot be implemented. This is one of the interesting problems concerning choreography modeling languages.

The second component of a choreography model is a set of service implementations. When the services interact within a composition, their collective global behaviors should "conform" to the specification. In the following, we explore two essential ingredients needed in defining the notion of conformance, the latter will be given in Subsection 4.1.

Clearly, the services must communicate with each other using a *messaging model*. Different messaging models have been used in the literature. Under one model the sender of a message waits for the receiver to consume the message from the channel before it continues. The model is simple and prohibits the sender from taking any further actions, including sending another message prior to the consumption of the first by the receiver. We call this model *synchronous messaging* in the spirit of service composition. In contrast, *asynchronous messaging* models allow the sender to continue its execution immediately after its completion of the send action. A decision to be made is how to handle the situation when new messages arrive before old messages are consumed. A natural approach is to use a *FIFO queue* for each receiver to store all its unconsumed messages in their arriving order. One can also place a limit on the size of FIFO queues, in which case, an incoming message sent to a full queue could cause one of several possible actions, including: overwrite the oldest message, delete itself, or block the sender's execution. A messaging model should clearly define the actions to be taken.

The second ingredient is how to formulate the *global behaviors of an execution of services* and compare them against a choreography. One straightforward approach is to use traces of the service executions modulo irrelevant actions. This has been studied in mostly automata based choreography models. The other is to employ the notion of *bisimulation* between the generated global behaviors and choreography. Most process algebra based choreography models adopt this approach.

Table 1 summarizes some selected choreography modeling languages in the three categories. Rows in the table indicate specific elements in the global or local specifications. Messaging and activity mean whether a choreography/service implementation can include messaging actions and non-messaging activities (respectively). Here "Global" means choreography, "Local" means service implementation, "G/L" stands for both choreography and service implementation (in all models examined, the control flow constructs are the same for choreography and service implementation). For example,

Table 1. Summary of Choreography Models

	Automata			Petri nets	Process algebras		
	Mealy [10]	UML Collaboration Diagram [9]	Colombo [1]	IPN [16]	Bologna [11]	Global & Endpoint Calculi [12]	Chor & Role [25]
Global messaging	yes	yes	no	yes	yes	yes	yes
Local messaging	yes	yes	yes	yes	yes	yes	yes
Global activity	yes[1]	no	yes	no	no	yes[2]	yes
Local activity	yes[1]	no	yes	no	no	yes[2]	yes
G/L sequence	yes	yes	yes	yes	yes	yes	yes
G/L parallel	yes[1]	yes[1]	yes[1]	yes	yes	yes	yes
G/L choice	yes	no	yes	yes	yes	yes	yes[3]
G/L Recursion	yes	yes[2]	yes	yes	no	yes[3]	yes[3]
Messaging model	FIFO	FIFO	FIFO(1)	sync	sync	sync	sync
Semantics	trace	trace	trace	bisim	bisim	bisim	trace

[1]Can be extended to include the element   [2]Limited   [3]Dominated

in Colombo the global behavior specification could state that the "listen-to-music" activity in one service should happen before the "checkout" activity in another. The row "Messaging model" shows the model used for the languages, and the last row "Semantics" identifies whether the comparison of generated global behaviors and a choreography uses trace based semantics or bisimulation. Finally, two process algebra based modeling languages either model activities of particular types (shown as "Limited" in table) or require one service to control choice or iteration (shown as "Dominated").

In the remainder of the section, we give a short survey of choreography languages based on their underlying formalisms.

3.2 Automata Based Models

Automata based choreography models represent both choreographies and service implementations using finite state automata (or their variants). An advantage is that state machines explicitly capture a snapshot of a composite service execution as a "state" and (local/global) behaviors can be easily captured as sequences of states in which each state transition may be associated with a message or an activity.

At the service implementation level, send and receive are modeled as message actions since they are separate individual actions while the choreography level only the status of whether a message has happened (been sent) is of interest. This group of choreography modeling languages includes conversation protocols and Mealy services [10,19], UML collaboration diagrams [9], and the Colombo service composition model [1].

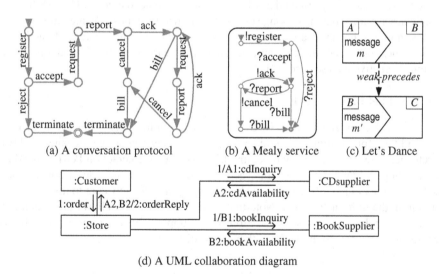

(a) A conversation protocol   (b) A Mealy service   (c) Let's Dance

(d) A UML collaboration diagram

Fig. 4. Automata based Choreography Modeling Languages

The use of conversations to specify choreographies was originally proposed in the IBM Conversation Support Project [20,21]. A formal model based on this idea was developed in [10] under which a conversation protocol is represented as finite state automaton over messages, and each service as a Mealy machine over the input/output messages of the service. An example of a conversation protocol is shown in Fig. 4(a), and a Mealy service in Fig. 4(b) where the leading symbol "!" denotes an action of sending a message and "?" a receiving action. Each service has an associated FIFO queue (of unbounded capacity) for storing unconsumed incoming messages. When services are executing, a virtual global *watcher* records the sequence of messages for all send actions. A *conversation* is the sequence of messages recorded by the watcher in a successful execution. A conversation protocol is *satisfied* if every conversation by the services is a word accepted by the conversation protocol automaton.

The automata based choreography modeling approach specifies a choreography through states and transitions. It is easy to use since this approach is commonly used to specify protocols and policies. The language *Let's dance* [30,31] provides a set of sequencing constraint primitives to allow a choreography to be specified in a graphical language. For example, Fig. 4(c) shows a message from A to B should "weak-precede" another message m', this means that B cannot send m' prior to A sending message m.

A variation of the conversation/Mealy model was studied in [9], which also uses Mealy services with unbounded FIFO queues. However, instead of conversation protocols, UML collaboration diagrams are used to specify choreographies. Fig. 4(d) illustrates a UML collaboration diagram which specifies that an "order" message is followed by "cdInquiry" and "bookInquiry" messages in any order, after their corresponding responses are made, "orderReply" can then be sent out.

Finally, another interesting variation is the Colombo model used to study an automated composition problem for semantic web services [1]. Similar to the UML model, the local services are represented as Mealy services (extended to allow OWL-S like semantic descriptions) but the message queues are limited to at most one message (size 1). Choreographies, however, are represented by finite state automata over only activities without messages. The model is an extension of the earlier "Roman" model for composing interactive web services [2].

3.3 Petri-net Based Models

Petri nets are another widely used tool to model, among other things, flow of control, and therefore a suitable candidate for choreography modeling languages. In [16], a Petri-net based choreography modeling language called Interaction Petri Nets (IPN) was developed. IPN treats a messaging action as a transition firing in describing a choreography. For example, Fig. 5 shows a choreography in IPN equivalent to the UML collaboration diagram in Fig. 4(d). Note that the use of Petri nets allows the concurrent Store-CDSupplier conversations and Store-BookSupplier conversations to be explicitly separated, in contrast to the UML collaboration diagram.

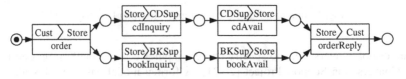

Fig. 5. Interaction Petri Nets

In [16], the technical problem studied concerns the local enforcement of an IPN choreography. In their study, the local services are represented by "behavior interfaces" that are Petri nets with "input/output" places. The services communicate with each other in the synchronous messaging model, rather than FIFO queues in automata based languages discussed in Subsection 3.2.

3.4 Process Algebra Based Models

Recently, there have been several efforts in developing choreography modeling languages using process algebras [11,8,12,25]. Common in these studies are that both choreographies and service implementations are specified in (slightly different) process algebras, with a key difference being the separation of sending and receiving a message at the local level but not at the global level, similar to the automata and Petri nets based models discussed in Subsections 3.2 and 3.3. All these approaches use the synchronous messaging model for communication.

In [11], process algebras, called the "Bologna" model in Table 1, for choreographies and service implementations (the latter are often called orchestration in process algebra based languages) were developed. The Bolonga model does not include recursion in choreography and service implementation specifications. The semantics of satisfaction of a choreography by an execution of service implementations is defined through a bisimulation between the two algebras. Global Calculus and Endpoint Calculus [12] was an attempt to provide a theoretical model for WS-CDL; they also include detailed operations and parameter passing. The semantics connecting the Global and Endpoint Calculi is also based on bisimulation. The concept of dominant role for choice and loop structures, which allows the "projection" of each choreography by inserting additional synchronization communications, was developed in Chor & Role [25]. In their model, a trace based semantics is used instead of bisimulation. Table 1 shows the basic elements available in these process algebra based languages.

4   Design and Analysis Problems

In this section, we define several key research problems concerning reasoning, design, analysis, and verification of choreographies and service implementations. In particular, we focus on the two challenges raised in Section 2 and discuss specific technical problems around the challenges.

In reasoning, we study the problem of "conformance", i.e., whether service implementations only generate global behaviors consistent with a choreography. As illustrated in Fig. 3, service design is to generate service implementations from a choreography such that the global behaviors of services are completely captured by the choreography. This "realizability" problem is important in understanding choreography specifications and thus addressing Challenge 1. A key technical problem in Challenge 2 focuses on the other direction, and demands the understanding of service implementations that realize a set of desirable choreographies. For this challenge, we formulate the "analysis" problem for service implementations.

Subsection 4.1 focuses on the conformance problem, Subsections 4.2 and 4.3 explore the problems of realizability and analysis, respectively. Subsection 4.4 outlines the main methodologies of verifying composite services.

4.1 The Conformance Problem

The *conformance* problem is stated as follows, assuming some fixed choreography modeling language $\mathcal{L}$: Given a choreography C in $\mathcal{L}$ and a set I of service implementations in $\mathcal{L}$, is it possible to determine if every possible execution of I always generates the behaviors allowed by C?

The conformance problem is fundamental in choreography design. It is very desirable that the problem is solvable for choreography modeling languages of interest. The problem has been studied for several choreography modeling languages.

The conformance problem is decidable for conversation protocols and Mealy services (with queues) when the queue size is bounded by some pre-determined constant, since the set of conversations of Mealy services with bounded queues is always a regular language [10]. It turned out that when the queue size restriction is removed, the problem becomes undecidable [18]; the key reason for this is that the class of finite state automata with (unbounded) FIFO queues are as computationally expressive as the class of Turing machines [7].

For process algebra based choreography languages, the problem was initially studied for the Bologna model without repetition [11]. The problem was further studied in a model extended with repetition in [8]. After projecting the choreography to local services, the checking procedure can be done locally without considering other services.

Given the known results, it appears that the conformance problem is decidable when queue sizes are bounded and undecidable for unbounded queues, in the choreography languages that have been proposed so far. In [19], it was observed that there are service compositions that need queues of size greater than 1 (possibly unbounded). It is interesting to identify classes of choreographies where the conformance problem is decidable for unbounded queues.

4.2 Realizing Choreographies

The choreography approach to service design raises several new interesting questions. A key problem is whether it is possible to turn a choreography into service implementations automatically (Fig. 3). In this subsection, we discuss this "realizability" problem and other related problems.

We fix some choreography modeling language $\mathcal{L}$ and let C be a choreography. We define the following notions. The choreography C is (*weakly*) *realizable* if there exists a set I of service implementations such that the behaviors of executing I coincides with (respectively, are contained in) C. Weak realizability is useful when realizability cannot be achieved. We will discuss this notion later in the subsection.

The *realizability* problem is stated as follows: For a given choreography modeling language $\mathcal{L}$, is every choreography C in $\mathcal{L}$ (weakly) realizable? Furthermore, if C is (weakly) realizable, it is desirable to construct service implementations.

Some choreographies are not realizable. Consider the choreography $C_1 = \{m_1 m_2\}$ where service s_1 sends a message m_1 to s_3 and s_2 sends m_2 to s_3. Obviously s_2 has no

Fig. 6. An non-realizable conversation protocol

way of knowing whether m_1 is sent. Thus C_1 is not realizable. Such a "missing connection" is a frequently cited reason for non-realizability (e.g., [18,31,12,25,16]). When FIFO queues are used, the reasons for non-realizability are sometimes not so obvious. Fig. 6 shows a choreography $C_2 = \{m_3 m_4 m_5, m_4 m_3\}$ over three services s_4, s_5, s_6 and messages m_3, m_4, m_5. Since every service has a FIFO queue, it was shown that every implementation that permits the two conversations in C_2 will also permit the conversation "$m_4 m_3 m_5$" that is not in C_2 [17].

Realizability for automata-based languages was studied for conversation protocols [18,19] and UML collaboration diagrams [9] with Mealy services and FIFO queues. For the case of conversation protocols, a sufficient condition for realizability was established in [18] which consists of three sub-conditions "lossless join", "synchronous compatible", and "autonomous". This condition was generalized to include message contents and "guarded automata" in [19]. For UML collaboration diagrams, a sufficient realizability condition is obtained in [9] which focuses on the predecessor of each *send* action. In both cases, it remains an open problem whether the realizability problem is decidable and/or a necessary and sufficient condition exists.

When queues are bounded or synchronous messaging is used (i.e., queue size is 0), the realizability problem becomes easier. For the case of conversation protocols and Mealy services, it was shown in [10] that the set of conversations of Mealy services with bounded queues is always a regular language (rather than context-sensitive for unbounded queues). This result leads to a decision procedure for realizability for bounded queues [17]. Furthermore, a necessary and sufficient condition can be formulated by modifying the sufficient condition in [18] for the unbounded queue case.

When a choreography is realizable, it is desirable to produce the service implementations. For the conversation protocols and Mealy service model, it was shown that the service implementations are simply projections of the choreography to the individual services [17]. The language Let's Dance contains a richer set of sequencing constraint primitives, projecting a choreography into local services also needs to consider the specific constraints [31]. (The referenced paper also includes a realizability checking algorithm.)

In the following, we briefly summarize recent work on realizability in process algebra and Petri nets based models, all of which assume synchronous messaging.

Realizability for process algebras was investigated primarily on the Global and Endpoint Calculi [12] and Chor & Role [25]. The main approach in these studies is to develop a "projection" operator which takes as input a choreography C and a participant service and produces an implementation for the service. The goal is to have the behaviors of the projected services to be identical to the choreography C. In the context of Global and Endpoint Calculi, a sufficient condition of realizability involving connectedness, well-threadedness, and coherence was obtained [12]. In Chor & Role, a different approach was taken which consists of two parts. First, the choreography algebra uses dominated choice and repetition. Then, the projection operator inserts additional messages so that the generated services can synchronize correctly on the performed activities [25]. Intuitively, the added messages allows the dominator to communicate its decision to others, thus avoiding the missing connection problem mentioned earlier.

If a choreography C is not realizable, sometimes one could further limit the service implementations (that are obtained from projecting the choreography) so that they weakly realize C. Naturally, it is necessary to require that the generated global behaviors are not trivial (e.g., a nonempty set of traces). In fact it is also ideal that the generated behaviors should be as "close" to C as possible. In [16], the problem of weak realizability was studied for the IPN model. The main idea is to introduce additional constraints on the service implementations so that the generated global behaviors are always allowed by the choreography. An algorithm was given for choreographies restricted to bounded Petri nets.

Before we end this subsection, it is worthwhile to mention the work of [1]. In their model, a choreography is a finite state automaton over observable (local) activities. Given a choreography C and a set of Mealy services (with "open" or configurable message channels), the choreography synthesis problem is to connect message channels among the services such that the set of observable activity sequences from executing the Mealy services is exactly the choreography C. It was shown there that the construction can be done in double exponential time complexity.

In spite of the studies on the realizability problem, there are many interesting open problems. For example, for the conversation/Mealy service model, are there restricted subclasses of Mealy services which allow unbounded queues such that the realizability problem is decidable? In general, in any choreography modeling language, if a choreography is not realizable, can we always find the "maximal" service implementations that weakly realize the choreography?

4.3 Analyzing Service Implementations

Subsection 4.2 discussed design problems in the top-down fashion, i.e., from choreographies to implementations. In this subsection, we focus the analysis problem, i.e., to characterize service implementations whose global behaviors are representable by choreographies.

The analysis problem may occur when one attempts to verify if given implementations e.g., a set of BPEL services, satisfy properties formulated over their global behaviors [18,19]. If the global behaviors of the implementation can be characterized by a choreography C, reasoning and verification can be performed on C that is expected to be simpler and more efficient. In practice, it is not uncommon that one starts with a set of choreographies (a choreography language) and hopes to constrain the implementations to those that realize some of the choreographies. (We note that a related but different issue concerns verification of localized properties, e.g., concerning two services, and has been studied variously in the literature. See, e.g., the survey [27] for details.)

The *analysis* problem is defined as follows. Let $\mathcal{L} = (\mathcal{C}, \mathcal{I})$ be a choreography modeling language where $\mathcal{C}$ is a collection of choreographies and $\mathcal{I}$ a collection of implementations. Can we decide if an arbitrarily given implementation in $\mathcal{L}$ realizes some choreography in C? Furthermore, what is the (largest) subset $\subseteq \mathcal{I}$ of implementations that realize some choreographies in C?

Several preliminary results concerning the analysis problem have been obtained. We begin with the conversation protocols and Mealy services model of [10]. While it is known that the computation power of Mealy services is Turing complete [7], the set of conversations of a set of Mealy services is nevertheless a context sensitive language (accepted by a quasi-realtime automaton with 3 queues) [10]. Reference [10] also gives examples of Mealy services with non-regular and non-context-free sets of conversations, which are not definable by conversation protocols. It further identifies two conditions on implementations which guarantee to produce regular sets of conversations (can be captured by conversation protocols). The first is when the queue sizes are bounded to some fixed number. In this case, each queue can be modeled as a finite state automaton and the composition can be characterized as some product machine of all Mealy services and queue automata, which turns out to be a finite state automaton. The second concerns the topology of the services and message channels. It was shown that when the graph of services and message links is a tree, the set of conversations is also a regular language.

The analysis problem was studied in [19] with C being the set of all conversation protocols. Motivated by the bounded queue case, the notion of "synchronizability" was formulated as follows. A set of Mealy services is *synchronizable* if its set of conversations does not change when unbounded queues are replaced with synchronous messaging (or bounded queues). A sufficient condition for synchronizability on Mealy services is identified which consists of synchronous compatible and autonomous sub-conditions.

As a final remark, the analysis problem focuses on the global behaviors of service implementations. At the first glance, this appears to simply produce the system traces. However, detailed system traces may not correspond to global behaviors permitted by choreographies, as it was shown in [10]. Secondly, having a logical representation of service behaviors is critical in many SOA applications, in fact, a key to business process design lies in the logical representations of both requirements and software processes [24].

Much of the analysis problem remains unknown. For example, is there a sufficient and necessary condition for synchronizability? Also, there are practical service implementations that are not synchronizable but they realize conversation protocols. Is it possible to characterize all conversation protocol-realizing implementations? It is also interesting to explore there problems for other choreography models.

4.4 Approaches to Verification

There have been many studies on verifying compositions of web services recently (see the survey [27]). Most of these studies treat service compositions as distributed systems and properties to be verified are thus formulated over the distributed systems. Clearly the technical results from these studied are valuable contributions to the understanding of the technology that SOA can provide.

On the other hand, due to many reasons, applications of SOA in many areas including in particular business process management demand a separation of at least logical and implementation levels in process development. Verification of system properties is not sufficient if the system properties cannot be mapped to properties at the logical level. In our framework of service design, this means that we ought to be able to verify properties over choreographies of service implementations. Here we give a sampler of results along this line of verification of choreography properties.

Service design can use the top-down approach starting from a choreography. In this case, verification of logical properties can be done on the specified choreography first and if the choreography is satisfactory, it can be considered for realization [18].

We now consider the second scenario: start with service implementations (e.g., a collection of BPEL services). References [15,28] studied the problem of checking if a single service implementation is consistent with a choreography or other services. In [23], a choreography representing the global behaviors is first obtained which is then used for verification. This approach is not applicable for the conversation/Mealy machine model since the global behaviors are not always representable as conversation protocols [19]. Instead, analysis on service implementations is performed first and if the implementations are synchronizable, a conversation protocol can be constructed and verified.

The verification problem for services is perhaps better understood. Still, a serious challenge is the verification of services with data (from infinite domains) included. Perhaps the semantic web services approach such as OWL-S [13] of describing service semantics (with data) could help developing feasible verification approaches.

5   Conclusions

Design of web services appears to have a new twist comparing with traditional software development: having a logical level specification of global behaviors that are not identical to system traces. Such a logical-implementation level separation played a fundamental role in the development of data management techniques in the early days. It may possibly turn out to be a fundamental design principle for SOA.

In this paper we examined one aspect of the logical-implementation separation, namely how choreographies are related to the (abstract) service implementations. While prior technical results help to identify main issues on this topic, more efforts are needed to understand the different concerns at each level and to develop techniques and tools for service design.

References

1. Berardi, D., Calvanese, D., De Giacomo, G., Hull, R., Mecella, M.: Automatic composition of transition-based semantic web services with messaging. In: Proc. 31st Int. Conf. on Very Large Data Bases (VLDB), pp. 613–624 (2005)
2. Berardi, D., Calvanese, D., De Giacomo, G., Lenzerini, M., Mecella, M.: Automatic composition of e-services that export their behavior. In: Orlowska, M.E., Weerawarana, S., Papazoglou, M.P., Yang, J. (eds.) ICSOC 2003. LNCS, vol. 2910, pp. 43–58. Springer, Heidelberg (2003)
3. Bhattacharya, K., Gerede, C., Hull, R., Liu, R., Su, J.: Towards formal analysis of artifact-centric business process models. In: Alonso, G., Dadam, P., Rosemann, M. (eds.) BPM 2007. LNCS, vol. 4714, Springer, Heidelberg (2007)

4. Bhattacharya, K., Guttman, R., Lymann, K., Heath III, F.F., Kumaran, S., Nandi, P., Wu, F., Athma, P., Freiberg, C., Johannsen, L., Staudt, A.: A model-driven approach to industrializing discovery processes in pharmaceutical research. IBM Systems Journal 44(1), 145–162 (2005)
5. Bloomberg, J.: The seven principles of service-oriented development. XML & Web Services (August 2002)
6. Business Process Execution Language for Web Services (BPEL), Version 1.1 (May 2003), http://www.ibm.com/developerworks/library/ws-bpel
7. Brand, D., Zafiropulo, P.: On communicating finite-state machines. Journal of the ACM 30(2), 323–342 (1983)
8. Bravetti, M., Zavattaro, G.: Towards a unifying theory for choreography conformance and contract compliance. In: Proceedings of 6th International Symposium on Software Composition (SC), Braga, Portugal. LNCS, pp. 34–50. Springer, Heidelberg (2007)
9. Bultan, T., Fu, X.: Specification of realizable service conversations using collaboration diagrams. In: Proceedings of the IEEE International Conference on Service-Oriented Computing and Applications (SOCA), Newport Beach, California, June 2007, pp. 122–130 (2007)
10. Bultan, T., Fu, X., Hull, R., Su, J.: Conversation specification: A new approach to design and analysis of e-service composition. In: Proc. Int. World Wide Web Conf. (WWW) (May 2003)
11. Busi, N., Gorrieri, R., Guidi, C., Lucchi, R., Zavattaro, G.: Choreography and orchestration conformance for system design. In: Ciancarini, P., Wiklicky, H. (eds.) COORDINATION 2006. LNCS, vol. 4038, pp. 63–81. Springer, Heidelberg (2006)
12. Carbone, M., Honda, K., Yoshida, N., Milner, R., Brown, G., Ross-Talbot, S.: A theoretical basis of communication-centred concurrent programming (2006)
13. OWL Services Coalition. OWL-S: Semantic markup for web services (November 2003)
14. Decker, G., Kopp, O., Leymann, F., Weske, M.: BPEL4Chor: Extending BPEL for modeling choreographies. In: Proceedings of IEEE International Conference on Web Services (ICWS) (2007)
15. Decker, G., Weske, M.: Behavioral consistency for B2B process integration. In: Krogstie, J., Opdahl, A., Sindre, G. (eds.) CAiSE 2007 and WES 2007. LNCS, vol. 4495, pp. 81–95. Springer, Heidelberg (2007)
16. Decker, G., Weske, M.: Local enforceability in interaction petri nets. In: Alonso, G., Dadam, P., Rosemann, M. (eds.) BPM 2007. LNCS, vol. 4714, pp. 305–319. Springer, Heidelberg (2007)
17. Fu, X.: Formal Specification and Verification of Asynchronously Communicating Web Services. PhD thesis, University of California at Santa Barbara (2004)
18. Fu, X., Bultan, T., Su, J.: Conversation protocols: A formalism for specification and verification of reactive electronic services. In: H. Ibarra, O., Dang, Z. (eds.) CIAA 2003. LNCS, vol. 2759, Springer, Heidelberg (2003)
19. Fu, X., Bultan, T., Su, J.: Analysis of interacting BPEL web services. In: Proc. Int. World Wide Web Conf. (WWW) (May 2004)
20. Hanson, J.E., Nandi, P., Kumaran, S.: Conversation support for business process integration. In: Proceedings of 6th IEEE Int. Enterprise Distributed Object Computing Conference (2002)
21. Hanson, J.E., Nandi, P., Levine, D.W.: Conversation-enabled web services for agents and e-business. In: Proceedings of the International Conference on Internet Computing (IC), pp. 791–796 (2002)
22. Hull, R., Su, J.: Tools for composite web services: A short overview. SIGMOD Record 34(2), 86–95 (2005)
23. Lohmann, N., Kopp, O., Leymann, F., Reisig, W.: Analyzing BPEL4Chor: Verification and participant synthesis. In: Proceedings of International Workshop on Web Services and Formal Methods (2007)

24. Nigam, A., Caswell, N.S.: Business artifacts: An approach to operational specification. IBM Systems Journal 42(3), 428–445 (2003)
25. Qiu, Z., Zhao, X., Cai, C., Yang, H.: Towards the theoretical foundation of choreography. In: Proceedings of 16th International World Wide Web Conference (WWW), pp. 973–982. ACM Press, New York (2007)
26. Ramakrishnan, R.: Database Management Systems. McGraw-Hill, New York (1997)
27. van Breugel, F., Koshkina, M.: Models and verification of BPEL (2006)
28. van der Aalst, W.M.P., Dumas, M., Ouyang, C., Rozinat, A., Verbeek, H.M.V.: Conformance checking of service behavior. ACM Transactions on Internet Technology (to appear, 2008)
29. Web Services Choreography Description Language Version 1.0 (December 2004), http://www.w3.org/TR/ws-cdl-10/
30. Zaha, J.M., Barros, A., Dumas, M., ter Hofstede., A.: Lets Dance: A language for service behavior modeling. In: On the Move to Meaningful Internet Systems: CoopIS, DOA, GADA, and ODBASE, pp. 145–162 (2006)
31. Zaha, J.M., Dumas, M., ter Hofstede, A.: Service interaction modeling: Bridging global and local views. In: Proceedings of IEEE International Enterprise Distributed Object Computing Conference (EDOC) (2006)

Controlling Petri Net Process Models

Jörg Desel

Angewandte Informatik
Katholische Universität Eichstätt-Ingolstadt, Germany
joerg.desel@ku-eichstaett.de
http://www.informatik.ku-eichstaett.de

Abstract. We present and compare existing formalisms that consider the control of Petri net process models in the area of business processes and web services. Control has the aim to force a process to behave in a desirable way. Process models that behave properly without any control are often called "sound". For process models that behave properly when being controlled, i.e., for controllable processes, there are various related notions, such as "relaxed soundness" and "weak soundness". We argue that both, the usual notion of sound behavior and the usual notion of control by message passing can be generalized. This way, control synthesis results obtained in the field of automation can be reformulated and reused for business process models and in the area of web services.

1 Introduction

In the last decades, research on Petri net analysis concentrated on the question whether a given Petri net model enjoys a desirable property or not. More recently, people study the question whether a given Petri net model *can* behave properly, if its environment behaves accordingly. This question only makes sense if there are notions of environment and of interface to the considered Petri net model. The environment might be formulated as a Petri net as well. So the problem depends on notions of Petri net modules that can be composed, together with interfaces between Petri nets that express at what parts of the model, and in which way, the interaction between models can take place, and on *proper* versus *not proper* behavior of a Petri net. In particular, proper behavior can be considered for the controlled Petri net in separation or for the Petri net within its environment.

Given a Petri net model N with an interface that allows composition with other net models N' via some operator $\oplus$, one therefore can ask:

1. Does $N \oplus N'$ behave properly for some net N'?
2. Does N behave properly when composed with some net N'?
3. Does $N \oplus N'$ behave properly for any net N'?
4. Does N behave properly when composed with any net N'?
5. Can N' be automatically generated (synthesized) from N such that $N \oplus N'$ behaves properly?
6. Can N' be automatically generated (synthesized) from N such that N behaves properly when composed with N'?

M. Dumas and R. Heckel (Eds.): WS-FM 2007, LNCS 4937, pp. 17–30, 2008.
© Springer-Verlag Berlin Heidelberg 2008

All these questions are tackled in various papers, assuming various composition operators ⊕ and various definitions of proper behavior. In this paper, we will frequently come back to these questions.

In this paper we concentrate on Petri net *process* models, where the term "process" refers to business processes. Distinguishing process models from arbitrary system models, characteristic properties of processes and their models include (see [3,10]):

– Process models have distinguished start and end states. Beginning with a start state, each run should eventually end with an end state. However, it is possible that the behavior of a process has loops, i.e., repetition of states.
– Whereas liveness (every activity can occur from every reachable state) is a desirable property for system models, process models should not be live, because in the end state no activity should be allowed to occur.
– Process models are considered to be embedded in information system models [8]. In contrast to process models, information system models should be live. The situation is comparable to operating systems and single user program executions. Each user program should eventually terminate, but the operating system – which is also an executable program – should not.
– Whereas a deadlock is a state without successor for general systems, end states are not considered deadlocks in process models. For information system and process models, deadlock freedom is desirable.
– Process models are based on single cases where each case corresponds to a single run of a process.
– As in reality, several cases can run concurrently. To reflect this situation, process models might also represent the concurrent run of several process instances, for example to investigate the usage of shared resources.

A process model may interact with its environment and, consequently, may have an interface to some other Petri net. This other Petri net influences the behavior of the process model in such a way that the process behaves properly. In this sense, the process model is *controlled* by the environment. This control happens by means of different kinds of stimulation, depending on the respective approach. Very often, the control also reacts on the behavior of the process. Therefore the control must have the possibility to observe the behavior of the process or at least some aspects of this behavior. Since thus information is flowing in both directions the process model also controls its environment.

Usually, not all elements of a process can be controlled and not all elements can be observed. In other words, it is useful to specify a process model together with its controllable and with its observable elements such that any composition of this net with a net representing the environment restricts to interaction via controllable and observable elements. This constitutes the interface definition of a Petri net process model.

The kind of interaction between a Petri net process model and a model of its environment varies in different approaches. Moreover, the elements of process models that can be controlled and those that can be observed are specified in various ways. Finally, there are different suggestions for desirable behavior and its specification.

In this paper, we compare some approaches and introduce some relations between them. In the first section, we provide a rough introduction to Petri net models of processes and we repeat the definition of soundness. The second section is devoted to behavioral properties that are related to the soundness property but require a suitable controlling net ensuring sound behavior. In particular, the control makes sure that a process does not run into a deadlock. We sketch a different approach in the third section where control of a process makes sure that places behave in a bounded way, i.e., that the number of tokens on a place does not grow arbitrarily. Finally, the fourth section establishes a relation to known results of controller synthesis in the field of discrete event systems. It is argued that the composition operation used there is more general than usual message passing, whence the results in this area can be transferred to business processes.

2 Petri Net Process Models

Unfortunately, the term "process" was and is used in the Petri net research community in an ambiguous way. Since more than 30 years, a process net is known to be an occurrence net representing a concurrent run of a net representing a system. This naming does not nicely match processes in the sense of business processes [8] and will be avoided in this paper.

One of the first approaches, starting in the late eighties, to model information systems and business processes with Petri nets was the INCOME project by the group of Wolffried Stucky in Karlsruhe, Germany. The INCOME tool developed in this project was successfully used in industrial practice by the spin-off PROMATIS. Relevant publications from this project include [14,18,19].

The process models used in INCOME are predicate/transition Petri nets (see Figure 1). These nets have distinguished input and output *transitions*, representing the start and the end action of a process. Using high-level tokens, data flow

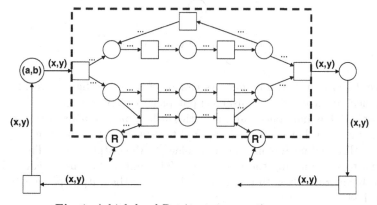

Fig. 1. A high-level Petri net representing a process

is thus thoroughly represented. In particular, processes of information systems including data bases are represented.

Therefore, (some) places represent data base relations (and tokens corresponding tuples), as the places R and R' in the example indicate. The interface of the process model to its environment is given by its input- and output transitions. In this way a process can be viewed as a refinement of a transition. Additionally, shared places model shared access to data bases.

A model of an information system preferably enjoys nice properties such as liveness and boundedness (an upper limit for the number of tokens). Within an information system model, processes can be identified [8], as in Figure 1. The model of the process, however, is not bounded because the initial transition can occur arbitrarily.

The INCOME approach concentrated on modelling and simulation of processes and information systems in early design phases. Analysis was performed on the level of the entire information system, i.e., the process net together with its environment was studied instead of the process net in separation. Therefore, according to the list of properties in the introduction, Question 3 was considered, because only the behavior of the composed model was of interest.

In the mid nineties, Wil van der Aalst came up with a different concept of a Petri net representation of a process [1,2,3]. His nets – called *workflow nets* – are place/transition nets, i.e., data aspects and control aspects are separated. A run of a workflow net represents a single case, no matter whether in reality several cases can run concurrently. These runs are assumed to behave without interference so that they all run properly provided a single case runs properly.

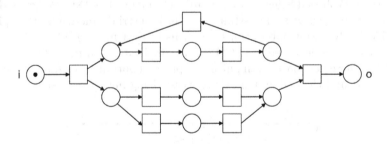

Fig. 2. A sound workflow net

Figure 2 shows a workflow net. As can be seen in the figure, workflow nets are assumed to have a distinguished input place i (representing that the event "case started" has happened) and a distinguished output place o (representing "case completed"). Formally, it is required that every net element of a workflow net is on a directed path from the input place to the output place. There is only one initial token, marking the input place. This initial marking is called **i**. The intended behavior ends with a marking where only the output place carries one token, called **o**.

Instead of analyzing the entire system model embedding the workflow net one can analyze the workflow net net in separation. So Question 4 from the introduction is considered. Proper behavior is formulated in terms of soundness [3]:

Definition 1. *A workflow net is sound if*
i) from every marking reachable from **i**, *the marking* **o** *is reachable, and*
ii) there are no dead transitions.

It can be shown that, as a consequence, **o** is the only reachable marking assigning a token to the output place (which was part of the original definition). Moreover, each sound workflow net is bounded.

A nice observation is that soundness is strongly related to the well-known notions of liveness and boundedness of general Petri nets [2]. Instead of representing the entire environment of an information system it suffices to add an additional transition moving the token from the output place to the input place, see Figure 3. This transition represents the behavior of the environment in a satisfactory way, as will be explained next.

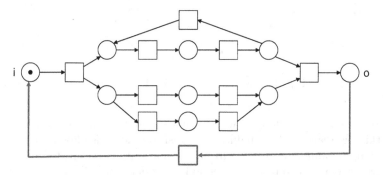

Fig. 3. The workflow net with an additional transition

If the workflow net is sound then the additional transition can always become enabled again (by the marking **o**) because of property i) of the definition of soundness. By property ii), every transition can always become enabled. Hence the extended net is live. It is bounded because its set of reachable markings coincides with the set of reachable markings of the workflow net. Conversely, liveness of the extended net implies that from each reachable marking a marking assigning a token to the output place is reachable. Boundedness implies that this marking must be **o** because otherwise tokens can be added arbitrarily to the net. Liveness also implies that the workflow net has no dead transitions. So soundness of the workflow net coincides with liveness and boundedness of the extended net. Therefore, the large amount of Petri net analysis techniques for liveness and boundedness can be applied for analyzing soundness of workflow nets. Moreover, if the workflow net happens to be free-choice [7] (which is often the case), the property soundness is decidable in polynomial time.

There are various more suggestions to model processes with Petri nets. For example, in [10] the reader can find examples of process nets with a behavior considering their past. If two transitions of a process strictly occur alternatingly, one in the first case, the other one in the second etc., different initial states are necessary. The initial marking of a process net has to have additional tokens that represent the necessary "memory" of the process.

3   Relaxed and Weak Soundness

In this section, we consider workflow nets that are not sound but behave in a proper (to be defined) way when being connected to a controlling environment. First let us consider an example:

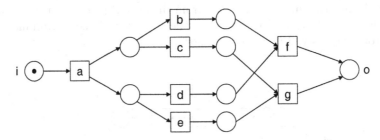

Fig. 4. A workflow net which is not sound

Figure 4 shows a workflow net which is not sound. By firing transitions a, b and e a marking is reached that enables no transition, i.e. a deadlock. In particular, the marking **o** cannot be reached from this marking. However, the net still has a positive property, formulated in the following definition [5]:

Definition 2. *A workflow net is relaxed sound if every transition occurs in some occurrence sequence leading from **i** to **o**.*

It is easy to verify that the occurrence sequences $abdf$ and $aceg$ of the example net both lead to the marking **o** and that every transition occurs in one of these sequences. Hence this net is relaxed sound.

The example net has two forward branching places representing a choice between b and c and a choice between d and e. Whenever one of the places is marked, both output transitions are enabled but firing one of the transitions disables the other one.

Generally, Petri net choices can represent quite different concepts:

– The choice is done within this process but the respective part of the process is not modelled. For example, two transition could represent two users that both could take care of a work item. Any solution is as good as the other one. This view relates to Question 4 of the introduction: Does N behave properly for any partner net N'? In a sound workflow net, we expect that any other component N' which decides which of the conflicting transition fires would not destroy the desired property.

- The choice depends on data of the case, which is not modelled. There are different suggestions how to handle data dependent choices. In the INCOME approach all relevant data is captured in the high-level tokens. This information can be reduced to *routing information* if the only purpose of this data is to decide choices. If one choice depends on data, another choice can depend on the same data as well, and this way deadlocks could be avoided. In our example, it might be the case that either transitions b and d or transitions c and e are chosen, whence the net can behave in a sound way. This view was originally taken in [5].
- Similarly, choices can depend on additional pre-conditions of the conflicting transitions which are not modelled first (see Figure 5). In other words, an embedding of the process net in a larger net is considered. With this view, we can ask whether there is an appropriate environment controlling the process net such that this net behaves soundly (Question 2 of the introduction). It is easy to see that putting tokens to the other new places instead yields the other sound run.

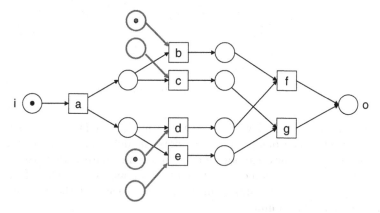

Fig. 5. Enforcing sound behavior by additional places

Now let us consider the next example, shown in Figure 6. This net is not even relaxed sound because there is no run leading from **i** to **o** which includes an occurrence of transition h. In this example net we have three conflicts. The addition of respective pre-conditions (Figure 7) shows that it is still possible to reach **o** from **i**.

Definition 3. *A workflow net, extended by input places to some of the conflicting transitions, is weakly sound if from every marking reachable from* **i**, *the marking* **o** *is reachable.*

Notice that this definition is very similar to i) in the definition of soundness. Actually, the original definition of weak soundness employs so-called open workflow

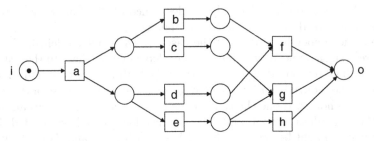

Fig. 6. A process net which is not relaxed sound...

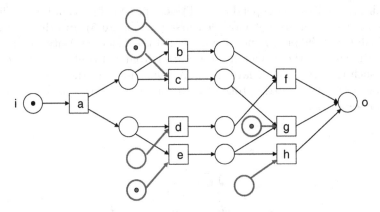

Fig. 7. ... together with pre-conditions

nets which contain the workflow net together with additional input places of some of the conflicting transitions [15,17]. Therefore the definitions of relaxed soundness and of weak soundness cannot be compared immediately. However, at least for nets in which no transition can occur more than once, every relaxed workflow net can be extended by accordingly marked places such that the resulting open workflow net is weakly sound.

Whereas relaxed soundness clearly corresponds to Question 2 of the introduction, one might argue that weak soundness refers to Question 1. There are other approaches, e.g. [13], where local and global soundness is explicitly distinguished. Therefore the work described in [13] definitely answers Question 1.

Whereas weak soundness does not explicitly refer to a controller, the closely related property controllability as used in [21], does. In the application context of web services, the property is called usability [16]. The term controllability is used in [6] to characterize relaxed soundness.

4 Weak Boundedness

Although soundness refers to liveness and boundedness, its derivates relax the liveness condition by assuming that the net remains live if, in case of conflicts, only the right transitions are chosen. In this section we introduce a related, but different approach, where liveness is guaranteed but boundedness needs additional control. This approach stems from the area of schedulability of concurrent programs on a chip [4], but can similarly be formulated for processes in our sense.

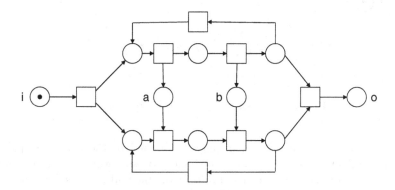

Fig. 8. A weakly bounded process net

The process net shown in Figure 8 can always reach the marking **o**. But, if the upper cycle occurs more often than the lower cycle, then there will be an arbitrary number of tokens in the places a and b, whence the net is not bounded. However, this effect can be avoided by firing transitions in the lower cycle at least as fast as those in the upper cycle.

Definition 4. *A workflow net is weakly bounded if there is a bound b such that, for each occurrence sequence from* **i** *to* **o***, there is a permutation of this sequence (leading from* **i** *to* **o** *as well) such that the token count on any place does not exceed b at any intermediate marking.*

Figure 9 shows a workflow net which is not weakly bounded. Due to place a the lower cycle cannot run faster than the upper cycle but to keep place b bounded it would have to run twice as fast. [4] contains sufficient and necessary conditions for weak boundedness of a net defined in the other application domain. Since this definition and the definition of workflow nets is not too different, these results should be transferable to the domain of business processes and web services.

The upper and the lower cycle of our example process could be viewed as separate processes which are both started by the occurrence of the only enabled transition in the figure. These processes communicate via message passing. In this sense, tokens on the places a and b can be viewed as requests. In this setting, it is an important question whether the lower process is able to serve all requests. For the weakly bounded example, the answer is positive. It is negative for the other example. Notice that this is not a negative property of any of the two subprocesses; both are fine in separation. Only their combination is ill. In the weakly bounded case, a scheduler – which is nothing else but an additional net

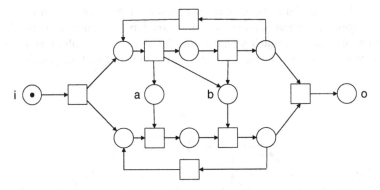

Fig. 9. A process which is not weakly bounded

module controlling processes – can only be applied to the combined process. Two independent schedulers of the two single processes would not work. In this sense, weakly bounded process nets are controllable and process nets which are not weakly bounded are not controllable.

5   Controller Synthesis

Based on previous work in discrete event systems [20,22,23,11], we give in [9] an overview on our work on controller synthesis. Processes (which are cyclic in our setting in [9]) are given in terms of Petri nets and communication is based on events, formalized by means of *event arcs*. The aim of this section is to show that the results can be translated to the area of business processes.

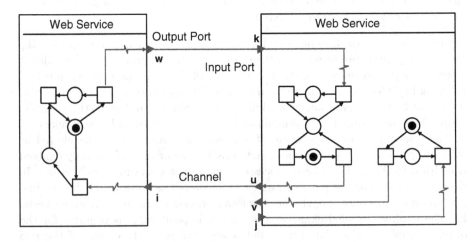

Fig. 10. Web service composition with event arcs

Figure 10 (taken from a presentation of Gabriel Juhás) shows how Petri nets representing web services communicate via event signals, formalized by event arcs. The meaning of an event arc is as follows: The occurrence rule for the source transition is the usual one. Assume it is enabled at a marking. If the target transition is enabled as well, both transitions occur coincidentally (in a step). Otherwise the source transition occurs alone, as usual. The target transition can only occur coincidentally with the source transition. See [12] for a translation of event arcs to nets using inhibitor arcs. This paper also provides a framework for controller synthesis on the basis of so-called open Petri nets.

The main result of [9] is an algorithm that provides for a given Petri net and a given specification another Petri net such that the behavior of the composed net matches the specification. So this approach provides a solution to Question 5 of the introduction. The specification is given in terms of a regular language (a regular expression, syntactically). The composition operator only uses event arcs. An event arc can only lead to a controllable event, and it can only start at an observable event. The composition of modules can be viewed as another module in the obvious way. The interface, i.e. the controllable and observable events, of the composed net is the set of transitions which are not controlled (observed, respectively) by one of the composed modules.

Instead of summarizing the result of [9] in more detail, we roughly explain why this result can be viewed as a generalization of the synthesis problem of workflow nets.

First, for workflow nets the desired property is that from each reachable marking the marking o can be reached. In other words, each run should end with one of the final transitions which put a token to the place o. If we abstract from tokens that do not enable any transition, we moreover require that no other transition is enabled after the occurrence of a final transition. Clearly, this can be expressed by means of a regular expression.

Second, the usual communication primitives used for process models and web services is message passing, formalized by a place in the post-set of a sending transition and in the pre-set of a receiving transition. This communication is

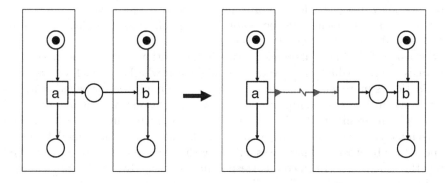

Fig. 11. Translating message passing in event arcs

purely asynchronous. In contrast, event arcs provide means to formalize synchronous aspects as well, but in an asymmetric way. However, Figure 11 shows how message passing can be modelled by means of event arcs: Instead of sending a message, a signal is sent which forces the receiver to create the message itself. Messages carrying data, modelled by high-level Petri nets, can be translated in a similar way because the event arcs can have high-level annotations, just as regular arcs. Similarly, overwriting of messages etc. can also be modelled by event arcs, in a similar way as they can be modelled by high-level Petri nets, see Figure 12.

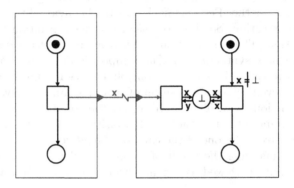

Fig. 12. Modelling overwriting of messages

6   Conclusion

Starting with a number of problems related to controllability of Petri nets in the introduction, we showed that, and how, different approaches to controlling Petri net process models are related but answer slightly different questions. The list of mentioned approaches is by far not complete. A first selection criterion was the popularity of the concepts in process modelling (soundness and relaxed soundness) or in web services (weak soundness and controllability/usability of open workflow nets). I added approaches which were (co-)developed in my research group and which might be usable to solve additional problems raised for process models and web service models.

Since one of the main differences between the mentioned approaches is the way modules interact which each other, one might ask whether asynchronous communication is more natural than synchronous communication or whether asymmetric synchronous communication, as provided by event arcs, is more natural than real synchronicity, etc. As shown before, message passing can be translated to asymmetric synchronous communication. Event arcs can also model mutual dependency between two processes, ensuring that each process can only proceed after the other one performed a corresponding activity (by sending an acknowledge via an event arc), see Figure 13.

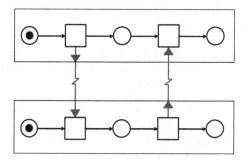

Fig. 13. Send and acknowledge of a message

So event arcs are quite general, and the quest for the right way of communication is not a matter of expressivity.

Considering a natural way to model communication, the level of abstraction plays a significant role. For example, web services are usually assumed to communicate strictly asynchronously. On a more technical level (i.e., on a lower layer) asymmetric communication turns out to be realized by means of synchronous communication primitives. I claim that the signal arc approach provides one of the most natural views of communication. As mentioned before, it can be restricted to mimic asynchronicity and it can be restricted to mimic synchronicity.

References

1. van der Aalst, W.M.P.: A class of Petri nets for modeling and analyzing business processes. Computing Science Report 95/26, Eindhoven Univ. of Technology (1995)
2. van der Aalst, W.M.P.: Verification of workflow nets. In: Azéma, P., Balbo, G. (eds.) ICATPN 1997. LNCS, vol. 1248, pp. 407–426. Springer, Heidelberg (1997)
3. van der Aalst, W.M.P., van Hee, K.: Workflow Management – Models, Methods and Systems. MIT Press, Cambridge (2002)
4. Liu, C., Kondratyev, A., Watanabe, Y., Desel, J., Sangiovanni-Vincentelli, A.: Schedulability analysis of Petri nets based on structural properties. In: Applications of Concurrency to System Design (ACSD), pp. 69–78. IEEE, Los Alamitos (2006)
5. Dehnert, J., Rittgen, P.: Relaxed soundness of business processes. In: Dittrich, K.R., Geppert, A., Norrie, M.C. (eds.) CAiSE 2001. LNCS, vol. 2068, pp. 157–170. Springer, Heidelberg (2001)
6. Dehnert, J.: Expressing the controllability of business processes. Petri Net Newsletter 61, 9–17 (2001)
7. Desel, J., Esparza, J.: Free Choice Petri Nets. Cambridge Tracts in Theoretical Computer Science, vol. 40. Cambridge University Press, Cambridge (1995)
8. Desel, J., Oberweis, A.: Petri-Netze in der Angewandten Informatik. Wirtschaftsinformatik 38(4), 359–367 (1996)
9. Desel, J., Hanisch, H.-M., Juhás, G., Lorenz, R., Neumair, C.: A guide to modelling and control with modules of signal nets. In: Ehrig, H., Damm, W., Desel, J., Große-Rhode, M., Reif, W., Schnieder, E., Westkämper, E. (eds.) INT 2004. LNCS, vol. 3147, pp. 270–300. Springer, Heidelberg (2004)

10. Desel, J.: Process modelling using Petri nets. Process-Aware Information Systems - Bridging People and Software through Process Technology, pp. 147–177. Wiley, Chichester (2005)
11. Hanisch, H.M., Rausch, M.: Synthesis of supervisory controllers based on a novel representation of condition/event Systems. IEEE International Conference on Systems, Man and Cybernetics 4, 3069–3074 (1995)
12. Heckel, R., Chouikha, M.: Control synthesis for discrete event systems – A semantic framework based on open Petri nets. Transactions of the SDPS 6(4), 63–104 (2003)
13. Kindler, E., Martens, A., Reisig, W.: Inter-operability of workflow applications: local criteria for global soundness. In: van der Aalst, W.M.P., Desel, J., Oberweis, A. (eds.) Business Process Management. LNCS, vol. 1806, pp. 235–253. Springer, Heidelberg (2000)
14. Lausen, G., Müller, H., Németh, T., Oberweis, A., Schönthaler, F., Stucky, W.: Integritätssicherung für die datenbankgestützte Software-Produktionsumgebung INCOME. In: Datenbanksysteme in Büro, Technik und Wissenschaft (BTW) Informatik-Fachberichte, vol. 136, pp. 152–156. Springer, Heidelberg (1987)
15. Martens, A.: On compatibility of web services. Petri Net Newsletter. Gesellschaft für Informatik 65, 12–20 (2003)
16. Martens, A.: On usability of web services. In: 1st Web Services Quality Workshop (WQW 2003), Rome, Italy (2003)
17. Martens, A.: Analyzing web service based business processes. In: Cerioli, M. (ed.) FASE 2005. LNCS, vol. 3442, pp. 19–33. Springer, Heidelberg (2005)
18. Oberweis, A., Scherrer, G., Stucky, W.: INCOME/STAR: methodology and tools for the development of distributed information systems. Information Systems 19(8), 643–660 (1994)
19. Oberweis, A., Sander, P.: Information system behavior specification by high-level Petri nets. ACM Transactions on Information Systems 14(4), 380–420 (1996)
20. Ramadge, P.J., Wonham, W.M.: The Control of Discrete Event Systems. Proceedings of the IEEE 77, 1, 81–98 (1989)
21. Schmidt, K.: Controllability of open workflow nets. In: Enterprise Modelling and Information Systems Architectures (EMISA), Gesellschaft für Informatik. LNI, vol. 75, pp. 236–249 (2005)
22. Sreenivas, R.S., Krogh, B.H.: On condition/event systems with disrete state realizations. Discrete Event Dynamic Systems – Theory and Applications 2, 1, 209–236 (1991)
23. Sreenivas, R.S., Krogh, B.H.: Petri net based models for condition/event systems. In: 1991 American Control Conference, vol. 3, pp. 2899–2904 (1991)

Extending Model Checking to Data-Aware Temporal Properties of Web Services

Sylvain Hallé, Roger Villemaire, Omar Cherkaoui, Jérôme Tremblay, and Boubker Ghandour

Université du Québec à Montréal
C.P. 8888, Succ. Centre-ville
Montréal, Canada H3C 3P8
halle@info.uqam.ca

Abstract. A "data-aware" web service property is a constraint on the pattern of message exchanges of a workflow where the order of messages and their data content are interdependent. The logic CTL-FO$^+$ expresses these properties by allowing temporal operators and first-order quantification over message content to be freely mixed. A "naïve" translation of CTL-FO$^+$ into CTL leads to a serious exponential blow-up of the problem that prevents existing validation tools to be used. In this paper, we provide an alternate translation of CTL-FO$^+$ into CTL where the construction of the workflow model depends on the property to validate. We show experimentally how this translation is significantly more efficient and makes model checking of data-aware temporal properties on real-world web service workflows tractable using off-the-shelf tools.[1]

1   Introduction

The phrase *web service validation* generally refers to the operation of checking the basic syntactical structure of the messages exchanged by a service for conformance to an interface description. It has long been known that to ensure a true interoperability of services, messages must also be sent and received in a proper sequence [2,18]. Therefore, workflow validation extends to conformance to a set of temporal constraints; depending on the authors, the approach has been called "operating guidelines", "behavioural properties" or "protocol of interaction".

A large amount of works have studied this question from various angles, mostly borrowing from model checking techniques. The external behaviour of web services can be modelled by the transmission or reception of messages identified by propositional letters standing for their names [9,12,16,26,22,35]. A possible refinement is to consider that the data exchanged in the messages of a web service can actually influence the control flow of that service [5,15,25,28,29]. A number of automated tools for the validation of the properties has been developed around this principle [32,8,30,24]; most of them use standard model checkers

---

[1] We gratefully acknowledge the financial support of the Natural Sciences and Engineering Research Council of Canada on this research.

M. Dumas and R. Heckel (Eds.): WS-FM 2007, LNCS 4937, pp. 31–45, 2008.

such as SPIN [23], NuSMV [10] or CWB [1] to validate the workflow models. The properties are expressed in Linear Temporal Logic (LTL), Computation Tree Logic (CTL), π-calculus, or a similar formalism [32, 12, 33].

These languages are called *propositional*: their atoms are propositional symbols over which first-order quantification is not allowed. For example, the CTL formula $\mathbf{AG}\,(a = x \rightarrow \mathbf{AF}\,b = x)$ correlates the values of state variables a and b at two different moments in time; it is a valid CTL formula when x is a static constant, but it cannot be used to express the same thing "for all x" unless the formula is repeated for every possible static value. This limited form of quantification is called *explicit*.

In contrast, there exist constraints where the sequence of messages and the data inside these messages are interdependent in such a way that first-order quantification is necessary; we call these properties "data-aware"; this concept was first introduced in [20]. We briefly show in Section 2 how these constraints arise naturally in a real-world web service scenario and are essential to validate. In Section 3, we present CTL-FO$^+$, a generalization of CTL that allows general first-order quantifiers to be freely mixed with temporal operators to express complex data-aware constraints. We show how it distinguishes itself from the few other methodologies suggested to model data-awareness; in particular, CTL-FO$^+$ model checking is decidable and PSPACE-complete.

There exist numerous ways to transform the CTL-FO$^+$ model checking problem back into classical CTL model checking to leverage existing workflow tools and standard model checkers; explicit quantification is one of them. Unfortunately, any such transformation results in an exponential blowup and shifts the original problem to the higher EXPTIME-hard class, unless $P = NP$. This result seems to suggest that data-aware properties are out of reach of existing tools.

However, in Section 4, we present a reduction of CTL-FO$^+$ to CTL that modifies the translation of a workflow into a finite-state system using the concept of "freeze quantification": the construction of the system becomes dependent on the property to validate. In Section 5, we compare this freeze quantification approach with the explicit quantification suggested above. Although both translations are ultimately exponential, we empirically demonstrate that freeze quantification is several orders of magnitude more efficient. We illustrate our claim by showing a technology chain using two off-the-shelf tools, the VERBUS [4] workflow translator coupled with the NuSMV [10] model checker to validate constraints on sample web service workflows. We conclude that despite the theoretical lower bound, it is nevertheless possible to model and validate data-aware properties in web services using existing technologies and a suitable reduction to CTL.

2   Data-Aware Web Service Properties

Our concern about capabilities of existing solutions to validate data-aware constraints comes from our observation that there exist real-world scenarios where such properties arise naturally.

We take as an example the User-Controlled Lightpath (UCLP) research project initiated by the CANARIE Consortium[2], which develops an environment that allows end users to self-provision and dynamically reconfigure optical network resources, called lightpaths, within a single domain or across multiple independent management domains. To this end, network resources from a specific provider are virtualized and exposed to the end user as instances of web services that implement functionality related to lightpath manipulation. Simply put, a *lightpath object* (LPO) is a point-to-point, high-speed optical link. In the UQAM-UO UCLP framework, each LPO is identified by a unique ID. The UCLP operations usually manipulate these IDs.

There are two main operations provided to manage LPOs. In order to build an end-to-end link, two adjacent LPOs can first be *concatenated*. The result of the concatenation operation is an LPO that is considered as one single link. In a dual manner, an LPO's bandwidth can be *partitioned* into links of equal bandwidth. This operation takes as input the reference to an LPO and returns an array of references to spawned lightpaths, each of the desired bandwidth. Typical partition and concatenate request and response XML messages are shown in Table 1.

Table 1. The concatenate request, concatenate response, partition request and partition response XML messages

```
<message>
  <operation>
    concatenateRequest
  </operation>
  <LPO-ID>i₁</LPO-ID>
  <LPO-ID>i₂</LPO-ID>
  ...
  <LPO-ID>iₙ</LPO-ID>
</message>

<message>
  <operation>
    partitionRequest
  </operation>
  <LPO-ID>i</LPO-ID>
  <bandwidth>b</bandwidth>
  <login>ℓ</login>
</message>
```

```
<message>
  <operation>
    concatenateResponse
  </operation>
  <LPO-ID>i</LPO-ID>
</message>

<message>
  <operation>
    partitionResponse
  </operation>
  <LPO-ID>i₁</LPO-ID>
  <LPO-ID>i₂</LPO-ID>
  ...
  <LPO-ID>iₙ</LPO-ID>
</message>
```

Once lightpaths are exposed as web services, operations for manipulating them can be called like any other web service invocation in a process expressed in a workflow language such as BPEL. However, these operations cannot be called arbitrarily.

---

[2] http://www.canarie.ca/canet4/uclp/. The software developed by all CANARIE funded development teams is freely available from their site http://www.uclpv2.ca.

To illustrate our point, we take the example of the partition operation, which takes as input the ID of some LPO x and returns new LPOs y, z corresponding to the results of the partition. It does not make sense to use x as an argument of a subsequent UCLP operation such as concatenate: although the LPO still physically exists, it has been logically superseded by its fragments y, z. The process could even have applied further operations on y and z, like concatenating them to other LPOs or further partitioning them. In this context, invoking, for example, a partition operation with x is at best semantically unsound and at worst plain dangerous for the reliability of the whole UCLP environment. We must therefore enforce the following constraint on any UCLP process:

UCLP Service Constraint 1. *Any LPO ID appearing in any partition request must be different from any LPO ID appearing in any future concatenate request.*

In that sentence, the first and third occurrences of the word "any" indicate a quantification over message content, while the second and fourth occurrences represent a quantification over messages in an execution sequence: data and temporal modalities are intertwined and the constraint is data-aware. Other data-aware constraints of technical nature can be easily found. We mention two of them which will be referred to in Section 5:

UCLP Service Constraint 2. *If two LPOs are the result of the same partition response, they cannot be involved together in any subsequent concatenate request.*

UCLP Service Constraint 3. *Every LPO occurring as an input of the concatenate operation must be of the same bandwidth.*

More details about UCLP and data-aware properties can be found in [20].

3   Formalizing Data-Aware Properties with CTL-FO$^+$

The previous properties express constraints on the data and sequentiality of messages exchanged by a workflow. Therefore, a suitable representation of this pattern of messages is a Kripke structure which contains state variables that represent the content of the messages that are sent or received. Discarding intermediate states where no message is received or sent, a path in the system corresponds to a possible sequence of messages in a service interaction. Properties about message sequences become properties on sequences of states that can then be expressed using temporal logics.

3.1   Syntax and Semantics of CTL-FO$^+$

The Computation Tree Logic with Full First-order Quantification (CTL-FO$^+$) is an extension of the well-known temporal logic CTL [11] aimed at describing sequentialities in a finite-state system while allowing full quantification over values of its state variables. Its syntax is defined as follows:

Definition 1 (Syntax). *The language CTL-FO⁺ (Computation Tree Logic with general first-order quantification) is obtained by closing CTL under the following construction rules:*

1. *If x is a variable or a constant, and y is either a variable, a constant or a state variable, then $x = y$ is a CTL-FO⁺ formula;*
2. *If φ and ψ are CTL-FO⁺ formulæ, then $\neg\varphi$, $\varphi \wedge \psi$, $\varphi \vee \psi$, $\varphi \rightarrow \psi$, $\mathbf{AG}\,\varphi$, $\mathbf{EG}\,\varphi$, $\mathbf{AF}\,\varphi$, $\mathbf{EF}\,\varphi$, $\mathbf{AX}\,\varphi$, $\mathbf{EX}\,\varphi$, $\mathbf{A}\,\varphi\,\mathbf{U}\,\psi$, $\mathbf{E}\,\varphi\,\mathbf{U}\,\psi$, are CTL-FO⁺ formulæ;*
3. *If φ is a CTL-FO⁺ formula and x is a free variable in φ, then $\exists x : \varphi(x)$ and $\forall x : \varphi(x)$ are CTL-FO⁺ formulæ.*

As usual [11], semantics can be defined in terms of the adequate set of operators $\exists$, $\mathbf{AF}$, $\mathbf{EX}$ and $\mathbf{EU}$, $\neg$ and $\vee$:

Definition 2 (Semantics). *Let $K = (S, I, R, L)$ be a Kripke structure, with S the set of states, I the set of initial states, $R \subseteq S^2$ the transition relation and L a labelling of states. Let $s_0 \in S$ be a state. Define a path $\pi = s_0, s_1, \ldots$ as a sequence of states in S such that $(s_i, s_{i+1}) \in R$ for every $i \geq 0$. Let $D_s(x)$ be the (finite) set of possible values for a quantified variable x in state s, p be some state variable in K and c_1 and c_2 be constants. We say the pair K, s_0 satisfies the CTL-FO⁺ formula φ if and only if it respects the following rules:*

$$K, s_0 \models p = c_1 \Leftrightarrow p \text{ is equal to } c_1 \text{ in state } s_0$$
$$K, s_0 \models c_1 = c_2 \Leftrightarrow c_1 \text{ is equal to } c_2$$
$$K, s_0 \models \neg\varphi \Leftrightarrow K, s_0 \not\models \varphi$$
$$K, s_0 \models \varphi \vee \psi \Leftrightarrow K, s_0 \models \varphi \text{ or } K, s_0 \models \psi$$
$$K, s_0 \models \mathbf{AF}\,\varphi \Leftrightarrow \text{for each } \pi = s_0 s_1 s_2 \ldots, K, s_i \models \varphi \text{ for some } i$$
$$K, s_0 \models \mathbf{EX}\,\varphi \Leftrightarrow \text{there exists } \pi = s_0 s_1 s_2 \ldots \text{ such that } K, s_1 \models \varphi$$
$$K, s_0 \models \mathbf{E}\,\varphi\,\mathbf{U}\,\psi \Leftrightarrow \text{there exists } \pi = s_0 s_1 s_2 \ldots \text{ such that } K, s_j \models \psi \text{ for some } j$$
$$\text{and } K, s_i \models \varphi \text{ for } i < j$$
$$K, s_0 \models \exists x\,\varphi(x) \Leftrightarrow \text{there exists } a \in D_{s_0}(x) \text{ such that } K, s_0 \models \varphi(a)$$

By extension, we write $K \models \varphi$ if the initial state s of K is such that $K, s \models \varphi$.

The values of the variables appearing in a CTL-FO⁺ formula are quantified according to specific elements of the XML message that is received or sent in the current state of the system. To indicate this, we add a subscript to the quantifier indicating the name of the element. A quantifier like $\forall_{\text{LPO-ID}}x$ therefore means "for all values x of elements named LPO-ID in the current message". Therefore, the domain of a variable depends on the content of the current message, which in turn depends on the current state of the system. By extension, we write $D(x)$ to designate the union of the $D_s(x)$ for all $s \in S$.

Using such notation, UCLP Service Constraint 1 becomes the following CTL-FO⁺ formula:

UCLP Formal Service Constraint 1

$$\mathbf{AG}\,(\forall_{operation}\,x_1 : x_1 = concatenateRequest \rightarrow$$
$$\forall_{LPO\text{-}ID}\,x_2 : \mathbf{AX}\,\mathbf{AG}\,(\forall_{operation}\,x_3 :$$
$$x_3 = partitionRequest \rightarrow \forall_{LPO\text{-}ID}\,x_4 : x_2 \neq x_4))$$

This formula states that at any time in any execution of the process, if the operation x_1 of the message is concatenateRequest, then for every LPO ID x_2 appearing in this message, we have that for every future message whose operation element value x_3 is partitionRequest, any value x_4 for its LPO ID is different from x_2. In other words, once an LPO has been concatenated, no further partition involves this LPO, which is indeed equivalent to UCLP Service Constraint 1. UCLP Service Constraints 2 and 3 can be formalized into similar CTL-FO$^+$ formulæ.

We are only aware of a limited number of works related to data-awareness in temporal properties. CTL-FO$^+$ is reminiscent of EQCTL that extends CTL by allowing existential quantification over *state variables* [27]. EQCTL is not closed under negation; therefore, universal quantification cannot be obtained; moreover, CTL-FO$^+$ quantifies over *values* and is closer to true first-order quantification. QCTL [31] extends CTL by including first-order quantification and monadic second-order quantification over arbitrary *algebraic data structures*. Such expressiveness is not required in our case. Specifications using XQuery on traces (SXQT) are defined in [34], but the approach allows the validation of one specific trace at a time; graph transformation rules [21] allow the description of data modifications but lack the ability to express temporal modalities; a logic called CTL-FO is introduced in [14], but its general model checking problem is shown to be undecidable. CTL-FO$^+$ generalizes CTL-FO by allowing free use of the existential quantifier.

3.2   Model Checking CTL-FO$^+$ Properties

Now that we have shown how data-aware properties can be expressed in CTL-FO$^+$, the next question is how to efficiently perform the model checking of these formulæ. We first establish the complexity of the problem with the following theorem.

Theorem 1. *Let $K = (S, I, R, L)$ be a Kripke structure modelling a particular web service and φ be a CTL-FO$^+$ formula. The problem of deciding whether $K \models \varphi$ is PSPACE-complete.*

Proof. PSPACE-hardness is obtained by reduction to the Quantified Boolean Formula (QBF) problem [17]; it suffices to observe that a QBF is by definition a CTL-FO$^+$ formula. A model checking algorithm can be devised in a straightforward manner from the classical CTL model checking algorithm. This algorithm performs a structural recursion on the formula and computes a set of states depending on the top-level operator. It suffices to add an additional case to the algorithm when the top-level operator is a quantifier of the form $\exists x\,\varphi(x)$. The algorithm simply calls itself on $\varphi(x)$ for every possible value of the variable x and computes the union of all sets of states returned by each such call. Every recursive call of the algorithm returns a subset of S and the height of the stack is bounded by $|\varphi|$, the length of φ. Since domains are considered finite, the total space consumed is polynomial in $|\varphi|$.   □

Although CTL-FO$^+$ is a generalization of CTL-FO mentioned above, we apply it on a simpler model of workflows that makes its model checking decidable. In particular, since all UCLP properties only involve equality between values, finitely many symbols are needed to handle infinite domains. This result shows that CTL-FO$^+$ is a generalization of CTL, whose model checking is in P. Therefore, existing web service tools and model checkers cannot be used as is to validate data aware properties. However, one can easily use the semantics definition of the existential operator and explicitly enumerate all possible values $k_1, k_2, \ldots, k_n$ in the domain D of the quantified variable. The universally quantified formula $\forall x : \mathbf{AG}\,(a = x \rightarrow \mathbf{AF}\,b = x)$ hence becomes:

$$\mathbf{AG}\,(a = k_1 \rightarrow \mathbf{AF}\,b = k_1) \wedge \mathbf{AG}\,(a = k_2 \rightarrow \mathbf{AF}\,b = k_2)$$
$$\wedge \cdots \wedge \mathbf{AG}\,(a = k_n \rightarrow \mathbf{AF}\,b = k_n)$$

The resulting expression is a plain CTL formula where all references to data are now static, which amounts to extending the message alphabet. This approach has already been suggested in Section 1 and has been called "explicit quantification". However, the next theorem shows that this construction is unlikely to be optimal.

Theorem 2. *If there exists a polynomial reduction of CTL-FO$^+$ model checking to CTL model checking, then $P = NP$.*

Proof. Suppose that that for every Kripke structure K and every CTL-FO$^+$ formula φ, there exists a polynomial translation of K into a Kripke structure K' and a polynomial translation of φ into a CTL formula φ'. Since CTL model checking is in P [11], and that P $\subseteq$ PSPACE [17, sect. 7.4], then from Theorem 1 PSPACE $\subseteq$ P, which can be true only if P $=$ NP.   □

4   An Efficient Reduction of CTL-FO$^+$ to CTL

Theorem 2 seems to indicate that in fact, *any* attempt to use standard model checkers to validate data-aware workflow properties is "doomed" to an exponential blow-up of the original problem, and not only the explicit quantification method suggested above. In this section, we show an alternate translation of the CTL-FO$^+$ model checking problem to CTL which, while still in EXPTIME, performs much better.

The method employed to achieve this result uses a technique called "freeze quantification" where additional variables can be added to a Kripke structure that can be used to "freeze" the value of a state variable at some point in the execution for future reference. It has been originally developed in [3] for timed transitions systems and further studied in [13]. [19] used this technique to reduce a subset of XPath to CTL. We proceed in two steps: first, we show how to convert a Kripke structure $K = (S, I, R, L)$ and a CTL-FO$^+$ formula φ to a Kripke structure $K_\varphi = (S', I', R', L')$; then, we show how a CTL-FO$^+$ formula φ can be translated to a CTL formula φ' and show that φ is true for K if and only if φ' is true for K_φ, thereby reducing the problem of CTL-FO$^+$ model checking to CTL model checking.

4.1   Transforming a Kripke Structure

Set of system states. The principle consists in adding to the original Kripke structure one system variable for each distinct quantified variable appearing in the CTL-FO$^+$ formula to validate. These variables are called the "freeze" variables, since they are intended to capture the value of some part of a message at a given point in the execution of the workflow. For example, to validate UCLP Formal Service Constraint 1, four additional variables are needed corresponding to the variables x_1 to x_4 in the CTL-FO$^+$ formula. At the start of any execution sequence, these variables take a special value noted $\#$ that indicates they have not yet taken any "real" value.

The domain of each freeze variable is dependent on the message part on which they are defined; in the previous example, the freeze variable x_1 is defined on operation elements; its domain is the set of all values appearing inside such elements somewhere in the process. In contrast, the freeze variable x_2 is defined on elements of name LPO-ID; its domain is the set of all possible values that can occur in this part of any message during the process. The computation of the domain of each variable is an easy task that can be statically computed on the original BPEL process; most web service validation tools can perform it automatically.

Formally, if we let $D(x_1), D(x_2), \ldots, D(x_n)$ be the respective domains of freeze variables $x_1, x_2, \ldots, x_n$, the set S' of states in K_φ is defined as $S' = S \times D(x_1) \times D(x_2) \ldots D(x_n)$. That is, the new Kripke structure is simply the extension of the original system to the n freeze variables. Consequently, we say that state $s' \in S'$ is an *extension* of $s \in S$ if all the non-freeze variables have the same values in both states; conversely, s is the (unique) *restriction* of s'.

The initial state of K_φ is defined uniquely by choosing the state s for which all non-freeze variables are identical as in the initial state of K, and where all freeze variables take the value $\#$.

Transition relation. We then define the transition relation of K_φ in the following way. In all states of the system where no message is sent or received, the transitions are left untouched. The internal variables of the model can change value in the same way as in the original Kripke structure, while all the freeze variables do not change. That is, if $s, t \in S$, $(s', t') \in S'$ and s' and t' are respective extensions of s and t such that all freeze variables have the same values in both s' and t', and s is a state where no BPEL communicating activity (invoke, receive or reply) occurs, then $(s, t) \in R$ if and only if $(s', t') \in R'$.

Let us now consider the case of a state of the model where a message is either sent or received. Such a state is exploded in the resulting Kripke structure into two phases: in the first phase, the non-freeze variables can change according to the original transition relation as described previously, while the freeze variables stay the same. Once these changes are made, the system enters into a "freezing" phase where the roles are reversed: the non-freeze variables keep their values, and some freeze variables can change in a specific way.

In the freezing phase, a freeze variable can stay undefined, or take the value of some part of the *current* message. It is important to remark that the variables can only be assigned values corresponding to the message part on which they are defined. Consider for example the sequence formed of a partitionRequest and a partitionResponse XML messages as shown in Table 1. In the first message of the pattern, variable x_1 can only take the value "partitionRequest", since x_1 is defined in UCLP Formal Service Constraint 1 as a variable on root element names. In the same way, x_2 can only take the value i, since x_2 is defined as a variable on elements of name <LPO-ID>. In the second message, x_2 can take the values $i_1, \ldots, i_n$.

The actual value assigned to either of these special variables in each state is non-deterministic. In addition, each variable may or may not take a value –that is, variables can stay undefined. However, once a variable has taken a defined value, it keeps this value for the remainder of the execution trace.

The exit from the freezing phase is also non-deterministic. The system loops any number of times into the freezing phase of a given state and then comes out and resumes its execution as specified by the original transition relation.

Formally, let $s \in S$ be a state of the model where an `invoke`, `receive` or `reply` occurs and $s' \in S'$ be an extension of s. Let x_i be a freeze variable and $v \in D_s(x_i)$. Let $t \in S$ be a state such that $(s,t) \in R$ and $t' \in S'$. Then $(s',t') \in S'$ if and only if t' is an extension of s or an extension of t, $x_i = \#$ in s', $x_i = v$ in t' and for all $1 \leq j \leq n$, if $i \neq j$, x_j does not change between s' and t'. We must then show that these modifications preserves the behaviour of the original model.

Theorem 3. *Let π' be an execution in K_φ, and let π'' be the sequence of states in S obtained by taking the reduction of π'. There exists an execution π in K such that π'' and π are stuttering equivalent.*

Proof. By construction, every transition (s_1', s_2') in K_φ that does not enter or leave a freezing phase is the extension of some transition (s_1, s_2) in K. It remains to observe that any sequence of states $t_1, \ldots, t_i$ in a freezing phase in K_φ leaves all non-freeze variables unchanged; therefore, the reduction of that sequence is nothing but the repetition of the same state in K, i times. It follows that π'' is the same sequence of states as some execution π in K, with the possible exception that some states are repeated a finite number of times, thus leading to stuttering equivalence. □

4.2   Converting a CTL-FO⁺ Formula

Once the Kripke structure has been modified in the previously described manner, the conversion of a CTL-FO⁺ formula into a standard CTL formula becomes straightforward.

We define a linear embedding ω of CTL-FO⁺ into CTL formulæ. Let φ and ψ be CTL-FO⁺ formulæ, c be a constant in V, m and n be message part names in N, and the x_i be quantified variables in the CTL-FO⁺ formula. Translating the Boolean connectives and the ground equality testings is direct.

The quantification on variables becomes a quantification on some execution paths. In effect, a quantifier like $\forall x : \varphi(x)$ actually means "for all possible values x can take in the current state, $\varphi(x)$ holds". According to the Kripke structure K_φ defined previously, this simply amounts to asserting that in the current state, for all possible ways for x of changing from # to some definite value, φ is true, which becomes the following translation:

$$\omega(\forall_n x_i : \varphi) \equiv (x_i = \# \to \mathbf{AX}\,(x_i \neq \# \to \omega(\varphi))) \tag{1}$$

Similarly, a quantifier like $\exists x : \varphi(x)$ actually means "there exists a value x can take in the current state such that $\varphi(x)$ holds". According to the Kripke structure K_φ defined previously, this simply amounts to asserting that in the current state, there exists a way for x of changing from # to some definite value where φ is true. This becomes the following translation:

$$\omega(\exists_n x_i : \varphi) \equiv (x_i = \# \to \mathbf{EX}\,(x_i \neq \# \wedge \omega(\varphi))) \tag{2}$$

The translation of the CTL temporal operators is also direct, except for the next quantifiers $\mathbf{AX}$ and $\mathbf{EX}$. The next state state in K is not necessarily the next state in K_φ because of the possible freeze loops that may put two consecutive states in K arbitrarily far apart in K_φ. However, it is possible to work around this by asserting that the next state in K is mirrored by the next *non-freezing* state in K_φ. We obtain:

$$\omega(\mathbf{AX}\,\varphi) \equiv \mathbf{A}\,\gamma\mathbf{U}\,\omega(\varphi) \tag{3}$$
$$\omega(\mathbf{EX}\,\varphi) \equiv \mathbf{E}\,\gamma\mathbf{U}\,\omega(\varphi) \tag{4}$$

where γ is an additional Boolean variable that is true whenever the system is in a freezing phase, and false otherwise. Formula (3) hence asserts that in K_φ, as soon as the system gets out of the current freezing phase (if any), φ must be true.

Using this embedding, UCLP Formal Constraint 1 is recursively translated to the following CTL expression.

$$
\begin{aligned}
\mathbf{AG}\,(x_1 = \# \to (\mathbf{AX}\,(x_1 \neq \# \to \\
(x_2 = \# \to (\mathbf{AX}\,(x_2 \neq \# \to \\
x_1 = \text{partitionRequest} \to \\
\mathbf{AX}\,\mathbf{AG}\,(x_3 = \# \to (\mathbf{AX}\,(x_3 \neq \# \to \\
(x_4 = \# \to (\mathbf{AX}\,(x_4 \neq \# \to \\
x_3 = \text{concatenateRequest} \to x_2 \neq x_4))))))))))))))
\end{aligned}
\tag{5}
$$

We do not expect data aware constraints to be expressed directly in CTL in such a way. However, the translation from CTL-FO$^+$ to CTL can be automated, and the next theorem shows that the overall construction preserves the validity of the original problem.

Theorem 4. *Let K be a Kripke structure, φ be a CTL-FO$^+$ formula, K_φ be a converted Kripke structure and $\varphi' = \omega(\varphi)$. Then φ is true for K if and only if φ' is true for K_φ.*

We only sketch the proof here, which is done by induction on the structure of the formula. By Theorem 3, we know that reachability of states is preserved when converting K to K_φ. It remains to show that an assignment ρ of values to the freeze variables $x_1, \ldots, x_n$ is true for φ in K if and only if it is true for φ' in K_φ, which can be realized by observing the definition of the freeze transitions.

Contrarily to explicit quantification, the freeze quantification approach does not cause an exponential blow-up of the original formula. The embedding ω is linear: that is, if we denote by $|\varphi|$ the length of a CTL-FO$^+$ formula φ, then $|\omega(\varphi)| \in O(|\varphi|)$. It suffices to remark that each translation rule consumes at least one symbol of the original CTL-FO$^+$ formula and contributes a fixed number of symbols in the resulting CTL formula.

5   Experimental Results

To confirm the soundness of our approach, we conducted a set of experiments that involved the validation of UCLP constraints detailed in Section 2 on sample BPEL processes taken from real-world UCLP use cases. The goal of these experiments was to show that validating UCLP constraints can be effectively done using the freeze quantification solution presented in this paper. Furthermore, we also show that the explicit model checking approach quickly becomes inadequate for these properties.

5.1   Methodology

The experiments were made using only readily available and open source tools. NuSMV [10] was chosen as the model checker because of its robustness, good performance, and especially its capability of model checking CTL formulæ. VER-BUS [4] was chosen to generate the Kripke structure from the original BPEL processes; the choice was influenced mostly by its ability to model the content of variables and messages in a process and its capability to directly output the Kripke structure as an SMV file. Only minor bug-solving modifications were made to the original code of VERBUS to make it work in our situation. The modified version of VERBUS, a compiled copy of NuSMV, the BPEL modification routines and all the files used in the experiments are released under the GNU GPL.[3]

---

[3] All the material is available from
   http://www.teleinfo.uqam.ca/Members/halle_sylvain/uclp

The SMV files produced by VERBUS were then modified according either to the explicit quantification or the freeze approach. In the explicit quantification, no modification other than appending the desired CTL formula at the end of the file was made. In the freeze approach, freeze variables and freeze transitions were added throughout the file, and the corresponding CTL formula was also added at the end.

5.2   Results and Discussion

We then proceeded to this method successively with sample BPEL processes. Each process consisted in one concatenation and one partition of a given number of LPOs. For $n = 1$, the result of all operations in the process is deterministic: for example, the partition operation with LPO A always returns the same LPO IDs B, C, D. We then varied this number n of LPOs by making the operations non-deterministically return IDs taken from a set of possible values. This generalization of the process is a natural step to take, since a UCLP operation on an LPO is dependent of the global situation of the UCLP network and therefore need not return the same value in every invocation.

The validation times for the freeze and the explicit quantification approaches are presented in Table 2, for each UCLP formal constraint, for BPEL processes with n ranging from 1 to 4. Similarly, the size of the NuSMV file required to validate the process is shown in Table 3. All times have been obtained with NuSMV 2.4.0 on an AMD Athlon 2200+ CPU running under Windows XP. Since NuSMV takes several dozens of seconds only to display the explicitly quantified formulæ, this time was not included in the results.

Table 2. Validation time (in seconds) of sample BPEL processes with UCLP constraints, using respectively the freeze and the explicit quantification approach

Constraint	Freeze quantification					Explicit quantification				
	$n=1$	$n=2$	$n=3$	$n=4$	$n=5$	$n=1$	$n=2$	$n=3$	$n=4$	$n=5$
1	1.5	1.9	4.5	5.4	8.7	0.2	0.3	0.4	0.4	0.5
2	1.6	2.2	4.4	5.4	9.2	13	36	101	222	884
3	1.8	2.2	4.6	5.8	9.3	—	—	—	—	—

These figures confirm what was suggested in Section 3.2: using explicit quantification to produce the CTL formula quickly takes its toll on the validation time. As expected, the translation of the CTL-FO$^+$ formula is heavily dependent on n and grows exponentially. With UCLP operations returning only 5 different possible values, validation time takes almost 15 minutes. We could not get any times for UCLP Formal Constraint 3 since NuSMV crashed before reaching the end of the files, most probably due to their size. We did not dare to generate the formulæ for $n = 4$ and $n = 5$ that were expected to occupy more than 500 Mb each. Comparatively, the freeze approach requires only minimal modifications to the original NuSMV file produced by VERBUS; most importantly, these

Table 3. File size (in kilobytes) of the NuSMV files for the validation of sample BPEL processes with UCLP constraints, using respectively the freeze and the explicit quantification approach

Constraint	Freeze quantification					Explicit quantification				
	$n = 1$	$n = 2$	$n = 3$	$n = 4$	$n = 5$	$n = 1$	$n = 2$	$n = 3$	$n = 4$	$n = 5$
1	30.3	30.5	30.6	30.7	30.8	237	299	368	445	529
2	33.9	34.0	34.2	34.3	34.5	10542	18156	29249	47939	70509
3	34.8	35.0	35.1	35.3	35.5	111597	198831	329075	—	—

modifications are constant and do not depend on n. The increase in the file size is only due to the addition of the non-deterministic transitions required when incrementing n. Validation time, no matter the property, exhibits the same behaviour and grows much more reasonably: the 884 seconds required to validate property 2 with $n = 5$ in the explicit quantification is improved by a factor 80 and falls to less than 10 seconds using the freeze approach.

These trends do not hold for UCLP Formal Service Constraint 1 where the explicit quantification approach fares better than the freeze approach. This can be explained by the fact that the addition of freeze variables and transitions imposes an initial overhead on the Kripke structure that the explicit quantification does not have. Since in this situation, the CTL formulæ to validate are only a few hundred kilobytes long, they can be considered too small to represent a serious load on the model checker.

6   Conclusions

In this paper, we have shown that the composition of User-Controlled Lightpath resources is subject to constraints involving both the sequentiality of messages and the content of these messages. We have demonstrated how current traditional model checking approaches to the validation of web service workflows are insufficient for the validation of UCLP scripts subject to these kinds of constraints. We have demonstrated by empirical testing on real-world BPEL processes how an extension of CTL called CTL-FO$^+$ can be used to effectively model these complex workflow properties; we showed how a suitable reduction of CTL-FO$^+$ to CTL can be used to validate them in reasonable time compared to classical approaches.

The success of this project opens the way for future developments. First, we plan to integrate the automated generation of freeze variables and transitions directly into VERBUS. Second, it is possible to expand the range of expressiveness of CTL-FO$^+$ formulæ by taking into account not only the values inside XML messages exchanged by a BPEL process, but also their hierarchical organization into trees, thereby embedding into CTL-FO$^+$ a subset of a tree language like XPath.

References

1. The Edinburgh concurrency workbench
2. Alonso, G., Casati, F., Kuno, H., Machiraju, V.: Web Services, Concepts, Architectures and Applications. Springer, Heidelberg (2004)
3. Alur, R., Henzinger, T.A.: A really temporal logic. J. ACM 41(1), 181–204 (1994)
4. Arias-Fisteus, J., Fernández, L.S., Kloos, C.D.: Applying model checking to BPEL4WS business collaborations. In: Haddad, H., Liebrock, L.M., Omicini, A., Wainwright, R.L. (eds.) SAC, pp. 826–830. ACM, New York (2005)
5. Berardi, D., Calvanese, D., De Giacomo, G., Hull, R., Mecella, M.: Automatic composition of transition-based semantic web services with messaging. In: Böhm,, et al. (eds.) [6], pp. 613–624
6. Böhm, K., Jensen, C.S., Haas, L.M., Kersten, M.L., Larson, P.-Å., Ooi, B.C. (eds.): Proceedings of the 31st International Conference on Very Large Data Bases, Trondheim, Norway, August 30 - September 2, 2005. ACM, New York (2005)
7. Bravetti, M., Núñez, M., Zavattaro, G. (eds.): WS-FM 2006. LNCS, vol. 4184. Springer, Heidelberg (2006)
8. Brogi, A., Canal, C., Pimentel, E., Vallecillo, A.: Formalizing web service choreographies. Electr. Notes Theor. Comput. Sci. 105, 73–94 (2004)
9. Bultan, T., Fu, X., Hull, R., Su, J.: Conversation specification: a new approach to design and analysis of e-service composition. In: WWW, pp. 403–410 (2003)
10. Cimatti, A., Clarke, E.M., Giunchiglia, E., Giunchiglia, F., Pistore, M., Roveri, M., Sebastiani, R., Tacchella, A.: NuSMV 2: An opensource tool for symbolic model checking. In: Brinksma, E., Larsen, K.G. (eds.) CAV 2002. LNCS, vol. 2404, pp. 359–364. Springer, Heidelberg (2002)
11. Clarke, E.M., Grumberg, O., Peled, D.A.: Model Checking. MIT Press, Cambridge (2000)
12. Decker, G., Zaha, J.M., Dumas, M.: Execution semantics for service choreographies. In: Bravetti, et al. (eds.) [7], pp. 163–177
13. Demri, S., Lazic, R., Nowak, D.: On the freeze quantifier in constraint LTL: Decidability and complexity. In: TIME, pp. 113–121. IEEE Computer Society, Los Alamitos (2005)
14. Deutsch, A., Sui, L., Vianu, V.: Specification and verification of data-driven web services. In: Deutsch, A. (ed.) PODS, pp. 71–82. ACM, New York (2004)
15. Duan, Z., Bernstein, A.J., Lewis, P.M., Lu, S.: A model for abstract process specification, verification and composition. In: Aiello, M., Aoyama, M., Curbera, F., Papazoglou, M.P. (eds.) ICSOC, pp. 232–241. ACM, New York (2004)
16. Foster, H., Uchitel, S., Magee, J., Kramer, J.: Model-based analysis of obligations in web service choreography. In: AICT/ICIW, p. 149. IEEE Computer Society, Los Alamitos (2006)
17. Garey, M.R., Johnson, D.S.: Computers and intractability, a guide to the theory of NP-completeness. W. H. Freeman, San Francisco (1979)
18. Greenfield, P., Kuo, D., Nepal, S., Fekete, A.: Consistency for web services applications. In: Böhm,, et al. (eds.) [6], pp. 1199–1203
19. Hallé, S., Villemaire, R., Cherkaoui, O.: CTL model checking for labelled tree queries. In: TIME, pp. 27–35. IEEE Computer Society, Los Alamitos (2006)
20. Hallé, S., Villemaire, R., Cherkaoui, O., Ghandour, B.: Model-checking data-aware temporal workflow properties with CTL-FO+. In: EDOC, pp. 267–278. IEEE Computer Society, Los Alamitos (2007)

21. Heckel, R., Mariani, L.: Automatic conformance testing of web services. In: Cerioli, M. (ed.) FASE 2005. LNCS, vol. 3442, pp. 34–48. Springer, Heidelberg (2005)
22. Hinz, S., Schmidt, K., Stahl, C.: Transforming BPEL to Petri nets. In: van der Aalst, W.M.P., Benatallah, B., Casati, F., Curbera, F. (eds.) BPM 2005. LNCS, vol. 3649, pp. 220–235. Springer, Heidelberg (2005)
23. Holzmann, G.J.: The SPIN Model Checker: Primer and Reference Manual. Addison-Wesley Professional, Reading (2003)
24. Johnson, J.E., Langworthy, D.E., Lamport, L., Vogt, F.H.: Formal specification of a web services protocol. Electr. Notes Theor. Comput. Sci. 105, 147–158 (2004)
25. Kazhamiakin, R., Pistore, M., Santuari, L.: Analysis of communication models in web service compositions. In: Carr, L., Roure, D.D., Iyengar, A., Goble, C.A., Dahlin, M. (eds.) WWW, pp. 267–276. ACM, New York (2006)
26. Koshkina, M., van Breugel, F.: Modelling and verifying web service orchestration by means of the concurrency workbench. ACM SIGSOFT SEN 29(5) (September 2004)
27. Kupferman, O.: Augmenting branching temporal logics with existential quantification over atomic propositions. In: Wolper, P. (ed.) CAV 1995. LNCS, vol. 939, pp. 325–338. Springer, Heidelberg (1995)
28. Lohmann, N., Massuthe, P., Stahl, C., Weinberg, D.: Analyzing interacting BPEL processes. In: Dustdar, S., Fiadeiro, J.L., Sheth, A.P. (eds.) BPM 2006. LNCS, vol. 4102, pp. 17–32. Springer, Heidelberg (2006)
29. Nakajima, S.: Model-checking of safety and security aspects in web service flows. In: Koch, N., Fraternali, P., Wirsing, M. (eds.) ICWE 2004. LNCS, vol. 3140, pp. 488–501. Springer, Heidelberg (2004)
30. Pistore, M., Roveri, M., Busetta, P.: Requirements-driven verification of web services. Electr. Notes Theor. Comput. Sci. 105, 95–108 (2004)
31. Rensink, A.: Model checking quantified computation tree logic. In: Baier, C., Hermanns, H. (eds.) CONCUR 2006. LNCS, vol. 4137, pp. 110–125. Springer, Heidelberg (2006)
32. Turner, K.J.: Formalising web services. In: Wang, F. (ed.) FORTE 2005. LNCS, vol. 3731, pp. 473–488. Springer, Heidelberg (2005)
33. van der Aalst, W.M.P., Pesic, M.: DecSerFlow: Towards a truly declarative service flow language. In: Bravetti et al.(eds.) [7], pp. 1–23
34. Venzke, M.: Specifications using XQuery expressions on traces. Electr. Notes Theor. Comput. Sci. 105, 109–118 (2004)
35. Zaha, J.M., Dumas, M., ter Hofstede, A., Barros, A., Decker, G.: Service interaction modeling: Bridging global and local views. In: EDOC, pp. 45–55. IEEE Computer Society, Los Alamitos (2006)

Analyzing BPEL4Chor:
Verification and Participant Synthesis

Niels Lohmann[1], Oliver Kopp[2], Frank Leymann[2], and Wolfgang Reisig[3]

[1] Universität Rostock, Institut für Informatik, 18051 Rostock, Germany
niels.lohmann@uni-rostock.de
[2] Institute of Architecture of Application Systems, University of Stuttgart, Germany
Universitätsstraße 38, 70569 Stuttgart, Germany
{kopp, leymann}@iaas.uni-stuttgart.de
[3] Humboldt-Universität zu Berlin, Institut für Informatik,
Unter den Linden 6, 10099 Berlin, Germany
reisig@informatik.hu-berlin.de

Abstract. Choreographies offer means to capture global interactions between business processes of different partners. BPEL4Chor has been introduced to describe these interactions using BPEL. Currently, there are no formal methods available to verify BPEL4Chor choreographies. In this paper, we present how BPEL4Chor choreographies can be verified using Petri nets. A case study undermines that our verification techniques scale. Additionally, we show how the verification techniques can be used to generate a stub process for a partner taking part in a choreography. This is especially useful when the behavior of one participant is intended to follow the corresponding requirements of the other participants. Thus, the missing participant behavior can be generated and the error-prone design of that participant can be skipped.

Keywords: BPEL4Chor, choreography, participant generation, Petri nets, service-oriented analysis and design.

1 Introduction

The Web Services Business Process Execution Language (WS-BPEL or BPEL for short, [1]) is the de facto standard to describe executable business processes as orchestrations of Web services. A *choreography* describes the interaction of several processes from a global perspective. In particular, it defines the order in which processes exchange messages. BPEL4Chor [2] is a choreography language based on BPEL. Each participant is associated with a *participant behavior description* (PBD) that describes the participant's behavior using abstract BPEL. The interconnection between the activities of different PBDs is formed by message links.

In this paper, we show how an existing tool chain [3,4] can be extended to analyze a BPEL4Chor choreography (Fig. 1). By mapping BPEL4Chor to Petri nets, we also provide a formal model for BPEL4Chor.

M. Dumas and R. Heckel (Eds.): WS-FM 2007, LNCS 4937, pp. 46–60, 2008.

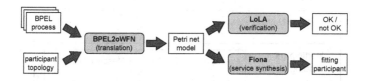

Fig. 1. Proposed tool chain to analyze BPEL4Chor choreographies

If two business partners agree on a choreography, but need a third business partner to achieve their goal, they also have to specify the behavior of the third party. We show how the behavior of the third party can be derived from existing participants in a choreography. The current algorithms assure deadlock-freedom for the synthesized participant if such a participant exists. We are aware that there are other possibilities for defining "proper interaction". Nevertheless, deadlock-free communication will certainly be part of any more sophisticated correctness definition, so the presented approach can be seen as a step towards a more sophisticated solution.

Section 2 introduces BPEL4Chor and open workflow nets (oWFNs), which are used to capture the semantics of BPEL4Chor. After presenting in Sect. 3 how BPEL4Chor can be translated into oWFNs, Sect. 4 shows how a BPEL4Chor choreography can be analyzed theoretically. Section 5 puts that analysis into practice and shows how the proposed tool chain is used to analyze a BPEL4Chor choreography and that it scales up to 1,000 participants. Finally, Sect. 6 concludes, compares the presented work with related work, and describes future research directions.

2   Background and Motivation

A choreography described by BPEL4Chor consists of (i) the participant topology, (ii) the participant behavior descriptions, and (iii) the participant groundings (cf. Fig. 2 and [2]). The participant topology lists all participants taking part in the choreography and all message links connecting activities of different participants. A message link states that a message is sent from the source of the message link to its target. Every participant has a certain type. For each participant type, a participant behavior description (PBD) defined in BPEL is given. In this description, port types and operations are omitted and thus the dependency on interface specifications such as WSDL [5] is removed. If the choreography has to be executed, every target of a message link has to be grounded to a WSDL operation so that the other participants can use the offered operation. This grounding is done after the choreography design itself, which enables choreography specification reuse. Since BPEL is used to specify the behavior of every participant, the development of executable BPEL processes following this behavior can be done by using the PBD of a participant as a basis and adding missing information. Other languages can be used to provide implementations of local behavior, but using BPEL is a seamless choice based on BPEL4Chor.

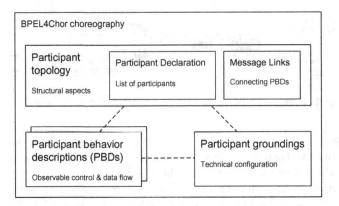

Fig. 2. BPEL4Chor artifacts ([2])

A choreography always describes the behavior of all participants. Thus, a *closed world* is assumed. Refer to the booking scenario in Fig. 3. A traveler requests booking of a flight at a travel agency. The travel agency requests a price quote from every airline in a set of airlines. The cheapest airline is selected and the tickets are ordered there. The airline replies with a confirmation and sends an electronic ticket directly to the traveler. There is no message going to an undefined participant. The observable behavior of all participants is specified. Note that BPMN [6] is used for visualization only. The choreography itself is specified using BPEL4Chor.

2.1 Open Workflow Nets

Open workflow nets (oWFNs) [7] are a special class of Petri nets. They generalize classical workflow nets [8] by introducing an interface for asynchronous message passing. Intuitively, an oWFN is a Petri net together with (i) an *interface*, consisting of input and output places, (ii) an initial marking m_0, and (iii) a set Ω of distinguished *final markings*. Final markings represent desired final states of the net and help to distinguish desired final states from unwanted deadlocks. Throughout this paper, we use the term 'deadlock' for a nonfinal marking which does not enable a transition (i. e., an unwanted blocking of the net). Figure 4 shows an oWFN modeling the traveler participant of the choreography depicted in Fig. 3.

The interplay of two oWFNs N and M is represented by their *composition*, denoted by $N \oplus M$. Thereby, we demand that the nets only share input and output places such that for some input places of N exist corresponding output places of M, and vice versa. The oWFN $N \oplus M$ can then be constructed by merging joint places and merging the initial and final markings. Merged places become internal to $N \oplus M$. Due to the closed world assumption in BPEL4Chor,

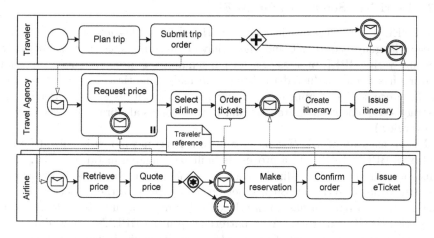

Fig. 3. Choreography of a Booking Scenario ([2])

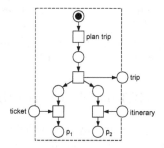

Fig. 4. An oWFN modeling the traveler participant. The interface consists of $P_{in} = \{ticket, itinerary\}$ and $P_{out} = \{trip\}$, depicted on the dashed frame. The traveler first plans the trip and then sends an order. Then, he concurrently receives a ticket and an itinerary. The set of final markings $\Omega = \{[p_1, p_2]\}$ consists of the single marking with one token on place p_1 and on p_2.

the composition of all oWFNs modeling services of a choreography results in a *closed* oWFN; that is, an oWFN with empty interface.

oWFNs provide a simple but formal foundation to model services and their interaction. They allow — like common Petri nets — for diverse analysis methods of computer-aided verification. The explicit modeling of the interface further allows to analyze the interaction behavior of a service [3,4]. An important property of an oWFN is whether it is possible to communicate deadlock-freely with it. An oWFN N is called *controllable*, if there exists an oWFN M such that $N \oplus M$ is free of deadlocks. Like the soundness property for workflow nets, controllability [9] can be regarded as a minimal correctness criterion for communicating services. Obviously, the net depicted in Fig. 4 is controllable.

2.2   Petri Net Semantics for BPEL

The BPEL [1] language provides an operational semantics defining the behavior of each language construct and the behavior of composites of constructs. To formally verify BPEL processes, a formal semantics is needed. Therefore, a lot of work has been conducted to define a formal semantics for the behavior of BPEL processes. The approaches cover many formalisms such as Petri nets, abstract state machines, finite state machines, process algebras, etc. (see [10] for an overview).

The translation of a BPEL process intro a Petri net model is guided by the syntax of BPEL. In BPEL, a process is built by plugging instances of language constructs together. Accordingly, each construct of the language is translated separately into a Petri net. Such a net forms a *pattern* of the respective BPEL construct. Each pattern has an interface for joining it with other patterns as is done with BPEL constructs. Also, patterns capturing BPEL's structured activities may carry any number of inner patterns as its equivalent in BPEL can do. The collection of patterns forms the *Petri net semantics* for BPEL. While the original semantics in [11] is feature complete (i. e., capturing both the standard as well as the exceptional behavior of a BPEL process), we only consider the positive control flow in this paper to ease the presentation. The presented approach can, however, be canonically enhanced to also model fault, compensation and exception handling of the participating BPEL processes.

3   Translating BPEL4Chor Choreographies into Petri Nets

To translate a BPEL4Chor choreography into a Petri net model, we extend the translation approach presented in [3]. Basically, the translation is enhanced to support *composition* and *instantiation*.

Composition. The tool chain presented in [3] is limited to the translation of a single process into a Petri net model. To translate BPEL4Chor, we translate the participating BPEL processes one by one and compose the resulting oWFNs. The information how input and output places of different processes are merged can be derived from the participant topology. As the composition of oWFNs is associative, the order of composition is not important. Furthermore, the resulting nets can be composed incrementally. Therefore, at most two nets have to be kept in memory during the translation process. Finally, structural reduction techniques can be applied already during the composition process. Not only the final composition, also the intermediate oWFNs can be reduced. This interleaving of structural reduction and composition does not only allow smaller nets, but also may speed up the translation process as the size of the composition grows more slowly.

Instantiation. The translation process is, however, not restricted to choreographies in which each process is instantiated just once. For instance, the choreography example presented in Fig. 3 models a choreography that communicates with a *set* of airlines. Again, the participant topology holds the necessary information about which process has to be instantiated. Admittedly, the topology does not provide the number of instances of each participant. We therefore demand an upper bound of instances to be specified for each participant set. While this upper bound may not be necessary when BPEL4Chor is just a means to *describe* choreographies, its definition is reasonable when such a choreography should be *analyzed*.

To introduce instantiation to the translation process, the following scenarios are possible:

i. message exchange between two uninstantiated participants (e. g., the trip order sent by the traveler to the agency),

ii. message exchange between an uninstantiated participant and one particular instantiated participant (e. g., the price request sent by the agency to an airline instance),

iii. message exchange between an uninstantiated participant and an arbitrary chosen instantiated participant (e. g., the e-ticket sent by the selected airline to the traveler), and

iv. message exchange between two instantiated participants (not present in our example choreography).

For an example of these scenarios, consider the BPEL code snippet of the agency process depicted in Fig. 5(a). For two airline instances, the resulting subnet is depicted in Fig. 5(b). The message trip sent by traveler to the agency is an example of the first scenario, as both services (traveler and agency) are uninstantiated. Therefore, the receipt of the trip message is modeled by a single transition, namely t_1. The price request sent to and the corresponding price quotes received from the airline instances are examples for the second scenario. Therefore, the communicating transitions (t_2–t_5) and the connected interface places (price.1, price.2, quote.1, and quote.2) are instantiated. The order sent to only one airline instance is an example for the third scenario.

Translating the example choreography. The presented translation approach was implemented in our compiler BPEL2oWFN[1]. BPEL2oWFN enables us to translate real-world BPEL choreographies into Petri net models. We translated the example choreography with five airline instances into a Petri net. The resulting net has 103 places and 81 transitions. Structural reduction simplified the net to 63 places and 41 transitions. The final marking of the composition is constructed canonically: it consists of the single state in which all participating services have completed faultlessly.

4   Analyzing BPEL4Chor Choreographies

In this section, we show how to analyze BPEL4Chor choreographies using Petri net models. We distinguish two analysis approaches: analysis of *closed* choreography models and analysis of *open* choreography models. A closed choreography

---

[1] BPEL2oWFN is available at www.gnu.org/software/bpel2owfn

(a) code snippet of the agency process   (b) resulting subnet of the agency oWFN

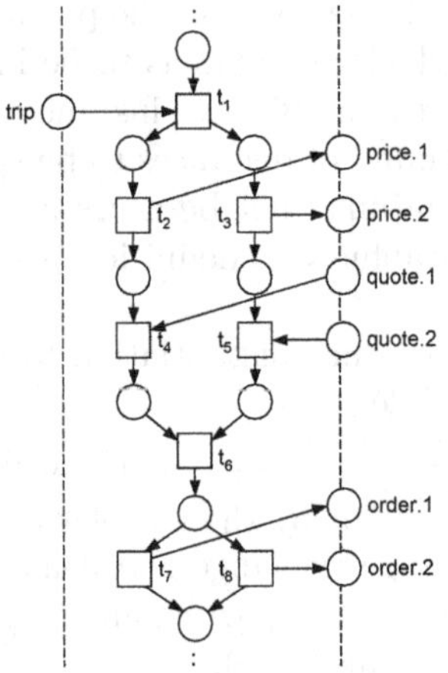

Fig. 5. Example for the instantiation of transitions and interface places. The BPEL process of the agency (a) is translated into an oWFN (b).

model (i. e., an oWFN with empty interface) can be analyzed in isolation and can be used to verify properties of a complete choreography. For example, deadlock-freedom or the absence of unwanted communication scenarios can be proven before the actual implementation and deployment of the participant services. In contrast, an open choreography model (i. e., an oWFN with nonempty interface) can be used during the design of the overall choreography. A choreography in which one participating service is missing can, for instance, be completed by synthesizing the missing participant service. This synthesized service is then guaranteed to participate deadlock-freely with the other participants.

4.1 Analyzing Closed Choreographies

Due to the closed-world assumption of BPEL4Chor, the resulting Petri net model of a completely specified BPEL4Chor choreography is a closed system; that is, a Petri net with empty interface. During the translation, each interface place of an intermediate oWFN, is merged with a corresponding interface place of another intermediate oWFN. Closed systems do not have an environment and thus their state space can be calculated and analyzed without considering the environment of the system. As Petri nets offer a broad variety of analysis methods, a lot of interesting properties can be investigated:

- Is the choreography free of deadlocks and livelocks? Will each participating service eventually reach a final state?
- Will a certain activity of a participant be executed? Does there exist a state in which more than one message is pending on a communication channel?
- What is the minimal/maximal number of messages to be sent to reach a final state of the choreography?

– Will a participant always receive an answer? Can a participant enforce the receipt of a certain message?

These questions can be formulated in terms of reachability or temporal logic properties and be checked using existing model checking tools.

Analyzing the example choreography. We analyzed the Petri net model of Sect. 3 with the Petri net verification tool LoLA [12], a state-of-the-art model checker which implements several state space reduction techniques. The unreduced state space consists of 3,843 states. The Petri net model contains an unwanted deadlock. We could map this deadlocking state of the model back to the participating services with the help of a *witness path*. A witness path is a transition sequence leading from the initial to the dead marking. The deadlock occurs in the choreography, when the agency's choice for an airline takes too much time, or when the message sent to the chosen airline is delayed. In this case, the timeout (i.e., the `onAlarm` branch) of all participating airlines ends their instances and the agency deadlocks waiting for a confirmation message from the chosen airline.

Correcting the example choreography. There are many ways to correct the deadlocking choreography. A straightforward attempt would be to replace the airline service's timeout by a message sent by the agency. This would, however, add an unrealistic dependency between the agency and the airline. To this end, we decided to keep the timeout, but at the same time ensure a response of the airline service even when a ticket order is received after the timeout.

Hence, we changed the choreography as follows (cf. gray shapes in Fig. 6). The airline's behavior does not change if the agency's ticket order is received before the timeout occurred and if the timeout occurs, the airline service's instance still

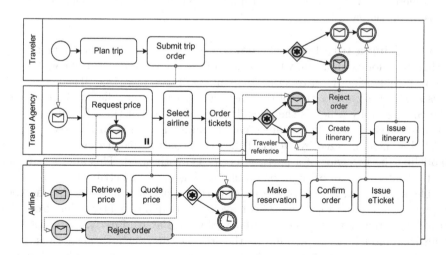

Fig. 6. Deadlock-free Choreography of a Booking Scenario. The two start events at the airline process denote a BPEL pick activity.

terminates. However, a new branch was added to the airline: this branch models the situation in which the agency's ticket order is received after the timeout. In this case, a new instance of the airline service is created which rejects the ticket order. The services of the agency and the traveler are adjusted to handle this rejection.

Analyzing the new example choreography. We translated the new choreography with five airline instances into a Petri net model. Due to the newly introduced activities, its structure and its state space have grown. The (structurally reduced) net has 113 places and 97 transitions. The model has 3,812 states and does not contain deadlocks except final states. With the help of LoLA, we could also verify that the choreography's participating services do not livelock and will always reach a final state.

4.2   Analyzing Open Choreographies

While the analysis of closed choreographies may help to find design flaws in the interaction between all participating services, Petri net models may also support the *design* of choreographies. To this end, controllability (cf. Sect. 2.1) is an important property. In [3], we presented an algorithm to decide controllability of an oWFN constructively. This algorithm is implemented in the tool Fiona[2]. If a partner exists such that the composition is deadlock-free, it is automatically generated.

Let $N_1, \ldots, N_{k-1}$ be the oWFNs of the already known participant services of an open choreography. Their composition, $N_1 \oplus \ldots \oplus N_{k-1}$, is an oWFN with nonempty interface. If this net is controllable, then there exists an oWFN N_k such that $N_1 \oplus \ldots \oplus N_{k-1} \oplus N_k$ is deadlock-free. Thus, Fiona can be used to "complete" a given open choreography by synthesizing the model N_k of the missing participant.

Synthesizing a traveler participant. Consider again the fixed choreography of Fig. 6. If, for example, only the services of the agency and the airline were specified, the blueprint of a traveler participant could be synthesized. If such a service exists (i. e., the composition of the existing services is controllable), it completes the choreography which is then deadlock-free by construction. To this end, the incomplete choreography is translated into an oWFN using BPEL2oWFN. This oWFN is then analyzed by Fiona. If the net is controllable, a service automaton modeling the behavior of a partner service is synthesized. This automaton can be translated into an oWFN, for example using the tool Petrify [13].

The synthesized oWFN of a traveler participant that completes the choreography is depicted in Fig. 7(a). This traveler participant slightly differs from the traveler participant in the new choreography (cf. Fig. 6). Firstly, there exists no transition modeling the planning of the trip, because such a transition is internal (i. e., not communicating), but the participant was synthesized based on the

---

[2] Fiona is available at www.informatik.hu-berlin.de/top/tools4bpel/fiona

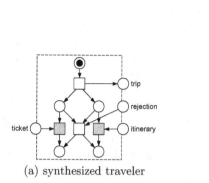
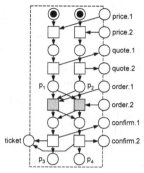

(a) synthesized traveler   (b) two synthesized airline instances

Fig. 7. Synthesized participants. (a) A traveler participant synthesized to fit in the new choreography. The gray transitions are concurrent, whereas in the choreography (cf. Fig. 6), the ticket is received *after* the itinerary. (b) Two synthesized airline instances to fit in the first choreography (cf. Fig. 3). The gray transitions synchronize the instances. The net has two final markings: $\Omega = \{[p_2, p_3], [p_1, p_4]\}$.

external behavior; that is, only the interaction of the service was taken into account. Secondly, the itinerary and the ticket can be received concurrently. This is due to the asynchronous communication model: messages can keep pending on the interface, so there is no order in which they have to be received. From this oWFN, an abstract BPEL process can be derived using existing approaches [14]. As this translation is out of scope of this paper, we do not present it here.

Limits of the participant synthesis. The presented approach allows to synthesize a participant that interacts deadlock-freely with the other participating services of the choreography if such a service exists; that is, if the open choreography is controllable. At present, it is, however, not possible to synthesize a *set* of services which complete a choreography.

As an example, consider again the first (deadlocking) choreography of Fig. 3. The choreography deadlocks because of the airline service's timeout mechanism. If we synthesize the airlines, the result will be a *single* oWFN modeling the behavior of *all* airline service's instances.

Figure 7(b) depicts the synthesized oWFN modeling two airline instances.[3] This service receives two price requests from the agency addressed to the different instances (input places price.1 and price.2) and sends two price quotes. Then, it waits to receive one ticket order (either on input place order.1 or order.2) and answers it accordingly. The resulting choreography would be deadlock-free. However, the airline's instances are not independent of each other. They are implicitly synchronized by the incoming arcs of the transitions receiving the orders. If this service had to be split into two services, explicit synchronization messages would have to be added to maintain deadlock-freedom. Still, the synthesized airline model can be seen as a starting point for further refinement.

---

[3] This structure of this oWFN was slightly adjusted to simplify the presentation.

Another issue of the participant synthesis are *causalities*. As sketched in the description of the generated traveler participant (cf. Fig. 7(a)), a generated participant might send and receive messages in different — mostly less constraint — orders. This might yield to synthesized services which send acknowledgment messages before actually receiving the corresponding request. In such cases, the causality between the request and the acknowledgment is ignored. In [15], we introduced behavioral constraints into the synthesis process to rule out such implausible behavior.

Each of the participating services of both choreographies are controllable. As the first choreography shows, their composition may still deadlock. Such deadlocking scenarios are not obvious even for small choreographies. Therefore, design and verification of deadlock-free choreographies with a larger number of participants and/or more complex participant services are even more challenging if not impossible to do manually.

5   Case Study

In the previous sections, we analyzed the first and the second choreography (cf. Fig. 3 and Fig. 6, resp.) with five airline instances. For these five airlines, the resulting models already had over 3,000 states. The states space grows dramatically when the number of airlines is further increased (cf. Table 1). For ten airlines, the model has over nine million states, and for larger numbers, the full state space could not be constructed due to memory overflow[4] (denoted as '—' in Table 1).

However, several state space reduction rules can be applied to reduce the size of the state space while still being able to analyze desired properties such as deadlock-freedom. In our particular example, we applied *symmetry reduction* and the *partial order reduction*, both implemented in LoLA (see [12] for further references). The symmetry reduction exploits the fact that all airline instances have the same structure. This regular structure induces symmetries on the net structure itself, but also on the state space of the choreography. Intuitively, the instances act of the airline service act 'similar' or 'symmetric'. During the state space construction, symmetric states are merged. The partial order reduction follows a different approach: as all instances run concurrently, any order of transitions of the airline instances are represented in the state space. These transition sequences introduce a lot of intermediate states. This is known as *state space explosion*. However, the actual order of independent actions is not relevant to detect deadlocks, for instance. To this end, partial order reduction tries to only construct one transition sequence (i. e., one order) of transitions of different airline instances to ease the state space explosion.

When each of the reduction techniques is applied in isolation, the state spaces grow more slowly, yet still exponentially in the number of airline instances. The combination of both techniques, however, yields a linear increase of states (cf. Table 1). Hence, we are able to verify properties of BPEL choreographies with

---

[4] The experiments where made with two gigabytes of memory.

Table 1. Net sizes (structurally reduced) and state spaces (full, reduced using symmetry reduction, reduced using partial order reduction, and reduced combining partial order reduction and symmetry reduction)

choreography	first example, cf. Fig. 3					second example, cf. Fig. 6				
airlines	1	5	10	100	1,000	1	5	10	100	1,000
places	20	63	113	1,013	10,013	19	63	113	1,013	10,113
transitions	10	41	76	706	7.006	12	52	97	907	9,007
states (full)	14	3,483	9,806,583	—	—	13	3,812	9,805,560	—	—
states (symmetry)	14	561	378,096	—	—	13	704	329,996	—	—
states (POR)	11	86	261	18,061	1,752,867	12	88	228	8,361	734,049
states (POR+symm.)	11	30	50	410	4,010	12	28	43	314	3,014

thousands of participating services. This shows that the presented approach can be used to analyze real-life examples.

6 Conclusion

In this paper, we presented an analysis of choreographies expressed in BPEL4Chor based on Petri nets. Models of choreographies with a lot of participating services contain a lot of concurrency which results in state space explosion. Our experiments showed that the combination of several reduction techniques allows to handle choreographies with thousand participants.

Deadlocks in choreographies can be very subtle. In the introductory example, each participant was correct (i. e., controllable) by itself, but the composition introduced deadlocks. We showed how our tool chain helps to detect deadlocks in a reasonable time and thus ensures that the choreography can be executed.

Since a choreography is a closed world, the analysis techniques allow a participant to be generated out of other participants, which speeds up the choreography design. If an airline and a travel agency agree on their behavior, the customer has to comply with it and can neither force the airline nor the travel agency to adapt their behavior to his wishes.

All things considered, the analysis and synthesis approach are independent of BPEL as input language as the approaches are based on the formal model of Petri nets. Therefore, the presented tool-chain (cf. Fig. 1) can be easily adapted to other service description languages.

6.1 Related Work

For analyzing BPEL4Chor choreographies, [16] presents a first approach for mapping BPEL4Chor to π-calculus. However, there was no formal mapping provided and it has not been shown whether the resulting π-formula can be verified in a reasonable period of time.

Choreographies themselves can be expressed by specifying (i) interconnection models and (ii) interaction models. An *interconnection model* captures the observable behavior of each participant in a choreography; that is, it defines an orchestration of the activities local to each participant. Activities of different participants are related in a choreography via message links tying together the local behavior into a global behavior. The basic messaging constructs are sending and receiving activities. BPMN [6] and BPEL4Chor are languages to express choreographies by interconnection models. An *interaction model* defines an ordering of the interactions of the processes on a global view. The basic messaging construct is the interaction activity, which models a message exchange between two participants. Current languages providing interaction models are Let's Dance [17] and WS-CDL [18]. Verification techniques are available for Let's Dance (cf. [19]) and WS-CDL (e. g. [20,21]). Since Let's Dance and WS-CDL provide interaction models, whereas BPEL4Chor provides interconnection models, the techniques cannot be directly applied to BPEL4Chor. [22] provides a formalization and a verification of BPMN models. However, BPMN does not originally support multiple instances of a participant as it is the case in BPEL4Chor.

[23] presents how to synthesize a BPEL processes which properly interacts with *one* given BPEL process. In contrast, we presented how to synthesize an oWFN out of n given BPEL processes.

6.2   Future Work

We plan to enhance and generalize the translation approach of [14] to synthesize a participant behavior description in BPEL instead of the oWFN only. For example, information about the participant topology has to be incorporated into the translation process to refine the resulting BPEL process.

Errors in choreographies can usually not be collated to a single participant, but to the combination of several participants. To this end, the repair of a erroneous choreography is nonlocal. We therefore plan to visualize the faulty scenario in the BPEL code of the affected participant(s) to support the designer in eliminating the detected problem.

In [9], the notion of *distributed controllability* was introduced. Distributed controllability focuses on synthesizing a set of services that interact deadlock-freely with a given service, and thus may allow to synthesize several independent instances of a participating service. This would ease the design of choreographies, because as soon as the first participant and a participant topology is specified, the blueprints of the remaining participants can be synthesized. We plan to further investigate the first theoretical results whether they can be integrated into our approach.

Acknowledgments. The authors wish to thank Gero Decker for the discussions we had on the subject. This work is funded by the German Federal Ministry of Education and Research (project Tools4BPEL, project number 01ISE08).

References

1. Alves, A., et al.: Web Services Business Process Execution Language Version 2.0. Technical report, OASIS (2007)
2. Decker, G., Kopp, O., Leymann, F., Weske, M.: BPEL4Chor: Extending BPEL for modeling choreographies. In: 2007 IEEE International Conference on Web Services (ICWS 2007), July 9-13, 2007, Salt Lake City, Utah, USA, pp. 296–303. IEEE Computer Society Press, Los Alamitos (2007)
3. Lohmann, N., Massuthe, P., Stahl, C., Weinberg, D.: Analyzing interacting BPEL processes. In: Dustdar, S., Fiadeiro, J.L., Sheth, A.P. (eds.) BPM 2006. LNCS, vol. 4102, pp. 17–32. Springer, Heidelberg (2006)
4. Lohmann, N., Massuthe, P., Stahl, C., Weinberg, D.: Analyzing interacting WS-BPEL processes using flexible model generation. Data Knowl. Eng. 64(1), 38–54 (2008)
5. Chinnici, R., Gudgin, M., Moreau, J.J., Weerawarana, S.: Web services description language (WSDL) version 1.2 part 1: Core language. World Wide Web Consortium, Working Draft WD-wsdl12-20030611 (2003)
6. OMG: Business Process Modeling Notation (BPMN) Specification. Final Adopted Specification, Object Management Group (2006), http://www.bpmn.org
7. Massuthe, P., Reisig, W., Schmidt, K.: An operating guideline approach to the SOA. Annals of Mathematics, Computing & Teleinformatics 1(3), 35–43 (2005)
8. van der Aalst, W.M.P.: The application of Petri nets to workflow management. Journal of Circuits, Systems and Computers 8(1), 21–66 (1998)
9. Schmidt, K.: Controllability of open workflow nets. In: Desel, J., Frank, U. (eds.) Enterprise Modelling and Information Systems Architectures, Proceedings of the Workshop in Klagenfurt, October 24-25, 2005, Lecture Notes in Informatics (LNI), vol. 75, pp. 236–249 (2005)
10. Breugel, F.v., Koshkina, M.: Models and verification of BPEL (2006), http://www.cse.yorku.ca/~franck/research/drafts/tutorial.pdf
11. Lohmann, N.: A feature-complete Petri net semantics for WS-BPEL 2.0. In: Dumas, M., Heckel, R. (eds.) WS-FM 2007. LNCS, vol. 4937, pp. 77–91. Springer, Heidelberg (2007)
12. Schmidt, K.: LoLA: A low level analyser. In: Nielsen, M., Simpson, D. (eds.) ICATPN 2000. LNCS, vol. 1825, pp. 465–474. Springer, Heidelberg (2000)
13. Cortadella, J., Kishinevsky, M., Kondratyev, A., Lavagno, L., Yakovlev, A.: Petrify: A tool for manipulating concurrent specifications and synthesis of asynchronous controllers. Trans. Inf. and Syst. E80-D(3), 315–325 (1997)
14. Lassen, K.B., van der Aalst, W.M.P.: WorkflowNet2BPEL4WS: A tool for translating unstructured workflow processes to readable BPEL. In: Meersman, R., Tari, Z. (eds.) OTM 2006. LNCS, vol. 4275, pp. 127–144. Springer, Heidelberg (2006)
15. Lohmann, N., Massuthe, P., Wolf, K.: Behavioral constraints for services. In: Alonso, G., Dadam, P., Rosemann, M. (eds.) BPM 2007. LNCS, vol. 4714, pp. 271–287. Springer, Heidelberg (2007)
16. Decker, G., Kopp, O., Puhlmann, F.: Service referrals in BPEL-based choreographies. In: 2nd European Young Researchers Workshop on Service Oriented Computing (YR-SOC 2007), pp. 25–30. University of Leicester (2007)
17. Zaha, J.M., Barros, A., Dumas, M., ter Hofstede, A.: Let's dance: A language for service behavior modeling. In: Meersman, R., Tari, Z. (eds.) OTM 2006. LNCS, vol. 4275, pp. 145–162. Springer, Heidelberg (2006)

18. Kavantzas, N., Burdett, D., Ritzinger, G., Lafon, Y.: Web Services Choreography Description Language Version 1.0. W3C Candidate Recommendation, W3C (2005), http://www.w3.org/TR/ws-cdl-10

19. Decker, G., Zaha, J.M., Dumas, M.: Execution semantics for service choreographies. In: Bravetti, M., Núñez, M., Zavattaro, G. (eds.) WS-FM 2006. LNCS, vol. 4184, pp. 163–177. Springer, Heidelberg (2006)

20. Busi, N., Gorrieri, R., Guidi, C., Lucchi, R., Zavattaro, G.: Choreography and orchestration conformance for system design. In: Ciancarini, P., Wiklicky, H. (eds.) COORDINATION 2006. LNCS, vol. 4038, pp. 63–81. Springer, Heidelberg (2006)

21. Corredini, F., De Angelis, A.P.: Verification of WS-CDL choreographies. In: 2nd European Young Researchers Workshop on Service Oriented Computing (YR-SOC 2007), pp. 13–18. University of Leicester (2007)

22. Puhlmann, F., Weske, M.: Investigations on soundness regarding lazy activities. In: Dustdar, S., Fiadeiro, J.L., Sheth, A.P. (eds.) BPM 2006. LNCS, vol. 4102, pp. 145–160. Springer, Heidelberg (2006)

23. Moser, S., Martens, A., Häbich, M., Mülle, J.: A hybrid approach for generating compatible WS-BPEL partner processes. In: Dustdar, S., Fiadeiro, J.L., Sheth, A.P. (eds.) BPM 2006. LNCS, vol. 4102, pp. 458–464. Springer, Heidelberg (2006)

Scalable Formalization of Publish/Subscribe Messaging Scheme Based on Message Brokers*

Qin Li, Huibiao Zhu, Jing Li, and Jifeng He

Software Engineering Institute, East China Normal University
3663 Zhongshan Road (North), Shanghai, China, 200062
{qli,hbzhu,jli,jifeng}@sei.ecnu.edu.cn

Abstract. Asynchronous communication is an important communication mechanism in service oriented architecture for developing dynamic large-scale applications among distributed services. Service systems which maintain large scalability and loose coupling properties need a convenient verification method for its asynchronous communication. Publish/Subscribe messaging scheme is a kind of asynchronous communication mechanisms supporting these properties. This paper provides a formal model for the publish/subscribe messaging scheme based on message brokers using π-calculus. Two patterns are provided to achieve the composition of message brokers, which generates a scalable system. Meanwhile, a complex publish/subscribe system can be simplified to an original one. From the original model reduced from the complex system, we can clearly analyze the behavior of the whole complex system and verify some properties of the publish/subscribe scheme. The composition and reduction can be applied to the service integration both within one enterprise and between enterprises.

1 Introduction

Asynchronous communication with publish/subscribe scheme [6] is receiving increasing attentions by the engineering field, especially in service oriented architecture [5]. With the development of distributed computation, the scale of web application becomes large and dynamic. Thousands of services with distinct locations and behaviors need asynchronous communication mechanisms to coordinate their interactions. Many application scenarios can only be implemented by using the publish/subscribe scheme.

Publish/Subscribe scheme has some brilliant advantages characterized by the full decoupling in space, time and synchronization. The participants are divided into two roles, the publisher and the subscriber. They interact with each other through some events. In the interaction paradigm, the subscribers declare their interests publicly in an event. Then when an event including the information which matches their registered interests has been published by a publisher, the subscribers will get their desired information. The participants have no idea of physical locations or infrastructures of each other, they even do not care how to contact each other. What is important for subscribers is that

---

* Supported by National Basic Research Program of China (No. 2005CB321904), Shanghai STCSM project (No. 06JC14058) and Shanghai Leading Academic Discipline Project (No. B412).

M. Dumas and R. Heckel (Eds.): WS-FM 2007, LNCS 4937, pp. 61–76, 2008.

once the useful information for them is ready, they consume it whenever they need. The publishers provide the information but have no reference to their consumers. That is exactly what we need in some service oriented scenarios. In this paper we call the event just as message in that we define a common type of messages which is capable to simulate the event exchanged among the services involved in the interactions.

To carry out the publish/subscribe messaging scheme in service oriented architecture, a messaging service is needed for central management and control. The message broker infrastructure is a good choice to fit the need.

Message broker is a special message-oriented middleware [1]. It acts like a broker between communicating entities, providing routing and filtering services for interaction messages. It has application logic components and queue systems to route and transmit the messages. A message broker not only routes messages, but also transforms and filters them, and even processes them for particular needs. It can coordinate distributed and loosely coupled applications and carry out some business workflow. For these reasons, message brokers are widely used for the integration of enterprise applications [9,11]. There are various message broker products available for industrial uses, such as IBM WebSphere Message Broker [3] and Microsoft Biztalk Server [13].

Recent researches on the publish/subscribe scheme seem like a burst. A variety of engineering researches mainly focus on the application issues of publish/subscribe scheme and the optimization of its performance. For example, the application of publish/subscribe in peer-to-peer networks [21], the scoping model for distributed publish/subscribe systems [7], access control of publish/subscribe systems [2], bounded delay for publish/subscribe systems [19] and so on. These researches improve the functions, security and performance of publish/subscribe systems but do not propose a formal model to simplify the verification of the properties. Some formal methods such as Petri nets have been used by some researches for modeling and analyzing other asynchronous communication mechanisms [4,20]. However, it is seldom applied to the publish/subscribe scheme.

This paper uses the message broker infrastructure to implement the publish/subscribe scheme. The formal method π-calculus is used for modeling and verifying of this scheme. The formalization facilitates the analysis of the model's behavior from the view of operational semantics. It helps to demonstrate that the message broker infrastructure has the capability to implement the publish/subscribe scheme with a satisfactory scalability. To demonstrate the scalability of the model, two patterns are proposed to compose the distributed systems. Then we prove that the large-scale composition of message brokers acts just as one unit observed from the outside of the whole system, which implies that the system is scalable and simplifiable with the two composition patterns. We also concentrate on the reliability of the publish/subscribe scheme to test the formal model.

The remainder of this paper is organized as follows. Section 2 gives a brief introduction of the formal method π-calculus. Section 3 presents the formalization of the message broker infrastructure which supports the publish/subscribe messaging scheme. Section 4 provides two patterns for the system composition and proves that the composed large-scale system can be treated as a whole one. The verification of the reliability property is given in section 5. Finally section 6 concludes the paper and mentions some further improvements.

2 π-Calculus

π-calculus is introduced by Robin Milner [14] and has been enhanced to support various applications [10,18]. It is widely used to formalize the issues in mobile network environment [15,16]. Mobility is the crucial feature of π-calculus that differs it from some static communication models. Mobility has the capability to change the connectivity of a network of processes, which is suitable to describe the dynamic mobile activities within web applications.

The basic syntax of π-calculus is

$$P := \sum_{i \in I} \pi_i.P_i \mid P_1 | P_2 \mid new\, a\, P \mid !P$$

$$\begin{aligned}
\text{where } \pi := x(y) && \text{receive } y \text{ along } x \\
\overline{x}\langle y \rangle && \text{send } y \text{ along } x \\
\tau && \text{unobservable action}
\end{aligned}$$

For the needs of formalizing the message broker, we extend some syntax structures to the original π calculus so as to clarify the model.

In our model, the content of the message transmitted among the processes is essential for the processing. The message must be dispatched to the corresponding place according to its content. So we distinguish the messages from channels using the following syntax:

$$\begin{aligned}
c\{\!| x |\!\} && \text{transmitting a message } x \text{ with a special format along } c \\
c(x) && \text{transmitting a channel } x \text{ along } c
\end{aligned}$$

In original π-calculus, only prefixing action π leads to the transitions of the processes. If π action does not happen, the process waits until it occurs. In our model, it is necessary to evaluate another kind of condition. They are not actions but decisions. That is, if a condition is satisfied, the process transfers to a corresponding branch. The syntax of the conditional choice is as follows:

$$P := \sum [b_i]P_i \qquad \forall i \neq j \ \bullet \ b_i \wedge b_j = false$$

where b_i is a boolean expression. Branch P_i will be chosen when b_i is satisfied. Note that only one boolean expression is true at a moment.

Moreover, some internal actions denoted by τ in original π-calculus which change the internal environment should be described as internal functions in our formalization. We use functions beginning with Greek symbols such as $\Phi()$, $\Psi()$ to denote this kind of internal actions.

3 Formalization of Publish/Subscribe Messaging

In this section we will give the formal definition of the publish/subscribe model implemented by message broker infrastructure.

3.1   Communication Model Definition for Participants

For a set of processes P_i, we introduce the notation $\overset{MB}{||}_{i \in \mathcal{N}} P_i$, which represents the asynchronous communication between P_i through a message broker MB. The definition of $\overset{MB}{||}$ can be described as follows:

$$\overset{MB}{||}_{i \in \mathcal{N}} (P_i) =_{df} (|_{i \in \mathcal{N}} E(P_i)) \mid MB(|\mathcal{N}|)$$

Where MB is a message broker, and $E(P_i)$ represents an enhanced P_i. $|\mathcal{N}|$ denotes the number of elements in set $\mathcal{N}$. If P_1 wants to send a message to P_2, the message is then actually sent from P_1 to broker MB. When P_2 receives a message from P_1, it is actually from MB. The benefits by introducing the broker is that the communication between participants is in an asynchronous way.

Let P_i be an arbitrary process using channel in_i and out_i to communicate with others. We enhance P_i by adding a middleware to it so that it can consume the service of the message broker MB. The enhanced process is denoted by $E(P_i)$. $E(P_i)$ contains a communicating middleware CM paralleled with P_i.

$E(P_i)$ is defined as follows:

$$E(P_i) =_{df} new\ in_i, out_i(\{c_i/c, c_i'/c', out_i/d, in_i/d'\}CM \mid P_i)$$

$$CM =_{df} \overline{on}\langle c \rangle.CM'$$

$$CM' =_{df} d\{\!|off|\!\}.\overline{lost}\langle c \rangle.0 + c'\{\!|m_1|\!\}.\overline{d'}\{\!|m_1|\!\}.CM' + d\{\!|m_2|\!\}.\overline{c}\{\!|m_2|\!\}.CM'$$

The channels c and c' are the external ports of CM communicating with MB while d and d' are its internal port for P_i. The enhancing method $E(P_i)$ hides the communication channels in_i, out_i of P_i and exchanges messages with MB using the channels c_i and c_i'. The motivation for introducing CM is to make a general purpose model for the integration.

Two channels on and $lost$ are held by MB and each instances of middleware CM. They are used to make the clients plug into a message broker and get off freely. Initially, CM in $E(P_i)$ sends its communication channel c_i, acting as an identifier of P_i, along on to register to the messaging service. Then P_i can send messages to the message broker along channel c_i. The corresponding c_i' which is used for receiving messages is also known by MB through easy computations. When P_i wants to get off, it sends out

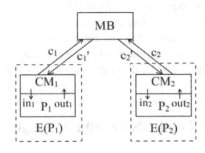

Fig. 1. Asynchronous communication between P_1 and P_2 through a message broker

a signal off. Receiving the signal, CM' in $E(P_i)$ sends its communication channel c_i along $lost$. MB saves no message for P_i and offers it no services whenever P_i has got off. Each P_i has its own communication channels which are different from others.

The structure of the model is illustrated in Figure 1.

3.2   Model for Message Broker

The message broker MB can be defined as follows:

$$MB(k) =_{df} new\ I(DM(k) \mid QM(k))$$

I represents all channels between DM and QM except external channels on, $lost$ and all channels registered by clients. on and $lost$ are the public channels we mentioned above used for the registrations of the clients. The parameter k denotes the number of clients engaged in the message broker.

According to the definition, the broker consists of two modules: the dealer module and the queue manager. We use DM and QM to denote them. DM is responsible for solving the registering and disconnecting requests from clients and creating a process for each client to manage the conversations. QM manages the message queues that store the messages for the recipients. Each queue corresponds to a recipient that has established a connection with the broker.

Message queues are necessary in the model in order to support the asynchronous communication. Messages can be stored temporarily in the queue, and when the consumer is ready to receive them, it can get them one-by-one from the queue. A general queue is defined as follows:

$$Queue(\phi) =_{df} in\{\!|m|\!\}.Queue(\langle m \rangle) + free\{\!|off|\!\}.0$$

$$Queue(\langle k \rangle \hat{\ } \overrightarrow{w}) =_{df} in\{\!|m|\!\}.Queue(\langle k \rangle \hat{\ } \overrightarrow{w} \hat{\ } \langle m \rangle) + \overline{out}\{\!|k|\!\}.Queue(\overrightarrow{w})$$
$$+ free\{\!|off|\!\}.0$$

The notation ϕ represents the queue is empty. $\overrightarrow{w}$ is a sequence of messages stored in the queue, while k, m are single messages. $\hat{\ }$ is a sequence linking notation. Channel in receives a message while channel out sends a message out. The channel $free$ is used to terminate the $Queue$ process for the management. The length of $\overrightarrow{w}$ can be limited to $n - 1$ so that the queue has its capacity of n. The broker creates a distinct queue for each recipient. We use the renaming method to instantiate the general queue model.

When the dealer module DM receives a register request from $E(P_i)$ along channel on, it creates an instance of process $Deal$ to listen to the communication channels of $E(P_i)$. The QM creates an instance of $Queue$ to deliver the messages to P_i. The responsibility of process $Deal$ is to implement the messaging logic of the publish/subscribe scheme. It analyzes the content of the messages from its client and routes them to the correct instances of $Queue$ for the recipients. Then the recipient can get the message sent to it from the $Queue$ instantiated for it.

The definitions of DM and QM are as follows, assume they have capacities of n:

$$DM(0) =_{df} on(u).(\overline{add}\langle u \rangle.\{u/in, g(u)/kill\}Deal \mid DM(1))$$

$$DM(k) =_{df} on(u).(\overline{add}\langle u \rangle.\{u/in, g(u)/kill\}Deal \mid DM(k+1))$$
$$+ lost(v).(\overline{g(v)}\{\!|off|\!\}.\overline{del}\langle v \rangle \mid DM(k-1)) \qquad\qquad 1 \leqslant k < n$$

$$DM(n) =_{df} lost(v).(\overline{g(v)}\{|off|\}.\overline{del}\langle v \rangle \mid DM(n-1))$$

$$QM(0) =_{df} add(u).(\{f(u)/in, u'/out, h(u)/free\}Queue(\phi) \mid QM(1))$$

$$QM(k) =_{df} add(u).(\{f(u)/in, u'/out, h(u)/free\}Queue(\phi) \mid QM(k+1))$$

$$+del(v).(\overline{h(v)}\{|off|\} \mid QM(k-1)) \qquad\qquad 1 \leqslant k < n$$

$$QM(n) =_{df} del(v).(\overline{h(v)}\{|off|\} \mid QM(n-1))$$

From the definition, we can see the interactions along the channels on and $lost$. The interactions are described by the mobile feature of π-calculus. A client $E(P_i)$ sends its communication channel c_i along channel on to the DM. DM makes the reaction and tells QM to create an instance of $Queue$ for P_i with the action $\overline{add}\langle c_i \rangle$. The instance has its channels renamed, where $f(u)$ represents the channel figured out with the channel it received (generally denoted by u, in the example here u is replaced by c_i). Like $f()$, the functions $g()$, $h()$ are one-to-one functions that map the received channel name to a new unique name relevant with the original one. u' is generated from u as we mentioned before. The two channels are corresponding to the client's communication channels. The motivation of introducing these functions is to guarantee the distinction of the names of channels. An instance of $Deal$ is also created with its channels renamed according to c_i. The detail of $Deal$ is left to the next part because it involves the routing logic of publish/subscibe scheme. Here it is only certain that it has free names of channels in and $kill$, where in is the input channel and $kill$ is used to terminate the $Deal$ process when the client cancels the messaging service. When receiving c_i along $lost$ channel, which means the client wants to quit, the instance of $Deal$ and $Queue$ should be terminated to release the system resources. DM completes this task by sending a signal off along $g(c_i)$ to cancel the $Deal$ instance for P_i and telling QM to delete the message queue for P_i using the action $\overline{del}\langle c_i \rangle$.

3.3   Model for Publish/Subscribe Scheme

In publish/subscribe scheme, the messaging logic is a little different from other asynchronous communication mechanisms. The messages in publish/subscribe system is called events. We choose topic-based events routing in our model because it has widely used by applications. The significant advantage of topic-based event pattern is the topic hierarchies that can easily achieve the access control. The messaging logic of topic-based publish/subscribe scheme is implemented by the process $Deal$. But at first, we should define the format of messages exchanging among the participants.

We define the messages in our model to be the following format:

$$Msg := \langle label \rangle values \langle /label \rangle; Msg$$

$$\mid \langle label \rangle Msg \langle /label \rangle; Msg$$

$label$ can be any identifier the user needs to denote the message's properties. The same $label$ in $\langle label \rangle$ and $\langle /label \rangle$ forms a pair. $value$ between the pair represents the value of the property denoted by the $label$. Msg format can be nested in the pair of $label$, which forms a hierarchy of information.

The format of the message looks like an XML document. It has almost the same description power as XML.

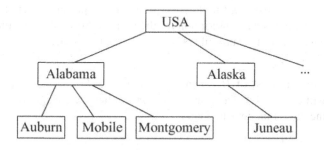

Fig. 2. Topic hierarchy expressed as a tree structure

In our model the message broker maintains a topic hierarchy. The topic hierarchy is usually represented as a tree structure. In the hierarchy, topics are classified by their characteristics. A main topic has some subtopics expressed as its children.

An example of topic hierarchy is showed in Figure 2. A publishing message matching this hierarchy is like follows :

$\langle type \rangle pub \langle /type \rangle$;
$\langle mark \rangle 0 \langle /mark \rangle$;
$\langle topic \rangle$
  $\langle USA \rangle \langle Alabama \rangle \langle Auburn \rangle values1 \langle /Auburn \rangle$;
    $\langle Mobile \rangle values2 \langle /Mobile \rangle$; $\langle Montgomery \rangle values3 \langle /Montgomery \rangle$;
    $\langle /Alabama \rangle$;
    $\langle Alaska \rangle \langle Juneau \rangle values4 \langle /Juneau \rangle$; $\langle /Alaska \rangle$;
      ⋮
  $\langle /USA \rangle$;
$\langle /topic \rangle$;

Here the label $mark$ is used to tell the message broker that the message is fresh. It will work in the composition conditions which we discuss in section 4. Some methods are required to access the information in the message. Let m be a message with the defined format, then $m@label$ gets the value of $label$ contained by m.

For example, a message subscribing the information about Alabama state will be formatted as :

$\langle type \rangle addsub \langle /type \rangle$;
$\langle topic \rangle USA \backslash Alabama \langle /topic \rangle$;

When processing the subscribing message, message broker registers the subscription. Once the above publishing message arrives, it sends the information of the topic $Alabama$ and all its subtopics to the subscriber.

We use the notation TH to represents the data structure of the topic hierarchy. Several functions are defined to access or modify this data structure to implement the subscription logic. Formally:

$$TH = \{(\hat{t_1}, C_{t_1}), (\hat{t_2}, C_{t_2}), \cdots, (\hat{t_n}, C_{t_n})\}$$

Where $\hat{t}_i$ is a path from *root* to the node t_i, and C_{t_i} represents a set of channels of the subscribers who make a subscription for the topic t_i. So we define a function Π to return the channel set of the subscribers corresponding to a topic.

$$\Pi(t_i, TH) = C_{t_i}$$

The computing process of Π depends on the data in TH. When TH changes, the result of Π will change too. The changes of TH implies the changes of subscriptions. Now we define three functions to update TH.

Let $TH = \{\cdots, (\hat{t}_i, C_{t_i}), \cdots\}$, then:

$\Psi(\hat{t}_i, c, TH) = TH'$ where $TH' = \{\cdots, (\hat{t}_i, C_{t_i} \cup \{c\}), \cdots\}$

$\Omega(\hat{t}_i, c, TH) = TH''$ where $TH'' = \{\cdots, (\hat{t}_i, C_{t_i} - \{c\}), \cdots\}$

$\Phi(c, TH) = TH'''$

where $TH''' = \{(\hat{t}_1, C_{t_1} - \{c\}), \cdots, (\hat{t}_i, C_{t_i} - \{c\}), \cdots, (\hat{t_n}, C_{t_n} - \{c\})\}$

The function of Ψ is to register a subscription for topic t_i from the subscriber identified by its communication channel c. The function of Ω is to cancel the subscriber's subscription for t_i. And the function of Φ is to remove all the subscriptions made by c from the TH.

We should also define a transformation function σ for the published message m so that it can be filtered to fit our needs.

$$\sigma(t_i, m) = m_{t_i}$$

Since m has a hierarchy structure which is represented by a tree and t_i is a node of the tree, then m_{t_i} contains m's subtree which starts with root t_i.

The *Deal* process is defined as follows:

$Deal =_{df} in\{\!|m|\!\}.$

$\quad ([m@type = pub] *_i (\overline{f(C_{t_i})}\{\!|m_{t_i}|\!\}).Deal$

$\quad +[m@type = addsub]\Psi(m@topic, in, TH).Deal)$

$\quad +[m@type = caclsub]\Omega(m@topic, in, TH).Deal)$

$\quad +kill\{\!|off|\!\}.0$

Where for all $t_i \in m@topic:$ $C_{t_i} = \Pi(t_i, TH)$ $m_{t_i} = \sigma(t_i, m)$

The notation $*_i(\overline{f(C_{t_i})}\{\!|m_{t_i}|\!\})$ represents the output event repeats until all topics in $m@topic$ have been processed.

Let $C = \{c_1, c_2, \ldots, c_n\}$, then $\overline{f(C)}\{\!|m|\!\} =_{df} \overline{f(c_1)}\{\!|m|\!\}.\overline{f(c_2)}\{\!|m|\!\}.\cdots.\overline{f(c_n)}\{\!|m|\!\}$

With the conditional choice we mentioned in section 2, the incoming messages are classified according to their *type* label. If the *type* label values *pub*, which means it is a publishing event message, the following branch of *Deal* will compute the results of Π and σ, then route the corresponding messages to correct queues. If the *type* label values *addsub*, which means it is a subscribing event message, the following branch will modify the TH to change the subscription. The third branch will be done if the *type* label values *caclsub*.

The invalid message handling is out of our consideration in this paper. If the message brokers receive the invalid messages, it simply neglects them.

When a client quits the communication model, the broker should remove all its subscriptions in the topic hierarchy. We add this logic to the definition of DM.

$$DM(k) =_{df} on(u).(\overline{add}\langle u\rangle.\{u/in, g(u)/kill\}Deal \mid DM(k+1))$$
$$+lost(v).(\Phi(v, TH).\overline{g(v)}\{\!|off|\!\}.\overline{del}\langle v\rangle \mid DM(k-1)) \qquad 1 \leqslant k < n$$
$$DM(n) =_{df} lost(v).(\Phi(v, TH).\overline{g(v)}\{\!|off|\!\}.\overline{del}\langle v\rangle \mid DM(n-1))$$

4   System Composition

This section will consider the composition of the communication units implemented by our message broker infrastructure.

First, we extends our model by adding two external ports named l and r to the definition of DM. The extended DM is denoted by CDM.

$$CDM(k) =_{df} on(u).(\overline{add}\langle u\rangle.\{u/in, g(u)/kill\}Deal \mid CDM(k+1))$$
$$+lost(v).(\overline{g(v)}\{\!|off|\!\}.\overline{del}\langle v\rangle \mid CDM(k-1)) \qquad 1 \leqslant k < n$$
$$+l\{\!|m|\!\}.([m@type = addsub]CDM(k) + [m@type = caclsub]CDM(k)$$
$$+[m@type = pub]([m@mark = L-1]CDM(k)$$
$$+[m@mark < L-1] *_i (\overline{f(C_{t_i})}\{\!|m_{t_i}|\!\}).\overline{r}\{\!|m'|\!\}.CDM(k)))$$
$$CDM(n) =_{df} lost(v).(\overline{g(v)}\{\!|off|\!\}.\overline{del}\langle v\rangle \mid CDM(n-1))$$
$$+l\{\!|m|\!\}.([m@type = addsub]CDM(n) + [m@type = caclsub]CDM(n)$$
$$+[m@type = pub]([m@mark = L-1]CDM(n)$$
$$+[m@mark < L-1] *_i (\overline{f(C_{t_i})}\{\!|m_{t_i}|\!\}).\overline{r}\{\!|m'|\!\}.CDM(n)))$$

Here m' is a new message computed from m. The only difference between m' and m is that m' increases the value of label $mark$ by 1 for describing m' has been consumed by a CDM. L is a constant to limit the times of forwarding the publishing message. If the message has been forwarded for $L-1$ times, it should be considered as out of time. Then the broker stops forwarding it. Replacing m by m' and limiting the forwarding times are to prevent endless publishing in the composed system. The detail will be demonstrated later.

Then we should also add another branch to $Deal$ and rewrite it as $CDeal$.

$$CDeal =_{df} in\{\!|m|\!\}.$$
$$([m@type = pub]([m@mark = 1]Deal$$
$$+[m@mark = 0] *_i (\overline{f(C_{t_i})}\{\!|m_{t_i}|\!\}).\overline{r}\{\!|m|\!\}.CDeal)$$
$$+[m@type = addsub]\Psi(m@topic, in, TH).\overline{r}\{\!|m|\!\}.CDeal$$
$$+[m@type = caclsub]\Omega(m@topic, in, TH)\overline{r}\{\!|m|\!\}.CDeal)$$
$$+kill\{\!|off|\!\}.0$$

Note that the message sent along r in $CDeal$ is still m not m'.

Then the scalable MB is defined as follows:

$$CMB =_{df} new\, I(CDM \mid QM)$$

At last, we can consider the composition based on the extended model. Consider that each unit consists of a message broker and the clients registered to it, and maintains a topic hierarchy containing the subscription information of its own clients. There are two kinds of compositions among these units. One is called embedded pattern, which means one system is plugged in another as a client, such as a department belonging to the whole management system. The other one is named companion pattern, which means the two system are of the same level such as two cooperating units.

In the embedded pattern, the subsystem can be considered as a client. In other words, it can be considered as one of P_i and then we can apply the enhancing method to enable it suitable for the composition.

$$E(CMB) =_{df} new\, l, r(CM \mid CMB)$$

The embedded pattern can be written as :

$$\overset{MB}{\|}\, (\, \overset{CMB}{\|}\, (P_i), \overset{CMB}{\|}\, (P_j), \cdots, \overset{CMB}{\|}\, (P_n))$$

Then the subsystem can communicate with the whole system as a client. This composition approach is dynamic since the client message broker can get in/off the master broker without interfering other clients. The $mark$ label works in this pattern when a client broker receives a publishing message m from its master broker. It consumes the message in its client scope and then it sends the the message back with its $mark$ label valuing 1. Then the master will neglect the returning message as we defined in the $Deal$. Figure 3 depicts the structure of embedded pattern.

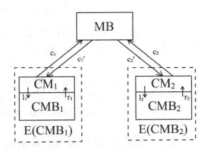

Fig. 3. The embedded pattern for system composition

The companion pattern requires the clients of each system can communicate with each other without knowing they are in different scopes.

According to the definition of $\overset{MB}{\|\,\|}$, the internal channels of the two systems should be hidden. Considering the concurrent messaging management, two queues should be added to the composite system. So we introduce the link component as follows.

$$CMB_1 \copyright CMB_2 =_{df} new\, l_1, l_2, r_1, r_2((CMB_1 \mid L_{1,2} \mid CMB_2) \mid L_{2,1})$$

$$L_{i,j} =_{df} \{r_i/in, l_j/out\}Queue(\phi)$$

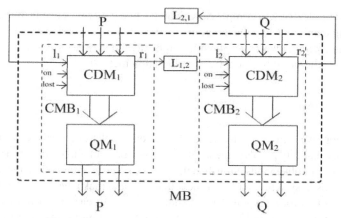

Fig. 4. The companion pattern for system composition

$$CMB_1 ©CMB_2© \cdots ©CMB_n =_{df}$$

$$new\, l_i, r_i((CMB_1 \,|\, L_{1,2} \,|\, CMB_2 \,|\, L_{2,3} \,|\, \cdots \,|\, L_{n-1,n} \,|\, CMB_n) \,|\, L_{n,1})$$

The companion pattern can be written as :

$$\overset{CMB}{||}\, (P_i)© \;\overset{CMB}{||}\, (P_j)© \cdots © \;\overset{CMB}{||}\, (P_n)$$

As the definition shows, the units form a cricoid chain. Here $L_{i,i+1}$ composes the channels between the units while $L_{n,1}$ connects the tail with the head of the chain. The cricoid structure lets messages exchange between distinct message brokers and finally get themselves to their recipients. It is easy to be implemented but somehow increases the propagation delay. Figure 4 demonstrates the structure of the composition.

With the link component, we can figure out a theorem for the composition. This theorem guarantees that the composite system using the companion pattern can be treated as a whole system with a single message broker.

Theorem : $\overset{CMB}{\underset{i\in I}{||}}\, (P_i) © \;\overset{CMB}{\underset{j\in J}{||}}\, (P_j) \approx \overset{MB}{\underset{k\in I\cup J}{||}}\, (P_k)$

With the definition of $\overset{MB}{||}$, the left side of the law can be deduced as:

$$(|_{i\in I}\, E(P_i)) \,|\, CMB © (|_{j\in J}\, E(P_j)) \,|\, CMB$$

$$= (|_{k\in I\cup J}\, E(P_k)) \,|\, (CMB©CMB)$$

And the right side of the law equals to:

$$(|_{k\in I\cup J}\, E(P_k)) \,|\, MB$$

Hence the theorem holds if the following lemma exists. This lemma can be proceeded via the concept of weak bisimulation.

Lemma: $CMB©CMB \approx MB$

The theorem can be extended to the case that more than two message brokers cooperate with each other. Therefore the companion pattern can be used freely to construct a large scale system.

Given a complex system composed with above two patterns, it can be finally simplified to a single unit by using the theorem. Then we can do the verification work only in the single unit without worrying about it will be invalid in the composite system. Time and energy can be saved by using the simplification method.

5   Verification

In this section, we will verify the reliability of our publish/subscribe communication scheme. The reliability property means that a subscriber can finally receive the message it needs if some publisher has published it. We do the verification both in the single unit and the composite system in order to show that they can make the same conclusion.

Let P_1, P_2 be processes willing to communicate with each other asynchronously. Then they are enhanced to $E(P_1)$ and $E(P_2)$ when getting into the message broker. $E(P_1)$ declares its communication channel p_1, p_1' to the broker through $\overline{on}(p_1)$ action. So does $E(P_2)$ with its communication channel p_2, p_2'. The system with our model is:

$$\overset{MB}{||}\ (P_1, P_2)$$

Assume P_1 is a publisher and P_2 is a subscriber (the role of P_1, P_2 can change to the opposite side freely). P_2 subscribes the topic t then P_1 publishes the information including the topic t to the message broker MB. The property we should verify is that P_2 can finally receive a message containing its desired topic information, which can be formally defined as follows:

Definition 5.1 (Reliability)

The system $\overset{MB}{||}\ (P_1, P_2)$ is reliable if $\exists tr \bullet \overset{MB}{||}\ (P_1, P_2) \overset{tr}{\Longrightarrow} \overset{MB}{||}\ (P_1', P_2'')$

$E(P_2) = \overline{p_2}\{\!|m_1|\!\}.E(P_2') \mid M$ where $m_1@type = addsub$, $m_1@topic = \hat{t}$

$E(P_1) = \overline{p_1}\{\!|m_2|\!\}.E(P_1') \mid M$ where $m_2@topic = \mathcal{T}$

$E(P_2') = p_2'\{\!|m_3|\!\}.E(P_2'') \mid M$ where $m_3@topic = tree(t)$

Here $\mathcal{T}$ represents the set of topics containing the topic that P_2 needs and M denotes the other actions we do not care about. The M implies that the processes can do other actions without waiting for the above useful actions. Assume $tr = \alpha_1 \cdots \alpha_n$, then $\overset{tr}{\Longrightarrow} =_{df} \overset{\alpha_1}{\Longrightarrow} \cdots \overset{\alpha_n}{\Longrightarrow}$. We use the notation $\alpha[\tau]$ to represent the action α is an internal action and is hidden for observers in the model.

According to the reaction rules in π-calculus, we can find a sequence tr like follows (we start with the initial situation where P_1 and P_2 are not plugged in the broker):

Initializing

$E(P_1)_{off} \mid MB \mid E(P_2)_{off}$

$\overset{on(p_1)add(p_1)[\tau]}{\longrightarrow} E(P_1) \mid (\{p_1/in, g(p_1)/kill\}Deal \mid DM(1))$

$\qquad \mid (\{f(p_1)/in, p_1'/out, h(p_1)/free\}Queue(\phi) \mid QM(1)) \mid E(P_2)_{off}$

$\overset{on(p_2)add(p_2)[\tau]}{\longrightarrow} E(P_1) \mid E(P_2)$

$$| (\{p_1/in, g(p_1)/kill\}Deal | \{p_2/in, g(p_2)/kill\}Deal | DM(2))$$

$$| (\{f(p_1)/in, p_1'/out, h(p_1)/free\}Queue(\phi)$$

$$| \{f(p_2)/in, p_2'/out, h(p_2)/free\}Queue(\phi) | QM(2)) \qquad (I)$$

For simplifying the representation, we use $Deal_1$ to denote $\{p_1/in, g(p_1)/kill\}$ $Deal$ and $Deal_2$ to denote $\{p_2/in, g(p_2)/kill\}Deal$ below. Similarly, the two queues are rewritten as $Queue_1$ and $Queue_2$.

Messaging

$$(I) \xrightarrow{p_2\langle\!\langle m_1\rangle\!\rangle} E(P_1) | E(P_2')$$

$$| (([m_1@type = pub]([m_1@mark = 1]Deal_2$$

$$\qquad +[m_1@mark = 0] *_i (\overline{f(C_{t_i})}\langle m_{t_i}\rangle).Deal_2)$$

$$+[m_1@type = addsub]\Psi(m_1@topic, p_2, TH).Deal_2$$

$$+[m_1@type = caclsub]\Omega(m_1@topic, p_2, TH).Deal_2) | Deal_1 | DM(2))$$

$$| (Queue_1(\phi) | Queue_2(\phi) | QM(2))$$

$$\xrightarrow{\Psi(m_1@topic,p_2,TH)[\tau]} E(P_1) | E(P_2') \qquad\qquad [m_1@type = addsub]$$

$$| (Deal_1 | Deal_2 | DM(2))$$

$$| (Queue_1(\phi) | Queue_2(\phi) | QM(2))$$

Note that the TH has changed to TH' after the function Ψ, where $(\hat{t}, p_2) \in TH'$.

$$\xrightarrow{p_1\langle\!\langle m_2\rangle\!\rangle} E(P_1') | E(P_2')$$

$$| (([m_2@type = pub]([m_2@mark = 1]Deal_1$$

$$\qquad +[m_2@mark = 0] *_i (\overline{f(C_{t_i})}\langle m_{t_i}\rangle).Deal_1)$$

$$+[m_2@type = addsub]\Psi(m_2@topic, p_1, TH).Deal_1$$

$$+[m_2@type = caclsub]\Omega(m_2@topic, p_1, TH).Deal_1) | Deal_2 | DM(2))$$

$$| (Queue_1(\phi) | Queue_2(\phi) | QM(2))$$

For $[m_2@mark = 0] \wedge [m_2@type = pub]$ is true and $C_{t_i} = \Pi(t_i, TH) = p_2$, $\sigma(t, m_2) = m_3$, then:

$$\xrightarrow{\overline{f(p_2)}\langle m_3\rangle[\tau]} E(P_1') | E(P_2')$$

$$| (Deal_1 | Deal_2 | DM(2))$$

$$| (Queue_1(\phi) | Queue_2(m_3) | QM(2))$$

$$\xrightarrow{p_2'\langle\!\langle m_3\rangle\!\rangle} E(P_1') | E(P_2'')$$

$$| (Deal_1 | Deal_2 | DM(2))$$

$$| (Queue_1(\phi) | Queue_2(\phi) | QM(2))$$

$$\overset{MB}{=}|| (P_1', P_2'')$$

Therefore we find a minimum sequence tr_0 that $\forall tr \supseteq tr_0$ satisfies Definition 5.1 :

$$tr_0 = p_2\{|m_1|\}.\Psi(m_1@topic, p_2, TH)[\tau].p_1\{|m_2|\}.f(p_2)\{|m_2|\}[\tau].p_2'\{|m_3|\}$$

Thus the verification of the reliability property is completed in single unit condition.

The composition situation of message brokers should be verified. For the first composition requirement as we mentioned in section 4, assume P_1, P_2 belong to different message brokers composed with the embedded pattern. To be a sample, we consider the structure illustrated by Figure 3 and let P_1 belong to CMB_1 using channels p_1 and p_1', P_2 belong to CMB_2 with channels p_2 and p_2' (the other situations with different topology is similar). We also add suffix to the topic hierarchy TH maintained by each broker. Then the definition of the reliability property can be rewritten as:

Definition 5.2: The composite system with embedded patterns is reliable **if**

$$\exists tr \bullet \overset{MB\ CMB}{||} (\overset{CMB}{||} (P_1), \overset{CMB}{||} (P_2)) \overset{tr}{\Longrightarrow} \overset{MB\ CMB}{||} (\overset{CMB}{||} (P_1'), \overset{CMB}{||} (P_2''))$$

Then we can also find a minimum sequence tr_1 that $\forall tr \supseteq tr_1$ satisfies Definition 5.2 :

$$tr_1 = p_2\{|m_1|\}.\Psi(m_1@topic, p_2, TH_2)[\tau].r_2\{|m_1|\}[\tau].c_2\{|m_1|\}.$$
$$\Psi(m_1@topic, c_2, TH)[\tau].p_1\{|m_2|\}.r_1\{|m_2|\}[\tau].c_1\{|m_2|\}.f(c_2)\{|m_3|\}[\tau].$$
$$c_2'\{|m_3|\}.l_2\{|m_3|\}[\tau].f(p_2)\{|m_3|\}[\tau].p_2'\{|m_3|\}.r_2\{|m_3'|\}.c_2\{|m_3'|\}$$

The details of the deduction are similar to the deduction for Definition 5.1.

For the companion pattern, considering the sample given in Figure 4. Assume P_1, P_2 belong to different message brokers. Then the definition of the reliability property can be rewritten as:

Definition 5.3: The composite system with companion pattern is reliable **if**

$$\exists tr \bullet \overset{CMB}{||} (P_1)ⓒ \overset{CMB}{||} (P_2) \overset{tr}{\Longrightarrow} \overset{CMB}{||} (P_1')ⓒ \overset{CMB}{||} (P_2'')$$

Then we can find a minimum sequence tr_2 that $\forall tr \supseteq tr_2$ satisfies Definition 5.3 :

$$tr_2 = p_2\{|m_1|\}.\Psi(m_1@topic, p_2, TH_2)[\tau].r_2\{|m_1|\}[\tau].l_1\{|m_1|\}[\tau].$$
$$p_1\{|m_2|\}.r_1\{|m_2|\}[\tau].l_2\{|m_2|\}[\tau].f(p_2)\{|m_3|\}[\tau].p_2'\{|m_3|\}.r_2\{|m_2|\}[\tau].$$
$$l_1\{|m_2|\}[\tau]$$

Thus the reliability property holds in all cases in our model.

6   Conclusion and Further Work

This paper has proposed a formal model to describe the publish/subscribe scheme implemented by message brokers. Scalability and loose coupling have been realized in the model. We have provided two patterns, embedded pattern and companion pattern, to compose individual systems and to simplify the composite systems. It is guaranteed that the properties verified in the single system is also holds in the composite system. To demonstrate that, we have verified the reliability property in our single model and showed that it holds in the composite system. Considering the services plugged in the message broker can be arbitrary processes subject to the same data transmitting protocol, the model can be useful in service integration with asynchronous interactions.

Based on the above work, we will focus on the following issues in our future work. Special routing and transforming logic of messages can be added to message brokers to achieve more powerful functions and more secure interactions. The security and performance issues [8,12] will be considered in the extension model. The definition of the model is expected to be translated for automatic verification with some workbenches for π-calculus [17]. We need to figure out an approach to realize the dynamic composition, which requires that any unit can connect to the whole system and can leave it without disturbing the other units' work. The dynamic composition will definitely make the whole model more flexible and useful.

References

1. Alonso, G., Kuno, H., Casati, F., Machiraju, V.: Web Services: Concepts, Architectures and Applications. Springer, Heidelberg (2003)
2. Belokosztolszki, A., Eyers, D.M., Pietzuch, P.R., Bacon, J., Moody, K.: Role-based access control for publish/subscribe middleware architectures. In: Proc. of DEBS 2003: Proceedings of the 2nd international workshop on Distributed event-based systems, pp. 1–8. ACM Press, New York (2003)
3. Davies, S., Cowen, L., Giddings, C., Parker, H.: WebSphere Message Broker Basics. IBM International Technical Support Organization (2005)
4. Devillers, R., Klaudel, H.: Synchronous and asynchronous communications in composable parameterized high-level petri nets. Fundam. Inf. 66(3), 221–257 (2005)
5. Erl, T.: Service-Oriented Architecture (SOA): Concepts, Technology, and Design. Prentice Hall PTR, Englewood Cliffs (2005)
6. Eugster, P.T., Felber, P.A., Guerraoui, R., Kermarrec, A.-M.: The many faces of publish/subscribe. ACM Computing Surveys 35(2), 114–131 (2003)
7. Fiege, L., Cilia, M., Muhl, G., Buchmann, A.: Publish-subscribe grows up: Support for management, visibility control, and heterogeneity. IEEE Internet Computing 10(1), 48–55 (2006)
8. Fiege, L., Zeidler, A., Buchmann, A., Kilian-Kehr, R., Mhl, G.: Security aspects in publish/subscribe systems. In: Proc. of DEBS 2004: the Third International Workshop on Distributed Event-Based Systems (2004)
9. Fowler, M.: Patterns of Enterprise Application Architecture. Addison-Wesley, Reading (2002)
10. Hennessy, M., Riely, J.: Information flow vs. resource access in the asynchronous pi-calculus. ACM Transactions on Programming Languages and Systems 24(5), 566–591 (2002)
11. Hohpe, G., Woolf, B.: Enterprise Integration Patterns. Addison-Wesley, Reading (2003)
12. Jerzak, Z., Fetzer, C.: Handling overload in publish/subscribe systems. In: Proc. of ICDCSW 2006: 26th IEEE International Conference Workshops on Distributed Computing Systems, Washington, DC, USA, p. 32. IEEE Computer Society Press, Los Alamitos (2006)
13. Microsoft Cooperation. Microsoft Biztalk Server (2006), http://www.microsoft.com/technet/prodtechnol/biztalk/2006/default.mspx
14. Milner, R.: Communicating and Mobile Systems: the π-Calculus. Cambridge University Press, Cambridge (1999)
15. Orava, F., Parrow, J.: An algebraic verification of a mobile network. Journal of Formal Aspects of Computing 4, 497–543 (1992)

16. Priami, C.: Stochastic analysis of mobile telephony networks. In: Brinskma, E., Nymeyer, A. (eds.) Proc. of PAPM 1997: 5th Int. Workshop on Process Algebra and Performance Modeling, pp. 145–171 (1997)
17. Victor, B., Moller, F.: The mobility workbench — a tool for the π-calculus. In: Dill, D.L. (ed.) CAV 1994. LNCS, vol. 818, pp. 428–440. Springer, Heidelberg (1994)
18. Walker, D.: Pi-calculus semantics of object-oriented programming languages. In: Ito, T., Meyer, A.R. (eds.) TACS 1991. LNCS, vol. 526, pp. 532–547. Springer, Heidelberg (1991)
19. Wang, J., Cao, J., Li, J., Wu, J.: Achieving bounded delay on message delivery in publish/subscribe systems, vol. 0, pp. 407–416 (2006)
20. Xia, F., Clark, I.: Algorithms for signal and message asynchronous communication mechanisms and their analysis. Fundam. Inf. 50(2), 205–222 (2002)
21. Zhu, Y., Hu, Y.: Ferry: An architecture for content-based publish/subscribe services on p2p networks, vol. 00, pp. 427–434 (2005)

A Feature-Complete Petri Net Semantics for WS-BPEL 2.0

Niels Lohmann

Universität Rostock, Institut für Informatik, 18051 Rostock, Germany
niels.lohmann@uni-rostock.de

Abstract. We present an extension of a Petri net semantics for the Web Service Business Execution Language (WS-BPEL). This extension covers the novel activities and constructs introduced by the recent WS-BPEL 2.0 specification. Furthermore, we simplify several aspects of the Petri net semantics to allow for more compact models suited for computer-aided verification.

1 Introduction

Recently, the emerging standard to describe business processes on top of Web service technology, the Web Service Business Execution Language (WS-BPEL), has been officially specified [1]. This specification is much more detailed and more precise compared to the predecessor specification [2]. Still, WS-BPEL is specified informally using plain English. To formally analyze properties of WS-BPEL processes, however, a *formal* semantics is needed. Therefore, many work has been conducted to give a formal semantics for the behavior of WS-BPEL processes. The approaches cover many formalisms such as Petri nets, abstract state machines, finite state machines, process algebras, etc. (see [3] for an overview). In addition to the possibility to analyze WS-BPEL processes, a formal semantics may also help to understand the original specification and to allow to find ambiguities.

The language constructs found in WS-BPEL, especially those related to control flow, are close to those found in workflow definition languages [4]. In the area of workflows, it has been shown that Petri nets [5] are appropriate both for modeling and analysis. More specifically, with Petri nets several elegant technologies such as the theory of workflow nets [6], a theory of controllability [7,8], a long list of verification techniques, and tools (see [9] for an overview) become directly applicable.

In this paper, we present an extension of the Petri net semantics of [10]. This extension is twofold: (1) we simplify several patterns of the original semantics that resulted in huge nets, and (2) we introduce novel Petri net patterns for the constructs introduced by WS-BPEL 2.0 such as new activities or handlers. Admittedly, we can only present a few aspects of this new semantics and refer to [11] where the complete semantics formalizing all activities of WS-BPEL.

The rest of this paper is organized as follows. In Sect. 2, we briefly introduce WS-BPEL, our formal model, and the basic concepts of the Petri net semantics

M. Dumas and R. Heckel (Eds.): WS-FM 2007, LNCS 4937, pp. 77–91, 2008.

we extend in this paper. Then, in Sect. 3, we show how several aspects of the semantics can be simplified. Section 4 is devoted to the presentation of patterns for some novel activities and constructs of WS-BPEL 2.0. Finally, Sect. 5 concludes the paper, summarizes related work, and gives directions for future work.

2   Background

2.1   WS-BPEL

The *Web Services Business Process Execution Language* (WS-BPEL) [1], is a language for describing the behavior of business processes based on Web services. For the specification of a business process, WS-BPEL provides *activities* and distinguishes between *basic activities* and *structured activities*. The basic activities are ⟨receive⟩ and ⟨reply⟩ to provide web service operations, ⟨invoke⟩ to invoke web service operations, ⟨assign⟩ to update partner links, ⟨throw⟩ to signal internal faults, ⟨exit⟩ to immediately end the process instance, ⟨wait⟩ to delay the execution, ⟨empty⟩ to do nothing, ⟨compensate⟩ and ⟨compensateScope⟩ to invoke a compensation handler, ⟨rethrow⟩ to propagate faults, ⟨validate⟩ to validate variables, and ⟨extensionActivity⟩ to add new activity types.

A structured activity defines a causal order on the basic activities and can be nested in another structured activity itself. The structured activities are ⟨sequence⟩ to process activities sequentially, ⟨if⟩ to process activities conditionally, ⟨while⟩ and ⟨repeatUntil⟩ to repetitively execute activities, ⟨forEach⟩ to (sequentially or in parallel) process multiple branches, ⟨pick⟩ to process events selectively, and ⟨flow⟩ to process activities in parallel. Activities embedded to a ⟨flow⟩ activity can further be ordered by the usage of *control links*.

Finally, the ⟨scope⟩ activity can add exception handling to an activity. For this purpose, there exist four kinds of handlers: a ⟨compensationHandler⟩ to compensate successfully executed scopes, ⟨faultHandlers⟩ to undo partial, unsuccessful executed scopes, a ⟨terminationHandler⟩ to control the forced termination of a scope, and ⟨eventHandlers⟩ to process message or timeout events. Though not listed as an activity, WS-BPEL's root element is the ⟨process⟩, which is in fact a special ⟨scope⟩ activity.

2.2   Open Workflow Nets

Open workflow nets (oWFNs) are a special class of Petri nets. They generalize the classical workflow nets [6] by introducing an interface for asynchronous message passing. oWFNs provide a simple but formal foundation to model services and their interaction. Open workflow nets—like common Petri nets—allow for diverse analysis methods of computer-aided verification. The explicit modeling of the interface further allows to analyze the communicational behavior of a service [12,13].

To model data flow and data manipulation, Petri nets can be extended to algebraic high-level nets [14]. Similarly, open workflow nets can be canonically extended to high-level open workflow nets (HL-oWFNs).

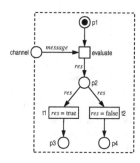

Fig. 1. A high-level oWFN

An example for a high-level oWFN is depicted in Fig. 1. Transition evaluate receives a *message* (variable names are written in an *italic* font) from place channel and evaluates it. The evaluation process itself is not explicitly modeled. Still, the *result* of this evaluation (either the value 'true' or 'false') is produced on place p2. Then, depending on this value, either t1 (the guard "*res* = true", written inside the transition, holds) or t2 (the guard "*res* = false" holds) can fire. Throughout this paper, we refrain from depicting the concrete underlying Petri net schema. The domains of the places can be canonically derived from the patterns and the respective WS-BPEL activity.

2.3   A Petri Net Semantics for WS-BPEL

Both the semantics of [10] and the extension presented in this paper follow a hierarchical approach. The translation is guided by the syntax of WS-BPEL[1]. In WS-BPEL, a process is built by plugging instances of language constructs together. Accordingly, each construct of the language is translated separately into a Petri net. Such a net forms a *pattern* of the respective WS-BPEL construct. Each pattern has an *interface* for joining it with other patterns as is done with WS-BPEL constructs (cf. Fig. 2). Also, patterns capturing WS-BPEL's structured activities may carry any number of inner patterns as its equivalent in WS-BPEL can do. The collection of patterns forms the *Petri net semantics* for WS-BPEL.

Both semantics consist of high-level patterns which completely model WS-BPEL's control and data flow. As the data-domains of the variables can be infinite, abstract (low-level) patterns are implemented in the respective compilers BPEL2PN [15] and BPEL2oWFN [11]. To simplify the presentation of the patterns, we use several graphical conventions, depicted in Fig. 3(a) and 3(b).

---

[1] The semantics of [10] is only defined for BPEL4WS 1.1. As, however, the concept of the semantics is version-independent, we use "WS-BPEL" without version number unless we want to distinguish the two different versions.

Fig. 2. The interface places of an activity: initial, final, stop, stopped, and fault. Marking the initial place starts an activity. Upon faultless completion of the activity, the final place is marked. The places stop and stopped model the termination of activities. Faults are signaled by marking the fault place.

(a) place copies   (b) read arcs

Fig. 3. Graphical conventions used to simplify patterns. (a) A dashed place is a copy of a place with the same label. (b) Read arcs are unfolded to loops.

3   Simplifying Existing Patterns

The original semantics [10] was designed to formalize BPEL4WS 1.1 rather than to create compact models that are necessary for computer-aided verification. Some patterns were easy to understand yet made use of quite "expensive" constructs such as reset arcs [16]. We improved these patterns and replaced them by less intuitive patterns with simpler structure. In particular, the setting of control links and the complex interplay of the fault, compensation, event, and (the newly introduced) termination handlers was condensed.

3.1   Links and Dead-Path-Elimination

Activities embedded in a ⟨flow⟩ activity are executed concurrently. However, it is possible to add control dependencies by the help of *links*. A link is a directed connection between a *source activity* and a *target activity*. After the source activity is executed, the link is set to true, allowing the target activity to start. As links express control dependencies, they may never form a cycle.

More precisely, when the source activity is executed faultlessly, the outgoing links are set according to their corresponding *transition conditions* which returns a Boolean value for each outgoing link. After the status of all incoming links of a target activity is determined, a *join condition*—again a Boolean expression[2]—is evaluated. If this condition holds, the target activity is executed. If, however, the condition is false, the activity is skipped. In this case, all outgoing links recursively embedded to the skipped activity are also set to false to avoid deadlocks.

---

[2] While transition conditions are expressions over arbitrary variable values, join conditions only evaluate the status of the incoming links.

This concept is called *dead-path-elimination* (DPE) and can be enabled for each target activity.

```
<flow>
  <links> <link name="AtoB"/> <link name="BtoC"/> </links>
  <activity name="A">
    <sources> <source linkName="AtoB"/> </sources>
  </activity>
  <if>
    <condition>...</condition>
    <activity name="B">
      <targets> <target linkName="AtoB"/> </targets>
      <sources> <source linkName="BtoC"/> </sources>
    </activity>
    <else> <activity name="E"/> </else>
  </if>
  <sequence>
    <activity name="C">
      <targets> <target linkName="BtoC"/> </targets>
    </activity>
    <activity name="D"/>
  </sequence>
</flow>
```

Fig. 4. An example for links and dead-path-elimination. ⟨activity⟩ is a placeholder for any WS-BPEL activity.

As an example, consider the ⟨flow⟩ of Fig. 4. Two scenarios are possible, depending on the condition of the ⟨if⟩ activity: If the condition evaluates to true, we have the execution order shown in Fig. 5(a). Firstly, A is executed and sets link AtoB to true, then B is executed and sets link BtoC. Finally, C and D are executed sequentially.

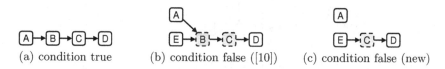

(a) condition true   (b) condition false ([10])   (c) condition false (new)

Fig. 5. Possible executions of the activities of the example in Fig. 4. Skipped activities are depicted with dashed lines. The executions (a) and (b) correctly model the specified behavior, whereas the execution (c) does neither skips nor executes activity B.

In case the condition evaluates to false, E is executed and, due to the DPE, activity B is skipped; that is, B has to wait until A has set its link AtoB. Then, B's outgoing link, BtoC, is set to false and C is also skipped. Finally, D is executed. This yields the execution order of Fig. 5(b). These two runs are correctly modeled by the semantics of [10] using a subnet in each pattern to bypass the execution of the activity and to set outgoing links to false.

However, if the branches to be skipped are more complex, the skipping of activities yields a complex model due to the DPE. In particular, skipping of activities and execution of non-skipped activities is interleaved which might result in state explosion problems. To this end, the new semantics differs from the described behavior of [1]: an *overapproximation* of the process's exact behavior is modeled. In the example, activity B is not skipped explicitly, but its outgoing link, BtoC, is set to false *directly* when E is selected. This yields the execution order of Fig. 5(c). Compared to the semantics of [10], two *additional* runs are modeled by the new semantics, namely A and D being executed concurrently, and D being executed before A. Due to the overapproximation, it may be possible that the resulting model contains errors that are not present in the WS-BPEL process. For example, activity A and D could be ⟨receive⟩ activities that receive messages from the same channel. If they are active concurrently, a "conflicting receive" fault would be thrown. However, static analysis of the WS-BPEL process can help to identify these pseudo-errors (see [13,11] for details). Figure 6 depicts another example for the direct setting of recursively embedded links (transition skip). Again, transition evaluate_JC and evaluate_TC only implicitly model the evaluation of the join and transition condition, respectively. An explicit model of the evaluation would require to take XPath expressions, XML variables, etc. into account and is out of scope of this paper.

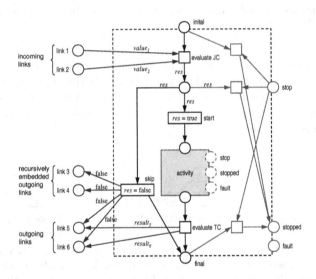

Fig. 6. Wrapper pattern of an activity that is source and target of links. Transition evaluate_JC evaluates the join condition. If the *result* is true, the embedded activity is started. Upon completion of the this activity, transition evaluate_TC evaluates the transition condition and sets the outgoing links accordingly. If, however, the join condition evaluates to false, transition skip does not only set all directly or recursively enclosed outgoing links to false.

3.2   Fault Handling and Termination of Scopes

As the ⟨scope⟩ activity not only embeds an activity, but can also contain event, fault, compensation, and termination handlers, it is WS-BPEL's most complex activity. This complexity is reflected by the big ⟨scope⟩ pattern of the semantics of [10]. Though termination handlers were not introduced in BPEL4WS 1.1, this pattern still had to be distributed to several subpatterns, one for each handler. In addition, a *stop component* which has no equivalent in WS-BPEL was added to the ⟨scope⟩ pattern. This pattern by itself consists of 32 places, 16 transitions, and also uses a reset arc [16].[3] The main purpose of this component is to model the interactions of the several subpatterns in case of fault and compensation handling, or during the termination of the scope. In particular, the stop component uses several status places to "distribute" control and data tokens to the correct subpattern. Thus, it is possible to signal faults to a unique place of the scope. However, faults occurring in the embedded activity can be handled by the fault handler of the respective scope whereas faults of the compensation handler have to be handled by the parent scope's fault handler. This separation of positive control flow inside the activities' patterns and the negative control flow organized in the stop component allowed comprehensible patterns. Still, the stop pattern introduced several intermediate states. In addition to this possible state explosion, the scope pattern of [10] could not be nested inside repeatable constructs such as ⟨while⟩ activities or event handlers[4]. To this end, we decided not to extend the existing scope pattern, but to create a new pattern optimized for computer-aided verification while covering the semantics specified by WS-BPEL 2.0.

The main idea of the new pattern is to use as much information about the context of the activities as possible. For example, we refrain from a single place to signal faults to avoid a stop component to distribute incoming fault tokens. Instead, we use static analysis to derive information of the activities from the WS-BPEL process. If, for example, an activity is nested in a fault handler, faults should be signaled to the fault handler's parent scope *directly*. This way, we decentralize the aspects encapsulated in the stop component, resulting in patterns which are possibly less legible yet avoiding unnecessary intermediate states.

The new scope pattern is depicted in Fig. 7. It consists of four parts modeling the different aspects of the scope.

- The **positive control flow** consists of the inner activity of the scope and the optional event handlers. It is started by transition initialize which sets the scope's state to Active. The scope remains in this state while the inner activity and the event handlers are executed. Upon completion, transition finalize sets the scope's state to !Active (the positive control flow is not active) and Successful (the embedded activity ended faultlessly). The latter state is later used by the compensation handler.
- The **negative control flow** consists of the fault handlers and a small subnet organizing the stopping of the embedded activity. It can be seen as the

---

[3] For verification purposes, this reset has to be unfolded (the connected place is bounded), resulting an even bigger subnet.

[4] The WS-BPEL 2.0 specification now actually demands activities in event handlers to be nested in a ⟨scope⟩ activity.

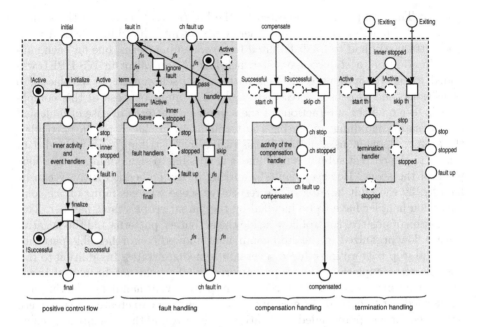

Fig. 7. The pattern for the ⟨scope⟩ activity. It consists of four parts modeling the different aspects of the scope: the positive control flow consisting of the embedded activity and the event handlers, the fault handlers, the compensation handler and the termination handler.

remainder of the former stop component, yet it is integrated more closely to the rest of the pattern. When a fault occurs in the inner activity or the event handlers, a token consisting of the fault's name is produced on place fault in. As the positive control flow is active, place Active is marked. Thus, transition term is activated. Upon firing, the scope's state is set to !Active, and the stop place of the inner activity and the event handlers is marked. Furthermore, the fault's name *fn* is passed to the fault handlers (place fsave). When the positive control flow is stopped (place inner stopped is marked), the fault handlers are started. If they succeed, place final is marked and the scope has finished.[5] If, however, the fault could not be handled or the fault handlers themselves signal a fault, place fault up is marked. This place is merged with the parent scope's or process's fault in place. Instead of using a reset arc to ignore any further faults occurring during the stopping of the embedded activity, transition ignore fault eventually removes all tokes from place fault in.

– The transitions pass, handle, and skip organize the fault propagation in case the compensation handler throws a fault. In this case, the fault is passed to the scope that called the faulted compensation handler. The **compensation handler** itself is not modeled by a special pattern, but its embedded activity

---

[5] The scope is left in state !Sucessful to avoid future compensation.

is directly embedded to the scope. The compensation of the scope is triggered by a ⟨compensate⟩ or ⟨compensateScope⟩ activity that produces a token on place compensate. If the positive control flow of the scope completed faultlessly before (i. e., place Successful is marked), transition start ch starts the compensation handler's activity. If the scope did not complete faultlessly or the compensation handler was already called, transition skip ch skips the embedded activity. In any case, place compensated is marked. This place is again merged with the calling ⟨compensate⟩ or ⟨compensateScope⟩ activity.

– The **termination handler** is a new feature of WS-BPEL 2.0 and is discussed in the next section. The termination behavior of BPEL4WS 1.1 can, however, be simulated by embedding a ⟨compensate⟩ activity to the termination handler.

The new scope pattern is more compact as the pattern from the semantics of [10]. It correctly models the behavior of a ⟨scope⟩ activity for both BPEL4WS 1.1 and WS-BPEL 2.0 processes. Furthermore, it is easily possible to reset the status places which allows for scopes embedded in repeatable constructs (cf. the ⟨forEach⟩ pattern in Fig. 8). Finally, due to the absence of a stop component which is connected to all subpatterns, it is easy to derive parameterized patterns for any constellation of handlers, for example, a pattern for a scope without any handlers, a pattern for a scope with just an event handler, etc.

3.3   Comparison

To compare the new patterns for scopes and dead-path-elimination with the old patterns, we investigated an example process described in [15]. This process models a small online shop consisting of 3 scopes, 2 links, and 46 activities. The authors of [15] translated it using the old Petri net semantics and report a net size of 410 places and 1069 transitions, and a state space consisting of 6,261,648 states (443,218 states using partial order reduction). We translated this process with our compiler BPEL2oWFN[6] which implements the new semantics. Using the new patterns, the resulting net has 242 places and 397 transitions. The smaller net structure also results in a smaller state space consisting of 304,007 states (74,812 states using partial order reduction).

With the presented simplified patterns, we can verify processes of realistic size. Furthermore, structural reduction rules can be applied to further reduce the net size and—due to less intermediate states—also the state space.

4   Modeling WS-BPEL's New Features

WS-BPEL 2.0 [1] clarified several scenarios and added or renamed a couple of activities. While most of the semantical details where already covered by the semantics of [10], the other changes are mainly of syntactic nature and can be modeled straightforwardly. For example, the new ⟨repeatUntil⟩ activity can

---

[6] Available at http://www.gnu.org/software/bpel2owfn

be easily modeled by a ⟨while⟩ activity with adjusted loop condition. As such resulting patterns are not very surprising, we focus on those features that are entirely novel. In particular, the parallel ⟨forEach⟩ activity with its complex completion and cancelation behavior cannot be simulated with existing features. Furthermore, a termination handler now allows to execute an arbitrary activity when a scope is forced to terminate. In this section, we present patterns for the ⟨forEach⟩ activity and the termination handler and refer to [11] for the complete collection of patterns.

4.1 Modeling the ⟨forEach⟩ Activity

The ⟨forEach⟩ activity allows to parallel or sequentially process several instances of an embedded ⟨scope⟩ activity. To this end, an integer counter is defined which is running from a specified start counter value to a specified final counter value. The enclosed ⟨scope⟩ activity is then executed according to the range of the counter. In addition, an optional *completion condition* specifies a number of successful executions of the ⟨scope⟩ activity after the ⟨forEach⟩ activity can be completed prematurely.

The semantics of the sequential ⟨forEach⟩ activity can be simulated by a ⟨while⟩ or a ⟨repeatUntil⟩ activity which encloses a ⟨scope⟩ activity and an ⟨assign⟩ activity that organizes the counter. As the resulting pattern is rather technical and straightforward, we refrain from a presentation. Instead, we focus on the parallel ⟨forEach⟩ activity.

To model the parallel ⟨forEach⟩ activity, the number of instances of the embedded ⟨scope⟩ activity—that is, the range of the counter—has to be known

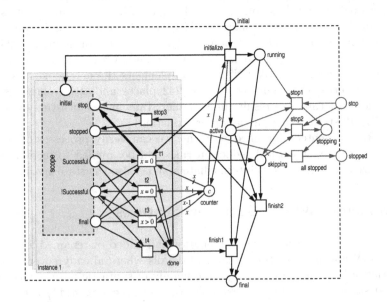

Fig. 8. The pattern for the parallel ⟨forEach⟩ activity

in advance. It can be derived using static analysis, for instance. Due to the expressive power of XPath, static analysis of WS-BPEL processes with arbitrary XPath expressions is undecidable. Thus, if no upper loop bound can be derived, this bound has to be given explicitly. However, for the case where the loop bound is received as a message, existing work [17] can be adapted to create an exact model in this case.

Figure 8 depicts the generic pattern for an arbitrary but fixed number of scope instances. All nodes in the grey rectangle (the scope pattern as well as transitions t1–t4 and stop3) are present for each instance, whereas the other nodes of the pattern belong to the ⟨forEach⟩ activity itself and exist only once. To simplify the graphical representation, we merge arcs from or to instanced places. For example, the arc from transition initialize to the place initial of the scope pattern represents a single for each instance. Likewise, transition finish1 is connected to the done places of all instances. In addition, the bold depicted arc connects each instance's t1 transition with *every* stop place of the instance's scope.

We now describe the possible scenarios of the parallel ⟨forEach⟩ activity and their respective firing sequences in the pattern of Fig. 8. Any scenario starts with the firing of transition initialize which initializes all embedded scope patterns and produces a token with the value b on place counter. This value describes the completion condition; that is, the number of scope instances that have to finish successfully to end the ⟨forEach⟩ activity prematurely. The ⟨forEach⟩ activity is now in state active and running.

- **Normal completion.** The instances are concurrently executing their embedded ⟨scope⟩ activities. When a scope completes, its final place is marked. In addition, either place Successful (the scope executed faultlessly) or place !Successful is marked (the scope's activity threw a fault that could be handled by the scope's fault handlers). In case of successful completion, transition t3 fires and resets the scope's state to !Successful and marks the instance's done place. Furthermore, the counter is decreased. If the scope was in state !Successful, transition t4 produces a token on the instance's done place without decreasing the counter. When all instances' scopes are completed, transition finish1 completes the ⟨forEach⟩ activity.

- **Premature completion.** When a sufficient number of scope instances have completed faultlessly, the ⟨forEach⟩ activity may complete prematurely; that is, it ends without the need to wait for the other still running scopes to complete. As mentioned before, the completion condition is modeled by the counter place. As this counter is decreased every time an instance's ⟨scope⟩ activity completed faultlessly, the counter value might reach 0. In this case, transition t3 is—due to its guard—disabled. Instead, transition t1 can fire which resets the scope as before and additionally sets the ⟨forEach⟩'s state to skipping. Furthermore, it produces a token on the stop place of every instance's scope.[7] Thus, all running scopes are stopped. Eventually, the stopped

---

[7] This is depicted by the bold arc. Transition t1 also produces a token on the stop place of the scope that just finishes.

place of all instances is marked—any tokens on the done places are also removed—and transition finish2 completes the ⟨forEach⟩ activity. Due to the asynchronous stopping mechanism, it is possible that other scopes complete while their stop place is marked. In this case, transition t2 behaves similarly to transition t1, but does not initiate the stopping sequence again.

– **Forced termination.** The ⟨forEach⟩ activity can—as all other activities— be stopped at any time by marking its stop place. Transitions stop1 and stop2 organize the stopping for the normal completion and the premature completion, respectively. The counter is not changed by the stopping mechanism, because its value is overwritten each time the ⟨forEach⟩ starts.

The ⟨forEach⟩ activity is mainly used to parallel or sequentially perform similar requests addressed to multiple partners and is thus an important construct to model service orchestrations or choreographies. To simplify the presentation of the pattern, we do not depicted the subnet that organizes the compensation of the instance's scopes.

4.2 Modeling Termination Handlers

By the help of a termination handler, the user can define how a scope behaves if it is forced to terminate by another scope. The termination handler is syntactically optional, but—if not specified—a standard termination handler consisting of a single ⟨compensate⟩ is deemed to be present.[8]

The termination handler is only executed if (1) the scope's inner activity has stopped, (2) no fault occurred, and (3) no ⟨exit⟩ activity is active. In the scope pattern of Fig. 7, these prerequisites are fulfilled if the places inner stopped, Active, and !Exiting (a status place of the process that is marked unless an ⟨exit⟩ activity is active) are marked. Then, transition start th invokes the termination

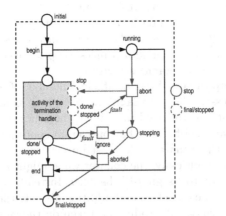

Fig. 9. The pattern for the termination handler

---

[8] This standard termination handler also models the behavior described in the BPEL4WS 1.1 specification.

handler. In any other case, place stopped is marked. Unlike the compensation handler, the termination handler's activity cannot be embedded directly to the scope, but needs a wrapper pattern, depicted in Fig. 9.

In the positive control flow, transitions begin and end start the embedded activity and end the termination handler, respectively. If the embedded activity throws a fault, it is not propagated to the scope's fault handler, because the scope is forced to terminate to handle a fault that occurred in a different scope. Thus, transition abort just stops the inner activity if a fault occurred, and transition ignore fault ignores further faults. When the inner activity is stopped, place done/stopped place is marked and transition aborted completes the termination handler similarly to transition end.

5   Conclusion

We presented a feature-complete Petri net semantics that models all data and control flow aspects of a WS-BPEL (version 1.1 or 2.0) process. The semantics is an extension of the semantics presented in [10]. To allow more compact model sizes, we simplified and reduced important aspects such as dead-path-elimination and the ⟨scope⟩ pattern. First experiments show that the resulting models are much more compact than the models presented in [15]. We further introduced patterns of the novel constructs such as the ⟨forEach⟩ activity and termination handlers. For computer-aided verification, we implemented a low-level version of the semantics in our compiler BPEL2oWFN which is used in several case studies [12,13]. We only presented a few patterns of the semantics in this paper. The complete semantics is published in [11].

As WS-BPEL is only defined informally, the correctness of the presented patterns can not be proven. However, we validated the Petri net semantics in various case studies. We translated real-life WS-BPEL processes into Petri net models and analyzed the internal (cf. [15]) and interaction (cf. [12,18,13]) behavior as well as the interplay of several WS-BPEL processes in choreographies (cf. [19]).

5.1   Related Work

Though many formal semantics for WS-BPEL were proposed (see [3] for an overview), to the best of our knowledge, no formal semantics of the new constructs of WS-BPEL 2.0 was proposed yet.

Ouyang et al. present in [20,21] a pattern-based Petri net semantics. This semantics models the behavior of the activities and constructs of BPEL4WS 1.1 with the semantics described an early specification draft of the WS-BPEL 2.0. Thus, the semantics adequately models the behavior of BPEL4WS 1.1 processes and avoids the ambiguities of the earlier specification [2]. However, constructs such as the ⟨forEach⟩ activity or termination handlers are not covered by this semantics. For detailed comparison between, see [22].

5.2   Future Work

The presented semantics is feature-complete; that is, it models all data and control flow aspect of a WS-BPEL process.[9] However, the instantiation of process instances and message correlation is not covered by the semantics. In future work, we want to add a instantiation mechanism to the semantics, allowing to analyze the complete lifecycle of process instances.

As WS-BPEL is just a part of the web service protocol stack (cf. [23]), the underlying layers such as WSDL, WS-Policy, etc. may also influence the behavior of the WS-BPEL process under consideration. In ongoing research, we plan to incorporate the information derived from these layers (e. g., fault types and policy constraints) to our semantics to *refine* the resulting models and allow for more faithful analysis results.

Acknowledgements. The author wishes to thank Christian Gierds, Eric Verbeek, Christian Stahl, Martin Znamirowski, and Simon Moser for valuable discussions and comments regarding the Petri net semantics. This work is funded by the German Federal Ministry of Education and Research (project Tools4BPEL, project number 01ISE08).

References

1. Alves, A., et al.: Web Services Business Process Execution Language Version 2.0. Technical report, OASIS (2007)
2. Andrews, T., et al.: Business Process Execution Language for Web Services, Version 1.1. Technical report, BEA, IBM, Microsoft (2003)
3. Breugel, F., Koshkina, M.: Models and verification of BPEL (2006), http://www.cse.yorku.ca/~franck/research/drafts/tutorial.pdf
4. Aalst, W.M.P.v.d., Hee, K.M.v.: Workflow Management: Models, Methods, and Systems. MIT Press, Cambridge, Massachusetts (2002)
5. Reisig, W.: Petri Nets. Springer, Heidelberg (1985)
6. Aalst, W.M.P.v.d.: The application of Petri nets to workflow management. Journal of Circuits, Systems and Computers 8(1), 21–66 (1998)
7. Martens, A.: Analyzing Web service based business processes. In: Cerioli, M. (ed.) FASE 2005. LNCS, vol. 3442, pp. 19–33. Springer, Heidelberg (2005)
8. Schmidt, K.: Controllability of open workflow nets. In: Desel, J., Frank, U. (eds.) Enterprise Modelling and Information Systems Architectures, Proceedings of the Workshop in Klagenfurt, October 24-25, 2005. Lecture Notes in Informatics (LNI), GI, vol. 75, pp. 236–249 (2005)
9. Girault, C., Valk, R. (eds.): Petri Nets for System Engineering – A Guide to Modeling Verification and Applications. Springer, Heidelberg (2002)
10. Stahl, C.: A Petri net semantics for BPEL. Techn. Report 188, Humboldt-Universität zu Berlin, Germany (2005)
11. Lohmann, N.: A feature-complete Petri net semantics for WS-BPEL 2.0 and its compiler BPEL2oWFN. Techn. Report 212, Humboldt-Universität zu Berlin, Berlin, Germany (2007)

---

[9] We do not model aspects that are not part of the WS-BPEL language itself such as XPath or XSLT.

12. Lohmann, N., Massuthe, P., Stahl, C., Weinberg, D.: Analyzing interacting BPEL processes. In: Dustdar, S., Fiadeiro, J.L., Sheth, A.P. (eds.) BPM 2006. LNCS, vol. 4102, pp. 17–32. Springer, Heidelberg (2006)
13. Lohmann, N., Massuthe, P., Stahl, C., Weinberg, D.: Analyzing interacting WS-BPEL processes using flexible model generation. Data Knowl. Eng. 64(1), 38–54 (2008)
14. Reisig, W.: Petri nets and algebraic specifications. Theor. Comput. Sci. 80(1), 1–34 (1991)
15. Hinz, S., Schmidt, K., Stahl, C.: Transforming BPEL to Petri nets. In: van der Aalst, W.M.P., Benatallah, B., Casati, F., Curbera, F. (eds.) BPM 2005. LNCS, vol. 3649, pp. 220–235. Springer, Heidelberg (2005)
16. Dufourd, C., Finkel, A., Schnoebelen, P.: Reset nets between decidability and undecidability. In: Larsen, K.G., Skyum, S., Winskel, G. (eds.) ICALP 1998. LNCS, vol. 1443, pp. 103–115. Springer, Heidelberg (1998)
17. Moser, S., Martens, A., Görlach, K., Amme, W., Godlinski, A.: Advanced verification of distributed WS-BPEL business processes incorporating CSSA-based data flow analysis. In: IEEE International Conference on Services Computing (SCC 2007), pp. 98–105. IEEE Computer Society Press, Los Alamitos (2007)
18. Lohmann, N., Massuthe, P., Wolf, K.: Operating guidelines for finite-state services. In: Kleijn, J., Yakovlev, A. (eds.) ICATPN 2007. LNCS, vol. 4546, pp. 321–341. Springer, Heidelberg (2007)
19. Lohmann, N., Kopp, O., Leymann, F., Reisig, W.: Analyzing BPEL4Chor: Verification and participant synthesis. In: Dumas, M., Heckel, R. (eds.) WS-FM 2007. LNCS, vol. 4937, pp. 46–60. Springer, Heidelberg (2007)
20. Ouyang, C., Verbeek, E., Aalst, W.M.P.v.d., Breutel, S., Dumas, M., Hofstede, A.H.M.t.: WofBPEL: A tool for automated analysis of BPEL processes. In: Benatallah, B., Casati, F., Traverso, P. (eds.) ICSOC 2005. LNCS, vol. 3826, pp. 484–489. Springer, Heidelberg (2005)
21. Ouyang, C., Aalst, W.M.P.v.d., Breutel, S., Hofstede, A.H.M.t.: Formal semantics and analysis of control flow in WS-BPEL. Sci. Comput. Program. 67(2-3), 162–198 (2007)
22. Lohmann, N., Verbeek, H., Ouyang, C., Stahl, C., Aalst, W.M.P.v.d.: Comparing and evaluating Petri net semantics for BPEL. Computer Science Report 07/23, Eindhoven University of Technology, Eindhoven, The Netherlands (2007)
23. Wilkes, L.: The Web services protocol stack. Technical report, CBDI Web Services Roadmap (2005), http://roadmap.cbdiforum.com/reports/protocols

From BPEL to SRML:
A Formal Transformational Approach[*]

Laura Bocchi[1], Yi Hong[1], Antónia Lopes[2], and José Luiz Fiadeiro[1]

[1] Department of Computer Science, University of Leicester
University Road, Leicester LE1 7RH, UK
{bocchi,yh37,jose}@mcs.le.ac.uk
[2] Department of Informatics, Faculty of Sciences, University of Lisbon
Campo Grande, 1749-016 Lisboa, Portugal
mal@di.fc.ul.pt

Abstract. The SENSORIA Reference Modelling Language (SRML) provides primitives for modelling business processes in a technology agnostic way. At the core of SRML is the notion of module as a composition of tightly coupled components and loosely coupled, dynamically discovered services. This paper presents an encoding of BPEL processes into SRML modules using model transformation techniques. The encoding provides the means to create high-level declarative descriptions of BPEL processes that can be used for building more complex modules, possibly including components implemented in other languages. The composition can be modelled and analysed as an ensemble, relying on the rich formal framework that is being developed within SENSORIA.

1 Introduction

The SENSORIA Reference Modelling Language (SRML) is a high-level modelling language for Service Oriented Architectures (SOAs) developed in the context of SENSORIA, an IST-FET Integrated Project on *Software Engineering for Service-Oriented Overlay Computers*. The goal of SRML is to provide a set of primitives that is expressive enough to model applications in the service-oriented paradigm and simple enough to be formalized. Through the notion of module, SRML provides primitives for modelling business processes as assemblies of (1) tightly coupled components that may be implemented using different technologies (including wrapped-up legacy systems) and (2) loosely coupled, dynamically discovered services.

The structure of a SRML module is illustrated in Fig. 1. Both the service provided and the external services required by the module are represented through what we call external interfaces, which are rich descriptions of the behaviour that can be observed of the interactions with these parties. The language primitives used for description and specification of service and component behaviour have been presented in [5].

---

[*] This work was partially supported through the IST-2005-16004 Integrated Project *SENSORIA: Software Engineering for Service-Oriented Overlay Computers*, and the Marie-Curie TOK-IAP MTK1-CT-2004-003169 *Leg2Net: From Legacy Systems to Services in the Net*.

M. Dumas and R. Heckel (Eds.): WS-FM 2007, LNCS 4937, pp. 92–107, 2008.
© Springer-Verlag Berlin Heidelberg 2008

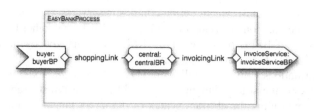

Fig. 1. The module *EasyBankProcess* has one component – *central* of type *centralBR* – which orchestrates the interactions with the external parties. The node *invoiceService* (of type *invoice-ServiceBP*) is an external-interface for a service required by the module. The node *buyer* (of type *buyerBP*) is the external interface for the provided service. The edges *shoppingLink* and *invoicingLink* provide the protocols that coordinate the interactions between the involved parties.

The interconnections between different parties are represented as wires labelled with interaction protocols [1].

SRML modules were inspired by the Service Component Architecture (SCA) [13]. SCA is a set of specifications that describe a middleware-independent model for building applications over SOAs. It provides a convenient framework to manage the deployment and configuration of service-oriented systems. In SCA, applications are built as assemblies of heterogeneous components and external services. SCA offers specific support for a variety of component implementations, namely for WS-BPEL [14]. More concretely, a BPEL client and implementation specification is defined that allows a component to be written is BPEL and deployed and assembled with other components written in any SCA implementation language.

In this paper, we present an encoding of WS-BPEL processes, including the WSDL interfaces with which they are associated, into SRML modules. As in SCA, the synthesis of high-level declarative descriptions allows existing BPEL processes to be used together with other components when defining models for composite services as SRML modules. The models consist of the assembly of a number of SRML modules that can be derived from existing components (implemented in BPEL or any other language for which an encoding into SRML has been provided), or for which an implementation still has to be provided. As a consequence, a given BPEL process can be used in the implementation of different composite services.

A basic difference between our encoding and the one provided through SCA results from the fact that, whereas SCA abstracts from the business logic provided by components, SRML provides a high-level declarative description of that business logic. Therefore, our encoding also addresses the orchestrations performed by BPEL processes within the assembly structures.

As a consequence, our encoding provides the means for WS-BPEL processes to be analysed, both individually and within composite services, by relying on the rich formal framework that is being developed within SENSORIA [15]. However, it should be clear that our aim is not to provide BPEL with yet another formal semantics and associated verification techniques, but only to the extent in which BPEL processes can be used in SRML to define composite services, possibly in conjunction with other service components implemented also in BPEL or in other languages.

The encoding of BPEL processes into SRML is formalized by means of model transformation rules based on triple graph grammars (TGG) [8]. The definition of model transformations with TGGs relies on: (1) *a source meta-model* representing the abstract syntax of the source language (e.g. BPEL) as a typed graph, (2) a *target meta-model* representing the abstract syntax of the target language (e.g. SRML) as a typed graph, (3) a third graph grammar — *the correspondence meta-model* — that connects related elements of (1) and (2) and is used to control the transformation process which, in general, is bidirectional. In our case, we provide directional transformation rules that specify only one direction – from BPEL to SRML.

The structure of the paper is as follows. Section 2 discusses the strategy of the encoding in more detail and presents an example. Section 3 presents the transformation rules for the module structure. Section 4 presents the encoding of the control flow. Finally, Section 5 presents final conclusions and discusses future work.

2   The Strategy of the Encoding

As described in [5], SRML provides mechanisms for assembling two modules via an external wire that establishes how the provides-interface *EX-P* of one module matches a requires-interface *EX-R* of the other module (Fig. 2). Assembly can be performed at design-time in order to define composite services (orchestrated systems), or dynamically, at run-time, through the discovery and binding mechanisms of the underlying SOA platform. In this paper, we do not address how SRML supports the dynamic aspects. The algebraic semantics of assembly is discussed in [6].

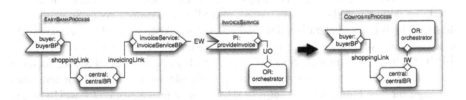

Fig. 2. The operation that assembles two modules into a module internalises the external wire EW that establishes a matching between the external interfaces (specifications) *invoiceService* (requires) and *PI* (provides)

The strategy of our encoding is precisely to abstract modules from BPEL processes, i.e. to identify the external interfaces (provides and requires) and the internal component that orchestrates the interactions involved, so that these BPEL-modules can then be used together with all other sorts of modules to define more complex services. In the resulting system, the original BPEL process will be connected with other components (possibly implemented in other languages like Java) through internal wires that establish the interaction protocols through which they communicate.

The encoding we propose involves both the module structure and the control flow involved in BPEL processes. A tool has been developed at the University of Leicester that provides semi-automated support [10] for this process. More precisely, it considers a subset of the BPEL constructs that concern service structure, produces a skeleton of a SRML module, and supports the manual definition of the missing aspects. The tool parses the XML tree representing the BPEL process with DOM and implements the transformation with a number of Java classes.

Our paper presents a more encompassing encoding than the one implemented by the tool. We encode structured activities (excluding scopes), control links and correlation sets. Table 1 shows which aspects of the BPEL control flow are considered in the encoding and which are supported by the tool. The encoding of the missing aspects is still work in progress. The main reason is that, as already explained, our aim is not to define yet another semantics for BPEL but to encode BPEL processes in a way that they can be used for defining SRML modules; as such, we have to take into account how the constructs provided by BPEL can be used within SRML. For instance, fault handling is a feature that, in SRML, is not handled at the same level of abstraction as the orchestration primitives (ditto for correlation sets). Therefore, we will consider the encoding of the throw primitive once we have extended SRML itself. The same applies to the constructs that relate to session handling, including correlation, which in SRML are treated as part of configuration management and treated in a fragment of the language that is still under construction.

Table 1. BPEL tags for control flow encoded in the tool and in this paper. BA stands for basic activity and SA for structured activity.

BPEL Tag/Construct	Tool	Encoding
Invoke , Receive, Reply, Assign (BA)	✓	✓
Wait, Empty, Exit (BA)	✗	✓
Throw (BA)	✗	✗
Sequence, Switch (SA)	✓	✓
Flow, While (SA)	✗	✓
Control Links, Scopes, Correlation Sets	✗	✗

The encoding of the SRML module structure from a BPEL process is in line with the one defined in [14] for embedding BPEL processes into SCA. The encoding of the control flow is inspired by the formal semantics of WS-BPEL in Petri Nets presented in [12]. The resulting approach is compositional because it describes any activity as a black box that is activated by the enclosing structured activity. This makes it easier to extend the encoding to the other types of BPEL activity.

To illustrate our approach we use a simple BPEL process — *easyBankProcess* – that receives an order from a buyer, uses an external service to create an invoice, and returns the invoice to the buyer. The following fragment defines the participants of the process and the links among them.

```
<process name="easyBankProcess"...
   <portType name="ShopPortType"> ...
   <portType name="InvoicingPortType"> ...
```

```
<portType name="BuyerPortType"> ...
<partnerLinkType name="invoicingLinkType">
    <role    name="invoiceService">    <portType    name="ns:InvoicePortType"/>
    </role>
</partnerLinkType>
<partnerLinkType name="shoppingLinkType">
    <role name="buyer"><portType name="ns:BuyerPortType"/></role>
    <role name="shop"><portType name="ns:ShopPortType"/></role>
</partnerLinkType>
<partnerLinks>
    <partnerLink name="invoicingLink" partnerLinkType="ns:invoicingLinkType"
        partnerRole="ns:invoiceService"/>
    <partnerLink name="shoppingLink" partnerLinkType="ns:shoppingLinkType"
        myRole="ns:shop" partnerRole="ns:buyer"/>
</partnerLinks>
```

The *partnerLinkType* elements define a link type between pairs of roles, each of which is associated with a certain *portType* element. A *portType* is a set of operations supported by a service. For example, *shoppingLinkType* defines a link type between two roles: *buyer*, of type *BuyerPortType*, and *shop*, of type *ShopPortType*. When only one role is specified, the other role can be associated with any *portType*, as in the case of *invoicingLinkType*. The *partnerLink* elements define an instance of *partnerLinkType* that specifies which of the roles belongs to the process (*myRole*) and to the partners (*partnerRole*).

The structure of the corresponding SRML module is illustrated in Fig. 1. Every partner role is represented as an external interface, either an EX-P (provides) or an EX-R (requires) interface, as discussed in Section 3. The central component represents all the roles assumed by the BPEL process (i.e., *myRole*). In the example, the SRML module has two external interfaces, *buyer* and *invoiceService*. The central component assumes the role of *shop* (i.e., port type *ShopPortType*) in *shoppingLink* and the generic role in *invoicingLink*.

Every role in the BPEL process is associated with a *portType* that declares a set of interactions:

```
<portType name="ShopPortType">                 <portType name="InvoicingPortType">
 <operation name="placeOrder">                  <operation name="doInvoice">
  <input message="ns:placeOrderInput"/>          <input message="ns:doInvoiceInput"/>
 </operation>                                     <output message="ns:doInvoiceOutput"/>
</portType>                                       </operation>
                                                </portType>

<portType name="BuyerPortType">
 <operation name="receiveBill">
  <input message="ns:receiveBillInput"/>
 </operation>
</portType>
```

In SRML, each external interface and component, to which we refer as nodes, is an instance of a business protocol or business role, respectively. The business role and protocols of the SRML *easyBankProcess* module are given below. The business role *centralBR* supports (1) the operation *PlaceOrder* of *shopPortType* and (2) the complementary interactions for *invoicePortType* and *buyerPortType*.

BUSINESS ROLE centralBR **is**

INTERACTIONS
  rcv shopPortType.placeOrder
    ⌂ placeOrderInput.product:Product
  s&r invoicePortType.doInvoice
    ⌂ doInvoiceInput.product:Product
    ✉ doInvoiceOutput.bill:Bill
  snd buyerPortType.receiveBill
    ⌂ receiveBillInput.bill:Bill

BUSINESS PROTOCOL buyerBP **is**

INTERACTIONS
  snd shopPortType.placeOrder
    ⌂ placeOrderInput.product:Product
  rcv buyerPortType.receiveBill
    ⌂ receiveBillInput.bill:Bill ...

BUSINESS PROTOCOL invoiceServiceBP **is**

INTERACTIONS
  r&s invoicePortType.doInvoice
    ⌂ doInvoiceInput.product:Product
    ✉ doInvoiceOutput.bill:Bill ...

Business roles and protocols declare a number of interactions in a way that is similar to BPEL port types. The specification of a node n defined in the encoding supports the interactions that: (1) correspond to an operation supported by the *portType* associated with n, (2) the complementary interactions (i.e., a send is complementary to a receive) of the operations supported by the node to which n is wired. The fragment of the BPEL process that models the control flow declares two variables, *order* and *bill*, and defines the orchestration as a sequence of one receive and two invocations:

```
<variables>
  <variable name="order" messageType="ns:orderData"/>
  <variable name="bill" messageType="ns:invoiceData"/>
</variables>
<sequence>
  <receive name="rcvOrder" partnerLink="ns:shoppingLink" operation="ns:placeOrder"
    portType="ns:ShopPortType" variable="order" createInstance="yes"/>
  <invoke name="askInvoice" partnerLink="ns:invoicingLink" operation="ns:doInvoice"
    portType="ns:InvoicePortType" inputVariable="order" outputVariable="bill"/>
  <invoke name="sndBill" partnerLink="ns:shoppingLink" operation="ns:receiveBill"
    portType="ns:BuyerPortType" variable="bill"/>
</sequence>
```

Both business roles and business protocols define causal relationships among the events that occur as part of the supported interactions. Business roles express this causality in terms of an orchestration, i.e. state-transition based description of the process through which a component reacts to and initiates such events. Business protocols provide specifications of provided or required behaviour in terms of properties (expressed in a temporal logic) that abstract such causal relationships from the processes that run in the co-parties. In the case of provides-interfaces, we provide a specification of the protocol offered to the co-party and, in the case of requires-interfaces, that of the protocol that the co-party is required to adhere to.

Because BPEL does not support such semantically reach external interfaces, we focus exclusively on how to extract the orchestration of the business role *centralBR* from a BPEL specification. As an example, we present the orchestration of the central business role of the SRML module that is derived from the activities of the BPEL process *easyBankProcess*. In the next sections, we will discuss in detail how the different elements of the module are synthesised.

BUSINESS ROLE centralBR **is**

INTERACTIONS

...

ORCHESTRATION

local   order.product:Product,
    start,exit,end,ra,rb,rc,rd,fa,fb,fc,fd:Boolean,
    na,nb,nc,cd:Natural
initialisation
    start=end=exit=false
    ra=rb=rc=rd=fa=fb=fc=fd=false
    na=nb=nc=nd=0
transition harness

> The local variables describe the state of the component: *order.product* and *bill.bill* are variables from the BPEL process; the others model control flow.

> The orchestration is described by transition rules.

    triggeredBy true
    guardedBy ¬start ∨ fa
    effects (¬start ⊃ start'∧ra')
       ∧ (fa ⊃ ¬fa'∧end')
transition transition_A (sequence)

> **triggeredBy** is a condition, typically a receive-event as in *transition_B*. When the condition is true the transition is triggered once the guard becomes true.

    triggeredBy true
    guardedBy (ra ∨ fb ∨ fc ∨ fd) ∧ ¬exit
    effects (ra ⊃ rb'∧¬ra')
       ∧ (fb ⊃ rc'∧¬fb')
       ∧ (fc ⊃ rd'∧¬fc')
       ∧ (fd ⊃ fa'∧¬fd')
transition transition_B (receive)

> **guardedBy** is a condition that identifies the states in which the transition can take place

    triggeredBy shopPortType.placeOrder⌂?
    guardedBy rb ∧ ¬exit
    effects ¬rb' ∧ fb'
       ∧ order.product'=shopPortType.placeOrder⌂.placeorderInput.product
transition transition_C (first invoke)

> The sentence **sends** describes the interaction events that are sent and the values taken by their parameters

    triggeredBy true
    guardedBy rc ∧ ¬exit
    effects ¬rc'
    sends invoicePortType.doInvoice⌂!
       ∧ invoicePortType.doInvoice⌂.doInvoiceInput.product=order.product
transition transition_C' (first invoke 2nd part)
    triggeredBy invoicePortType.doInvoice⊠?
    guardedBy
    effects fc' ∧ bill.bill'=invoicePortType.doInvoice⊠.doInvoiceOutput.bill
transition transition_D (second invoke)

> ⌂ and ⊠ identify request and reply events that may occur during conversational interactions.

    triggeredBy true
    guardedBy rd
    effects ¬rd' ∧ fd'
    sends buyerPortType.receiveBill⌂!
       ∧ buyerPortType.receiveBill⌂!.receiveBillInput.bill=bill.bill

3 Definition of the Module Structure

A BPEL process provides contextual information involving the external participants interacting with the process (i.e., the roles and port types wired to the business process through the partner links). In contrast, a SRML business role provides no information on the context in which it is used: the interface defines a set of interactions that is not partitioned according to the number of expected interacting parties. This is why, in order to preserve the contextual information in the encoding, we map BPEL processes not to business roles, but to modules that represent contextualized business roles.

The transformation rules, in line with the QVT standard for Model Transformation [11], are represented with the following syntax: the source and target (fragments of) meta-models are represented by UML class diagrams and the correspondence is represented by meta-relations. Following [9], meta-relations are represented as dashed wires with a diamond enclosing the constraints of the relation instance. The shadowed classes on the right hand side are the classes added to the model by the rule. The diamond for a relation instance created by the rule is shadowed as well.

Fig. 3 illustrates the transformation rule of the root element of a WSDL/BPEL (left hand side) that generates a SRML module (right hand side) having the same name of the BPEL process, the module central component and corresponding business role.

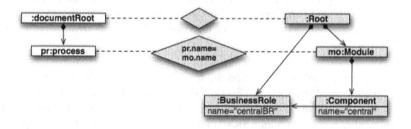

Fig. 3. Transformation rule generating the module

The application of the transformation rules in Fig. 3 to *myBankProcess* generates a module with name *myBankProcess* and one component named *central* of type *centralBP*. The set of other nodes that are wired to the central component is defined considering any *partnerLink* in the BPEL process. For any *partnerLink* element (representing a participant interacting with the business process) is created an external interface connected to the central component and the corresponding business protocol.

We discriminate between what must be encoded into an *EX-P* and into an *EX-R* by looking for the presence or absence of a *receive* operation having the *createInstance* attribute set to "*yes*", which is the mechanism used in BPEL to represent the invocation of a business process. The *partnerLink* associated with such operation is the one that, if it exists, invokes the service modelled by the BPEL process. Hence, an EX-P is created for such *partnerLink*. All the other *partnerLink* elements create an *EX-R* through the rule described in Fig. 4, which requires the absence of a *receive* operation having *createInstance* attribute set to "*yes*".

In the *myBankProcess* example, the rule described in Fig. 4 creates an *EX-R* named *invoiceService* of type *invoiceServiceBP*. The *EX-R* is connected to the central component with the wire *invoicingLink*. The rule for the *EX-P* interfaces creates an *EX-P* named *buyer* of type *buyerBP*, connected with the wire *shoppingLink*. The structure of the resulting module is the one presented in Fig. 1.

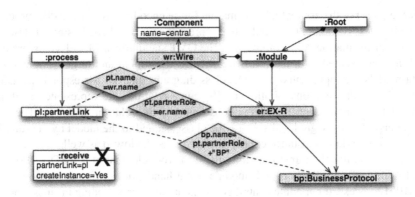

Fig. 4. Transformation rule generating a requires-interface and the corresponding wire that connects it to the central component. The rule that generates the external provides-interface is similar but, instead, requires the absence of a receive operation having *createInstance* attribute set to "*yes*".

Using the same method, we define the transformation rules for the set of interactions supported by all the nodes. Every node corresponds to a BPEL *portType* element. A node represents one or more port types and must support, for any operation in the *portType,* a corresponding SRML interaction. In addition, it must support the complementary interactions of the *portType* elements connected to the node through a *partnerLink.* We omit the details of the rules for the interactions and their parameters. Table 2 shows, for each WSDL operation type, the corresponding SRML interaction types/parameters and their complements. For example, the request-response operation is encoded as a *r&s* (i.e., receive and send) interaction, whose complementary element is an *s&r* interaction. The input parameters are encoded as △-parameters, which are the parameters for transmitting data when the interaction is initiated.

The current OASIS draft for WS-BPEL [2] specifies that some of the WSDL operations must not be supported by BPEL processors (i.e., *notification* and *solicit-response*); hence, we consider the supported operations only.

Table 2. WSDL operations and SRML interactions

WSDL	SRML	SRML (complementary)
one-way	*rcv*	*snd*
> input parameter	> △ parameter	> △ parameter
request-response	*r&s*	*s&r*
> input parameter	> △ parameter	> △ parameter
> output parameter	> ⊠ parameter	> ⊠ parameter

We encode the operation with name '*op*' of the *portType* '*pt*' as the interaction with name '*pt.op*'. Because any interaction event in SRML may occur at most once during a session, we have to define a family of interactions for each operation. This family defines an arbitrary number of interactions, each identified by an index (e.g., *pt.op[i]*). For each interaction we define a variable *pt.opB* (and also *pt.opE* for *r&s* and *s&r* interactions) of type *Natural* that is initially *0* and is incremented at each occurrence of the ⌂- (and ⊠-) event of the interaction *pt.op* and stores the index that must identify the next occurrence. In the example presented in Section 2, we omitted these indexes for readability, as each operation is invoked only once.

4 Transformation of Control Flow

The encoding of control flow into SRML has been inspired by the Petri Net-based semantics of WS-BPEL presented in [12]. Therein, a generic activity A is represented as a Petri net having: (1) an initial state r_A, in which the transition is ready to be executed, (2) a final state f_A, (3) the state s_A/c_A in which the activity starts/completes.

Fig. 5. A simplified version the Petri Net representation of a generic BPEL activity A [12], and the corresponding SRML transition. Additional statements have to be added to model the execution of the activity.

In the SRML encoding, the execution of the orchestration begins with a "harness" transition that uses a special boolean variable *start,* initially set to false. The harness triggers the activity A, corresponding to the root activity of the BPEL process, by setting *ra* to *true*:

```
transition harness
triggeredBy true
guardedBy ¬start ∨ fa
effects (¬start ⊃ start'∧ra') ∧ (fa ⊃ ¬fa'∧end')
```

4.1 Encoding Basic Activities

In a BPEL process, a parameter sent by an operation consists of a *Variable* element that has already been declared and assumed a meaningful value by means of an *Assign* activity. Fig.6. presents the transformation rule for creating a local variable in the orchestration of the SRML module from the corresponding variable in the BPEL process. The *DataType* object, defining the type of the variable, does not need to be created if an object already exists for the same type.

Some additional local variables have to be defined for handling the control flow:

- *start/end*, of type Boolean, is true when the process instance starts/ends.

- *exit*, of type Boolean, disables, when true, the execution of any transition. It is initially false. The value may be changed by the *Exit* activity.
- *ra* and *fa* for any activity *A*.

To improve readability, we present the transformation rules for activities by using a textual notation, showing the correspondence between the two languages. The generated transitions belong to the orchestration of the business role *centralBR*.

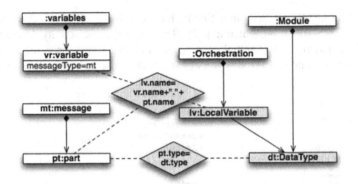

Fig. 6. Transformation rule for variables declaration. A BPEL variable refers to a message composed by parts. A local variable is created, for each part of each BPEL variable, in the orchestration of the business role typing the central component that is the only orchestration in the module.

Assign. The *assign* activity refers to a couple of variables and to a specific part of the message that types each variable. The *assign* activity in the BPEL code fragment below (on the left) is encoded into the SRML transition *transition_A* also shown below (on the right). The effects of the transition include the assignment of the part *formP* of the variable *fromV* to the part *toP* of *toV*.

```
<assign>
 <copy>
  <from variable="fromV" part="fromP"/>
  <to variable="toV" part="toP"/>
 </copy>
</assign>
```

```
transition transition_A
triggeredBy true
guardedBy ra ∧ ¬exit
effects ¬ra' ∧ fa'
         ∧ toV.toP'=fromV.fromP
```

Invoke. The *invoke* activity is used to invoke a service and may refer to either a one-way or request-response WSDL operation. The invocation, in BPEL, is modelled from the perspective of the invoked party and in SRML corresponds to either a *snd* or a *s&r* interaction of the central component. The BPEL code fragment below invokes a request-response operation.

```
<invoke      partnerLink="pl"      portType="pt"      operation="op"
       inputVariable="iv" outputVariable="ov"/>
```

The invoke statement above is transformed into the two SRML transitions below.

```
transition transition_A                    transition transition_A'
triggeredBy true                           triggeredBy pt.op[pt.opE]⊠?
guardedBy ra ∧ ¬exit                       guardedBy ¬exit
effects ¬ra' ∧ pt.opB'=pt.opB+1            effects fa'
sends pt.op[pt.opB]⊖!                        ∧ ov.p1'=pt.op[pt.opE]⊖.ov.p1 ∧ …
    ∧ pt.op[pt.opB]⊖.iv.p1=iv.p1 ∧ …        ∧ ov.pm'=pt.op[pt.opE]⊖.ov.pm
    ∧ pt.op[pt.opB]⊖.iv.pn=iv.pn            ∧ pt.opE'=pt.opE+1
```

The first part of the request-response is modelled by *transition_A* that sends the interaction event *pt.op[pt.opB]⊖!* where *pt* is the name of the *portType* and *op* is the operation. The parameters are assigned to the corresponding parts of the input variable *iv*. We assume, with no loss of generality, that the message type of *iv* consists of the parts *p1,...,pn*. The second part of the request-response is represented by *transition_A'* that receives the interaction event *pt.op[pt.opE]⊠?* and assigns the value of the output parameters (in all the *m* parts) to the output variable. We do not need to add a guard to enable *transition_Ab* after *transition_A* as SRML ensures that, *pt.op[i]⊠?* is always enabled after (and only after) *pt.op[i]⊖!*.

The invoke of a one-way operation, where the output variable is not specified, is transformed in *transition_A* where the effects include the statement *fa'*.

Receive and Reply. The *receive* activity refers to either a one-way or a request-response operation and it is encoded according to the transformation rule that follows.

```
<receive partnerLink="pl"        transition transition_A
    portType="pt"                triggeredBy pt.op[pt.opB]⊖?
    operation="op"               guardedBy ra ∧ ¬exit
    variable="v"                 effects ¬ra' ∧ fa' ∧ pt.opB'=pt.opB+1
    createInstance=…/>               ∧ v.p1'=pt.op[pt.opB]⊖.v.p1 ∧ …
                                     ∧ v.pn'=pt.op[pt.opB]⊖.v.pn
```

The *reply* activity refers to either a one-way or (the second part of) a request-response operation. In case of a one-way operation it is encoded according to the transformation rule that follows. The rule for the request-response is similar but it sends the interaction event *pt.op[pt.opE]⊠!*.

```
<reply partnerLink="pl"        transition transition_A
    portType="pt"              triggeredBy true
    operation="op"             guardedBy ra ∧ ¬exit
    variable="v"…/>            effects ¬ra' ∧ fa' ∧ pt.opB'=pt.opB+1
                               sends n.pt.op[pt.opB]⊖! ∧ n.pt.op[pt.opB]⊖.v.p1=v.p1
                                   ∧ … ∧ n.pt.op[pt.opB]⊖.v.pm=v.pm
```

Wait. The *wait* activity specifies a deadline (time interval or future instant of time).

```
<wait> <for>t</for>(<until>t</until>)</wait>
```

SRML provides a number of primitives for handling time [5], including the function *now* which returns the present time from a global clock. The *wait* activity is transformed into the transitions above:

```
transition transition_A (for)          transition transition_A (until)
triggeredBy true                       triggeredBy now≥t
guardedBy ra ∧ ¬exit                   guardedBy ra ∧ ¬exit
effects timeA=now ∧ ¬ra'               effects fa' ∧ ¬ra'


transition transition_A' (for)
triggeredBy now=timeA+t
guardedBy ¬exit
effects fa'
```

Exit and Empty. The *exit* activity terminates the execution of the process. It is encoded into *transition_A* below that gives the value true to the Boolean local variable *exit*. This disables any further transition. The *empty* activity performs no action. It is encoded into *transition_B* below.

```
transition transition_A (exit)         transition transition_B (empty)
triggeredBy true                       triggeredBy true
guardedBy        ra       ∧   ¬exit    guardedBy         rb      ∧        ¬exit
effects ¬ra' ∧ fa' ∧ exit'             effects ¬rb' ∧ fb'
```

4.2 Encoding Structured Activities

Sequence. The *sequence* activity is used to execute two activities in sequence, in the specified order. Let us suppose we have two activities A and B represented by two transitions *transition_A* and *transition_B*. We model the sequence activity X as the transition *transition_X*. We denote with rx, ra and rb the boolean variables that trigger the execution of X, A and B, respectively. The variables fx, fa and fb denote the end of the corresponding activity. The transition *transition_X* is executed three times: when the parent activity triggers X (by setting rx to true), when the enclosed activity A terminates (and sets fa to true) and, analogously, when B terminates.

```
<sequence            transition transition_X
   name="X">         triggeredBy true
   activity A        guardedBy (rx ∨ fa ∨ fb)  ∧ ¬exit
   activity B        effects (rx ⊃ ra'∧¬rx) ∧ (fa ⊃ rb'∧¬fa') ∧ (fb ⊃ fx'∧¬fb')
</sequence>
```

Flow. The *flow* activity executes the enclosed activities in parallel. We consider the case of two parallel activities with no loss of generality. The transition *transition_X* models the flow activity for A and B. The flow activity on the left side is transformed into *transition_X*. The transition is executed two times: when the parent activity triggers X (by setting rx to true) and when the enclosed activities A and B both terminate (i.e., synchronization).

```
<flow name="X">      transition transition_X
   activity A        triggeredBy true
   activity B        guardedBy (rx ∨ (fa ∧ fb)) ∧ ¬exit
</flow>              effects (rx ⊃ ra'∧ rb'∧¬rx') ∧ (fa ∧ fb ⊃ fx'∧¬fa'∧¬fb')
```

Switch. The *switch* activity executes one of two activities, depending on a condition. If all the conditions are false no activity is executed. The conditions are evaluated in the specified order. We consider a *switch* statement involving two conditions with no loss of generality. The switch activity on the left side is transformed into *transition_X*.

The transition is executed two times: when the enclosing activity triggers X (by setting rx to *true*), when one the enclosed activities terminates.

```
<switch name="X">                    transition transition_X
 <case>                              triggeredBy true
  <condition>       z1    </condition>  guardedBy (rx ∨ fa ∨ fb) ∧ ¬exit
  activity A                         effects (rx∧z1 ⊃ ra'∧¬rx')
 </case>                                ∧ (rx∧¬z1∧z2 ⊃ rb'∧¬rx')
 <case>                                 ∧ (rx∧¬z1∧¬z2 ⊃ fx'∧¬rx')
  <condition>       z2    </condition>    ∧ (fa∨fb ⊃ fx'∧¬fa'∧¬fb')
  activity B
 </case>
</switch>
```

Pick. The *pick* activity waits for a set of events, each associated to an activity, and executes (only) the activity associated to the first event that occurs. The events can be triggered by an external message or by an alarm. We consider, without loss of generality, a set of two events: one triggered by a message and one triggered by the alarm. The *Pick* activity on the left side is transformed into *transition_X* and *transition_X'*. First *transition_X* is executed: rx becomes *false* and the the present time is stored in the variable tX. Then *transition_X'* is executed when either $e1 ⌂?$ occurs or when the deadline expires and triggers the corresponding activity, A or B. Notice that, because of its guards, *transition_X'* is executed only once: before either A or B is triggered. $P\_e1[i] ⌂?$ is true if the event $e1[i] ⌂?$ occurred in the past. The transition *transition_X* is executed again when either fa or fb is *true; fx* is then set to *true*.

```
<pick name="X">         transition transition_X
 <onMessage       e1>   triggeredBy true
    A                   guardedBy (rx ∨ fa ∨ fb) ∧ ¬exit
 </onMessage>           effects (rx ⊃ ¬rx'∧tX'=now+t)
 <onAlarm>                 ∧ (fa ⊃ ¬fa'∧fx') ∧ (fb ⊃ ¬fb'∧fx')
   <for>          t
   </for>
    B                  transition transition_X'
 </onalarm>            triggeredBy e1[i]⌂? XOR now=tX
</pick>                guardedBy ¬ra ∧ ¬rb ∧ ¬exit
                       effects ra'=P_e1⌂? ∧ rb'=now=tX
```

While. The *while* activity iterates an activity A until a condition is true. The *while* activity on the left side is transformed into *transition_X*. The transition is executed the first time when rx is true and then when the execution of any enclosed activity terminates. During the first iteration rx is set to false. The condition determines either the execution of A or the end of *transition_X*. The end of a previous iteration ($fa=true$) determines either the end of *the while* activity or execution of the next iteration ($ra=true$), depending on the condition z.

```
<while name="X">        transition transition_X
 <condition>z          guardedBy (rx ∨ fa) ∧ ¬exit
 </condition>          effects rx ⊃ (¬rx'∧ ra'≡z ∧ fx'≡¬z)
  activity A              ∧ fa ⊃ (¬fa' ∧ ra'≡z ∧ fx'≡¬z)
</while>
```

5   Conclusions and Future Work

In this paper, we have discussed an encoding of WS-BPEL processes into SRML – the modelling language that is being developed within the SENSORIA project for supporting the engineering of complex services. In SRML, modules provide abstractions of composite services as provided through assemblies of components and externally services procured and bound at run-time.

SRML is inspired on SCA [13]. Like in SCA, the components used inside a module need not be homogeneous: they can be Java programs, BPEL process, wrapped-up legacy systems, and so on. SRML provides a language in which these components can be modelled as transition-based systems obtained through abstraction mappings. The purpose of this paper was precisely to illustrate the abstract encoding that we defined for BPEL-processes, which is richer than the one provided for SCA because we are able to encode the business logic operated by the component. We should stress that the purpose of the encoding is not to provide a new semantics for BPEL but to abstract from BPEL processes the SRML modules that allow them to be combined with other modules to define more complex services, avoiding having to develop required orchestrations from scratch. This is why the proposed encoding does not consider aspects that, like fault handling and correlation sets, are not directly relevant for the fragment of SRML that is concerned with composition. We are working on an extension of the encoding that considers some of the missing aspects in the context of the fragment of SRML that handles configuration management.

Our encoding is performed through model-transformation rules based on triple graph grammars. We present the design of some of the transformation rules that we developed so far. Their implementation is straightforward if using a tool for modeling graph transformations: we are using the Tiger tool environment [3], based on Eclipse Modelling Framework (EMF). The source WSDL/BPEL meta-model derives from the combination of the meta-model obtained from the XSD specifications of WSDL and the meta-model of WS-BPEL defined in the context of the Eclipse BPEL project[1]. The target SRML meta-model has been produced using the Eclipse Graphical Modelling Framework (GMF). The meta-models are modelled as EMF trees. In this way, it will be possible to easily implement the transformation rules using tools s.a. Tiger [3], which transform meta-models expressed in EMF.

Another strong point of our approach is that it will make it possible for the rich analysis framework being developed in SENSORIA [15] to be used for analysing and verifying properties of BPEL processes. The goal is to reason about the properties of modules assembled from possibly heterogeneous components, e.g. through model checking [7].

Acknowledgments

We would like to thank our colleagues in SENSORIA for many useful discussions, and our Leicester colleagues Reiko Heckel and Karsten Ehrig in particular for guidance in graph transformations and Tiger. Finally, we would like to thank the reviewers for extensive and profound comments and suggestions that have definitely improved the quality of this version.

---

[1] http://www.eclipse.org/bpel/

References

1. Abreu, J., Bocchi, L., Fiadeiro, J.L., Lopes, A.: Specifying and composing interaction protocols for service-oriented system modelling. In: Formal Methods for Networked and Distributed Systems. LNCS, Springer, Heidelberg (to appear, 2007)
2. Alves, A., et al.: Web Services Business Process Execution Language Version 2.0. Technical report, TC OASIS (2007), available from http://www.oasis-open.org/
3. Abreu, J., Bocchi, L., Fiadeiro, J.L., Lopes, A.: Specifying and composing interaction protocols for service-oriented system modelling. In: Formal Methods for Networked and Distributed Systems. LNCS, Springer, Heidelberg (to appear, 2007)
4. Alves, A., et al.: Web Services Business Process Execution Language Version 2.0. Technical report, TC OASIS (2007), available from http://www.oasis-open.org/
5. Biermann, E., Ehrig, K., Koehler, C., Kuhns, G., Taentzer, G., Weiss, E.: Graphical definition of in-place transformations in the Eclipse Modeling Framework. In: Nierstrasz, O., Whittle, J., Harel, D., Reggio, G. (eds.) MoDELS 2006. LNCS, vol. 4199, pp. 425–439. Springer, Heidelberg (2006)
6. Bisztray, D., Heckel, R.: Rule-level verification of business process transformation using CSP. In: Graph Transformation and Visual Modeling Techniques. Electronic Communications of the EASST (2007)
7. Fiadeiro, J.L., Lopes, A., Bocchi, L.: A formal approach to service-oriented architecture. In: Bravetti, M., Núñez, M., Zavattaro, G. (eds.) WS-FM 2006. LNCS, vol. 4184, pp. 193–213. Springer, Heidelberg (2006)
8. Fiadeiro, J.L., Lopes, A., Bocchi, L.: Algebraic semantics of service component modules. In: Fiadeiro, J.L., Schobbens, P.-Y. (eds.) WADT 2006. LNCS, vol. 4409, pp. 37–55. Springer, Heidelberg (2007)
9. Gnesi, S., Mazzanti, F.: On the fly model checking of communicating UML state machines. In: ACIS International Conference on Software Engineering Research, Management and Applications, pp. 331–338 (2004)
10. Grunske, L., Geiger, L., Lawley, M.: A graphical specification of model transformations with triple graph grammars. In: Hartman, A., Kreische, D. (eds.) ECMDA-FA 2005. LNCS, vol. 3748, pp. 284–298. Springer, Heidelberg (2005)
11. Hausmann, J.H.: Dynamic Meta Modelling: a semantics description technique for visual modelling languages. PhD Thesis, Faculty of Computer Science, Electrical Engineering, and Mathematics, University of Paderborn, Germany (2005)
12. Hong, Y.: WSDL and BPEL to SRML-P Language Transformation. MSc Dissertation, University of Leicester (2006)
13. Object Management Group, MOF QVT Final Adopted Specification (2007), available from: http://www.omg.org/docs/ptc/05-11-01.pdf
14. Ouyang, C., Verbeek, E., van del Aalst, W.M.P., Dumas, M., ter Hofstede, A.H.M.: Formal semantics and analysis of control flow in WS-BPEL (revised version). BPM Center Report BPM-05-15, BPMcenter.org (2005)
15. SCA Consortium Building Systems using a Service Oriented Architecture. Whitepaper version 0.9 (2005), available from: http://www.oracle.com/technology/tech/webservices/standards/sca/pdf/SCA_White_Paper1_09.pdf
16. SCA Consortium SCA Client and Implementation Model Specification for WS-BPEL. Version 1.00 (2007), available from:
    http://www.osoa.org/download/attachments/35/SCA_ClientAnd
    ImplementationModelforBPEL_V100.pdf?version=1
17. Wirsing, M., Bocchi, L., Clark, A., Fiadeiro, J., Gilmore, S., Hölzl, M., Koch, N., Pugliese, R.: SENSORIA: Engineering for Service-Oriented Overlay Computers (submitted, 2007)

Modeling Web Service Interactions Using the Coordination Language Reo

Samira Tasharofi[1,2], Mohsen Vakilian[1], Roshanak Zilouchian Moghaddam[1], and Marjan Sirjani[1,2]

[1] Department of Electrical and Computer Engineering, University of Tehran, Tehran, Iran
[2] School of Computer Science, Institute for Studies in Theoretical Physics and Mathematics (IPM), Niavaran Square, Tehran, Iran
stasharofi@ut.ac.ir,
{m.vakilian,r.ziloochian}@ece.ut.ac.ir,
msirjani@ut.ac.ir

Abstract. In this paper we propose an approach to derive the formal semantics of WS-BPEL processes compositionally using Reo and constraint automata. We map each WS-BPEL process into a Reo circuit and then construct the corresponding constraint automaton which shows the behavior of the process. The constraint automaton can be used for analyzing the process behavior. Our work covers the core part of the WS-BPEL language including basic and structured activities, correlation sets, variables, and links.

Keywords: Compositional Semantics, Constraint Automata, Reo, WS-BPEL, Web Services.

1 Introduction

Web service composition provides the mechanism to manage the complexity of execution of business processes which may be dynamic or static. For static composition of web services two main approaches are currently proposed. The first approach, referred to as web service orchestration, combines available services by adding a central coordinator (the orchestrator) that is responsible for invoking and combining the single sub-activities. The second approach, referred to as web service choreography, defines complex tasks via the definition of the conversation that should be undertaken by each participant (instead of using a central coordinator). Following this approach, the overall activity is achieved as the composition of peer-to-peer interactions among the collaborating services.

WS-BPEL [1] is a specification for web service orchestration that models the behavior of web services in a business process interaction. It has been revised by IBM and Microsoft and is a candidate for being the standard language for web service composition. The specification provides an XML-based grammar for describing the control logic required to coordinate web services participating in a process flow.

M. Dumas and R. Heckel (Eds.): WS-FM 2007, LNCS 4937, pp. 108–123, 2008.

There are some approaches for formal specification of web services and their composition [2,3,4,5]. One of the modeling languages that is used for modeling compositional construction of web services is Reo [6,7,8]. Reo [9] is a coordination language for modeling systems based on components. In this language the components are connected and coordinated through channels which are the simplest connectors. The Reo language has a strong formal basis and promotes loose coupling, distribution, mobility, exogenous coordination, and dynamic reconfigurability. Constraint automata [10] provide compositional formal semantics for Reo. The formal basis of Reo guarantees possibilities for both model checking and verification, as well as well-defined execution semantics of a web service composition [6]. Exogenous coordination of components in Reo by channels makes it suitable for modeling orchestration. In this modeling, web services play the role of the components (which may also be Reo circuits) and the orchestrator is the Reo circuit that coordinates them. In other words, Reo as a modeling language for service composition can provide service connectivity, composition correctness, automatic composition and composition scalability which are vital and valuable for modeling web services.

In this paper, each WS-BPEL process is mapped into a Reo circuit and consequently to its corresponding constraint automaton. The whole process can be compositionally built out of simple constructs while its constraint automaton can be used to formally analyze the behavior of WS-BPEL processes. In this work, we consider the core part of the WS-BPEL language which shows the main stream of the control flow including basic and structured activities, correlation sets, variables, and links. Some concepts of WS-BPEL which consist of scope, fault handling, event handling, and compensation handling are remained and will be subjected in future. In our approach, we visualize web services and their interactions by Reo (which shows the structure), while the analysis support is automatically provided by constraint automata (which capture the behavior).

The organization of this paper is as follows: Section 2 consists of a brief overview of WS-BPEL. Some description of Reo and constraint automata are provided in Section 3. In Section 4 we describe our mapping algorithm for translation of WS-BPEL to Reo and constraint automata. In order to show the applicability of our mapping, in Section 5 we investigate a case study. In Section 6, we consider related works on formal modeling of WS-BPEL. Finally, Section 7 contains our conclusion and future works.

2   WS-BPEL

The WS-BPEL [1] process model is layered on top of the service model defined by WSDL 1.1. A business process defines how to coordinate the interactions between a process instance and its *partners* (a participant, which itself is a process instance). In this sense, a WS-BPEL process definition provides the description of the behavior and interactions of a process instance relative to its partners and resources. Such a business process can be described in two different ways: either as an *executable business process* or as an *abstract process*.

Executable business processes, which are the focus of this paper, model actual behavior of a participant in a business interaction. Abstract business processes are partially specified processes that are not intended to be executed.

For the specification of the internal behavior of a business process, WS-BPEL provides two classes of activities which perform the process logic: *basic* and *structured*. Basic activities are those which describe elemental steps of the process behavior. Structured activities encode control-flow logic, and can contain other basic and/or structured activities. The set of basic activities includes: <invoke> (invoke an operation on a service), <receive> (wait for a message from a partner), <reply> (send a response to a request), <assign> (update variables and partner links), <wait> (specify a delay for a certain period of time or until a certain deadline is reached), <empty> (do nothing and provide a synchronization point in a <flow>), and <exit> (end the business process instance).

Structured activities prescribe the order in which a collection of activities is executed. A structured activity can be nested within other structured activities-for various control-flow patterns. These activities include: <sequence> (sequential processing), <if> (conditional behavior), <while>, <repeatUntil> (repetitive execution), <forEach> (processing multiple branches), <pick> (selective event processing), and <flow> (parallel and control dependencies processing).

The <link> concept in WS-BPEL can be used to define an order between two concurrent activities in a flow in a sense that the target activity of a link can not start before the source activity of the link has either been executed or has been skipped. The *join condition* which is a boolean expression (with default value of true) and defined on the source activity of a link determines the possibility of execution of the activity, i.e., if it is evaluated to true, the source activity of the link must be executed; otherwise, it must be skipped.

A <portType> construct defines the <operation>s (a grouping of a related set of messages that are exchanged) that a web service supports. This construct is used in <partnerLinks> construct for specifying the shape of a relationship with a partner by defining the portTypes used in the interactions.

The notion of *correlation* is used to determine the exact *instance* of the partner process when sending a message. The standard mechanism to do this is to carry a business token in messages in a conversation for correlation. A set of correlation tokens is shared by all messages in the correlated group. In a business conversation, with several partners, the originator sends the first message, starts the conversation and defines the correlation tokens in the <correlationSet>. The rest of participants are followers and bind their <correlationSet>s by an incoming message containing the values of the properties in the <correlationSet>. Correlation can be used on every messaging activity (<receive>, <reply>, <onMessage>, <onEvent>, and <invoke>).

3   Reo and Constraint Automata

Reo is an exogenous coordination language based on a calculus of channels [9]. Reo consists of components that are connected via connectors which coordinate their activities. Primitive connectors are channels which have two ends. There are two types of channel ends: *source* and *sink*. A source channel end accepts data into its channel, and a sink channel end dispenses data out of its channel. The channel can be defined by users which allows an open-ended set of different channel types, each with its own policy for synchronization, buffering, ordering, computation, data retention/loss, etc. Some basic types of channels, used in this paper are: Synchronous Channel (*Sync*), Synchronous Drain (*SyncDrain*), FIFO1, Filter, and Lossy Synchronous Channel (*LossySync*).

A *Sync* channel has a source and a sink. Writing a message succeeds on the source of it if and only if taking of a message succeeds at the same time on its sink. A *SyncDrain* has two sources. Writing a message succeeds on one of the sources of it if and only if writing a message succeeds on the other source. The *FIFO1* channel has a source and a sink. It maintains a buffer with capacity of one. Writing a message succeeds on the source of a FIFO1 if and only if its buffer does not contain any messages. Taking of a message, which makes the buffer empty, succeeds on the sink of it if and only if its buffer already contains a message. The Filter channel behaves like the *Sync* except that it loses all data that do not match the specified pattern of the Filter. A *LossySync* channel has a sink and a source. The source always accepts all data items. If the sink does not have a pending read or take operation, the *LossySync* loses the data item, otherwise the channel behaves as a *Sync*.

Complex connectors are constructed through composition of simpler ones by applying *join* operation. Whereas, the internal behavior of complex connectors can be abstracted away with the aid of *hide* operation. A component can write data items to a *source* node that it is connected to. The write operation succeeds only if all source channel ends coincident on the node accept the data item, in which case the data item is written to every source end coincident on the node. A *source* node, thus, acts as a *replicator*. A component can obtain data items, by an input operation, from a *sink* node that it is connected to. A take operation succeeds only if at least one of the sink channel ends coincident on the node offers a data item; if more than one coincident channel end offers data items, one is selected nondeterministically. A *mixed* node nondeterministically selects and takes a suitable data item offered by one of its coincident sink channel ends and replicates it into all of its coincident source channel ends. A sink or mixed node, thus, acts as a nondeterministic *merger*.

Constraint automata (CA) [10] are proposed as compositional semantics for Reo, based on timed data streams [11]. Each element of a timed data stream is a pair of time and a data item, where the time indicates when the data item is being input or output. A transition fires if it observes data item in a port of the component and according to the observed data, the automaton may change its state.Therefore, the automata-states stand for the possible configurations (e.g., the contents of the FIFO-channels of a Reo-connector) while the automata-transitions represent the possible data flow and its effect on these configurations.

Definition 1 (Constraint Automata). A constraint automaton is a tuple $A = (Q, Names, \longrightarrow, Q0)$ where:

Q is a finite set of states, $Names$ is a finite set of names(e.g. I/O ports of a component), $\longrightarrow$ is a finite subset of $Q \times 2^{Names} \times DC \times Q$, called the transition relation of A, and $Q0 \subseteq Q$ is the set of initial states. DC is data constraint that plays the role of guard for transition. For example, $d\_A = d\_B$ is a data constraint that imposes the observed data on ports A and B must be equal.

Figure 1 shows the five Reo channels we used in this paper (mentioned above) and their corresponding constraint automata and also the constraint automaton of the merger node.

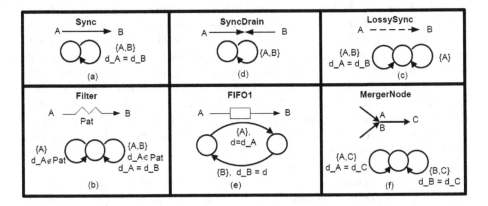

Fig. 1. Constraint automata for some basic Reo channels, and merger node

We may put a Reo connector (circuit) in a box to make a component out of it. The inner nodes become hidden and the source or sink nodes which are the interfaces of a component and its environment are called (input or output) ports. A component has well-defined behavior and interface and can be reused. We also used two Reo circuits, Exclusive Router (XR) and Shift Lossy FIFO $(ShiftLossyFIFO)$. The (XR) has an input port and two output ports, when a data item arrives at input, it flows to only one of the outputs depending on which is prepared to consume it. The $(ShiftLossyFIFO)$ behaves like an ordinary FIFO1, except that if it is full, the arrival of a new data item overwrites the existing data item.

4   Mapping Algorithm

Here, we present a mapping to transform a WS-BPEL process into a Reo circuit. Each basic and structured activity in WS-BPEL processes is mapped into a Reo circuit that models the behavior of the activity and can be considered as a reusable component.

For each component we consider two special ports called **start** and **end**. An activity is started whenever data is ready at the **start** port and the **end** port is fired whenever the corresponding activity is done. These **start** and **end** ports are used to make an activity be executed atomically. We use a FIFO1 and a SyncDrain to make a pattern to prevent a Reo circuit from restarting while it has not finished its current job (its **end** node has not yet been fired). The circuitry of this pattern can be seen in Fig. 5 and parts (a), (c), (e) and (g) of Fig. 4.

In WS-BPEL, the interaction between services is accomplished by message passing. To model this interaction in Reo, ports to send or receive messages are added to Reo components, and Sync channels connect corresponding ports between communicating components.

In the following, different concepts of WS-BPEL are explained briefly. Then, Reo circuits of each of these WS-BPEL activities are shown. Note that scope, fault handling, event handling, and compensation handling features of WS-BPEL are ignored in this paper for the sake of simplicity. They will be considered in our future development.

4.1 Variable

The Reo circuit and constraint automaton related to variable are depicted in Fig. 2.a and Fig. 2.b respectively. In the Reo circuit of variables, two ShiftLossyFIFO

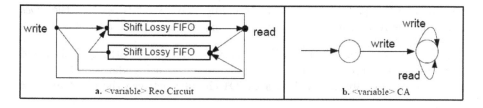

Fig. 2. Reo mapping of variable

channels are used in the form of a loop back. A write operation overwrites the values of both channels. An auxiliary ShiftLossyFIFO channel is used to restore the data of the other ShiftLossyFIFO channel whenever it is read. Actually, a restoring transition (which fires internally and is not observable from the outside) is needed between two consecutive reads. But as we are intended to model only the I/O behavior by hiding internal interactions from the constraint automaton, it is not appeared in the constraint automaton.

4.2 Basic Activities

Invoke. Generally the <invoke> activity is used to call services for specific operations. There are two forms of <invoke>, one-way invocation which requires only the **inputVariable**, and request-response invocation which requires both of **inputVariable** and **outputVariable**. Once the mapping of receive and one-way invocation are determined, the mapping of a request-response invocation could be easily obtained by considering a request-response invocation, as a <sequence> of a one-way invocation and a receive. The `initiate` attribute on a <correlation> specification is used to indicate whether the correlation set is being initiated. The Reo circuits of one-way invocation for `initiate=yes` is depicted in Fig. 4.a. For other values of `initiate` the circuits are slightly different.

Receive. The <receive> activity causes a blocking wait for a matching message. The `partnerLink` and the desired `operation` of the partner should be specified in <receive>. In addition, the `variable` in which the message is to be stored should be mentioned. Reo circuit of the <receive> activity for `initiate=yes` attribute of correlations set is illustrated in Fig. 4.c.

Reply. The <reply> activity, sends a message in reply to the received message. Therefore, a <reply> activity can be easily modeled as a <sequence> of a <receive> and an <invoke> activity.

Assign. The <assign> activity can be used to update the values of variables with new data. <assign> is a <sequence> of several <copy> constructs that copy one value each (Fig. 4.e). The desired part of the source variable is extracted from its Reo component using a Filter channel.

Wait. The <wait> construct specifies a delay for a given time period or until a certain time has passed. In the corresponding Reo circuit (Fig. 4.g), the *clock* component is responsible to announce finishing of the given period.

Empty. The <empty> construct is an activity that does nothing. This could be useful for synchronization of concurrent activities using <links>. This trivial activity can be easily modeled by a FIFO1 channel between the `start` and `end` nodes.

Exit. The <exit> construct is used to immediately end the business process instance. To model this construct in Reo we use an <empty> activity whose `end` signal is connected to the `end` node of the business process by a Sync channel.

4.3   Structured Activities

Sequence. The <sequence> construct defines a collection of activities to be performed sequentially. The Reo circuit and corresponding constraint automaton of the <sequence> construct are shown in Fig. 5.a and Fig. 5.b respectively.

If. The <if> construct is to provide conditional behavior. This activity is much like the `if-then-else` statements in regular programming languages in which a list of conditions are examined in order to find the first matching branch to execute. An <if> activity consists of one <condition>, optionally several <else if> elements and an optional <else> element. The Reo circuit and constraint automaton of <if> are depicted in Fig. 5.c and Fig. 5.d, respectively. In these figures, just one <else if> element is included. Additional <else if> elements can be added following the same pattern as the first one.

While, Repeat Until, For Each. The <while> construct indicates that an activity is to be repeated while a certain success criteria is met. The Reo circuit and the constraint automaton for the <while> activity are shown in Fig. 5.e and Fig. 5.f. The component for <repeatUntil> activity can be made using <while> component. The <forEach> activity executes its contained activity for a specified number of times and can be made using <while> activity.

Pick. The <pick> activity blocks and waits for a suitable message to arrive or for a time-out alarm to go off. When one of these triggers occurs, the associated activity is performed and the <pick> completes. The constraint automaton in Fig. 5.h, shows the behavior of the <pick> Reo circuit.

Flow. The <flow> construct specifies one or more activities to be executed concurrently. Figure 5.i models a <flow> of two processes. As shown in this figure, the start signal of the <flow> activity, *replicates* to the start signals of the given two activities to execute both concurrently. Finally, the end signal of the <flow> activity is issued whenever both of its containing activities have raised their end signals. As mentioned in Section 2, links can be used within concurrent activities to define arbitrary control structures in a way that the target activity of a link can not start before either its source activity is completed or skipped according to the value of *join condition.* As shown in Fig. 3, by using a FIFO1 and

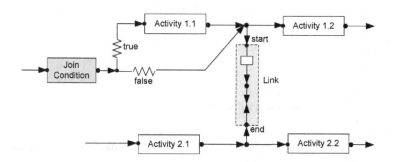

Fig. 3. Reo circuit depicting the use of <link> construct

a SyncDrain it is guaranteed that Activity 2.2 (target of the link) can not start either before Activity 1.1 (source of the link) is completed or skipped (after executing Activity 2.1). More precisely, if the output of the component *Join Condition* which is responsible for evaluating the join condition of Activity 1.1 is true, Activity 2.2 starts after Activity 1.1 is completed; otherwise, Activity 2.2 starts after Activity 1.1 is skipped. The filter channels with *true* and *false* filters determine the directions.

4.4   Trends for Adding Scope, Fault and Event Concepts

In order to incorporate scope, fault, and event concepts, the pattern used for each WS-BPEL activity must be extended so that it includes additional ports of *terminate* input port and *fault* output port. The *terminate* input port is used for terminating the executing activity when the process it belongs to must be terminated, e.g., a fault has occurred. On the other hand, enabling the *fault* output port stands for occurrences of fault within the activity. The detailed descriptions of mapping of these features are out of scope of this paper.

5   The Purchase Order Example

In this section, a typical process description [1] for handling a purchase order in WS-BPEL is mapped into Reo to demonstrate how the proposed mapping algorithm works in real world. On receiving the purchase order from a customer, the process initiates two paths concurrently: calculating the final price for the order, and selecting a shipper. While some of the processing can proceed concurrently, there are control and data dependencies between the two paths. In particular, the shipping price is required to finalize the price calculation. When the two concurrent paths are completed, invoice processing can proceed and the invoice is sent to the customer. The following is some parts of the code from the WS-BPEL description of the purchase order:

```
<sequence>
  <receive operation="sendPurchaseOrder" variable="PO" ...> </receive>
  <flow>
    <links> <link name="ship-to-invoice" /> </links>
    <sequence>
      <assign>
        <copy>
          <from>$PO.customerInfo</from>
          <to>$shippingRequest.customerInfo</to>
        </copy>
      </assign>
      <invoke operation="requestShipping" inputVariable="shippingRequest"
        outputVariable="shippingInfo" ...>
          <sources><source linkName="ship-to-invoice" /></sources>
      </invoke>
      <receive ... operation="sendSchedule" variable="shippingSchedule"/>
    </sequence>
    <sequence>
      <invoke operation="initiatePriceCalculation" inputVariable="PO".../>
      <invoke operation="sendShippingPrice" inputVariable="shippingInfo" ...>
        <targets><target linkName="ship-to-invoice"/></targets>
      </invoke>
      <receive ... operation="sendInvoice" variable="Invoice" />
    </sequence>
  </flow>
</sequence>
```

The circuit shown in Fig. 6 demonstrates the result of mapping the WS-BPEL process into Reo. However, the circuit is not an exact Reo circuit. Some notations

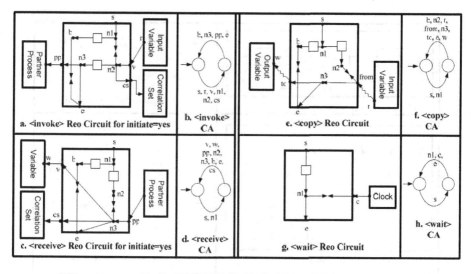

Fig. 4. Basic Activities

are used to keep the circuit concise. For example, a <receive> is represented by a box whose label is composed of "Receive" and the name of the activity. All other similar elements like <invoke> and <copy> are represented in the same manner. Other activities such as <assign> and structured activities are represented by a box containing other boxes as the inner activities or elements. Besides, the type of activity (<sequence>, <assign>, ...) is written in the upper left corner of the box. The complete Reo circuits of these boxes can be obtained in a straightforward way by using the mapping of each construct in Fig. 4 and Fig. 5. Therefore, all the activities inside a <flow> box, are executed in parallel. And, all of the activities inside a <sequence> box, are executed in the order the start and end nodes of them are connected to each other.

By sending the start signal to the purchase order component, the <sequence> component called "shippingSequence" and "invoiceSequence" get started (the upper left and right <sequence> respectively in Fig. 6). By starting the "shipping Sequence" construct, the first inner <assign> activity ("assignShippingRequest") is started and after its completion, <invoke> and <receive> activities will be initiated respectively, and completion of them completes the execution of the part of code mentioned above.

There is a tool [12] that automatically transforms WS-BPEL specification to its corresponding Reo circuit using our mapping algorithm and finally to constraint automaton. This constraint automaton can be analyzed by the tools presented in [13] and [14]. [14] enables us to check occurrences of deadlock and live-lock and also reachability in a constraint automaton. On the other hand, temporal properties can be checked using the tool introduced in [13]. These properties are noted in BTSL formula [15] which combines CTL operators with a special path modality $\langle\alpha\rangle$ and its dual $[\alpha]$ that allow to reason about the data streams observable at the network nodes by means of a regular expression α.

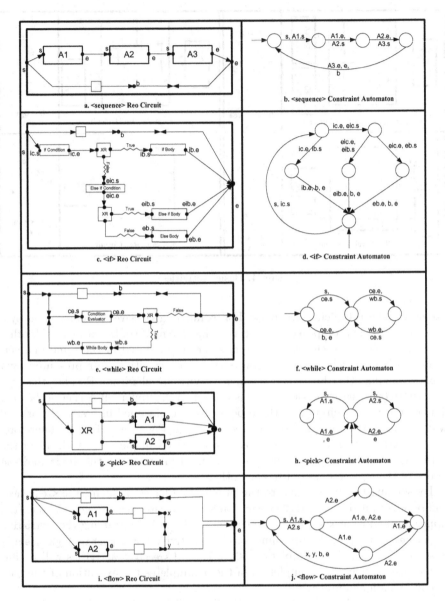

Fig. 5. Structured Activities

The BTSL model checking procedure relies on a combination of known methods for model checking CTL-like logics and automata-based approaches for linear time logics.

Figure 7 illustrates the constraint automaton of the case study. Having obtained the corresponding constraint automaton, several properties can be checked. This is one of the most important benefits of mapping WS-BPEL into

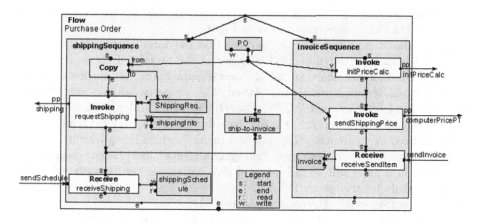

Fig. 6. Purchase Order Circuit

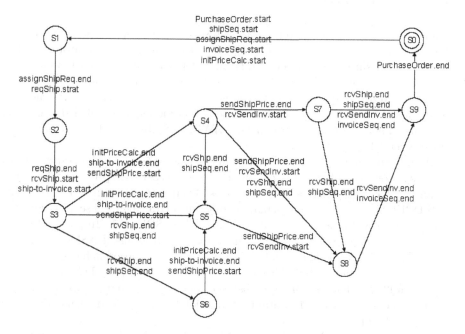

Fig. 7. Constraint automaton for purchase order

Reo that is, the ability of checking several properties formally. For instance, one might be interested in finding out whether or not the <invoke> activity "requestShipping" is executed before the <invoke> activity "sendShippingPrice". A <link> has been used to enforce the proper ordering and its mapping is presented in Fig. 6. In this case, no *join condition* is defined on the source activity of the link. So, it has its default value of true and the *Join Condition* component (presented in Fig. 3) does not appear in Fig. 6.

Using constraint automata, we can check that the order imposed by the <link> construct is satisfied in the actual behavior of the process. That is, it suffices to check whether the `start` signal of "`sendShippingPrice`" is issued only after the `end` signal of "`requestshipping`" raised. This property can be formulated as $\forall[(\neg reqShip.end)^*]\neg\exists\langle sendShipPrice.start\rangle true$ in BTSL logic. Another property can be insuring about that the purchase order process after receiving proper answers from two partners, Shipping and Invoice (which is equivalent to completion of its two child activities, "`shippingSequence`" and "`invoiceSequence`", executing in a flow) will be finished and give proper answer to customers. The BTSL formula for this property is:

$\forall[(true^*;shipSeq.end;(\neg PurchaseOrder.end)^*)\cap$
$(true^*;invoiceSeq.end;(\neg PurchaseOrder.end)^*)]\forall\langle PurchaseOrder.end\rangle true$

6   Related Work

Some well-known problems related to web services are how to specify them in a formal and expressive enough language, how to compose them (automatically), and how to ensure their correctness. Formal methods are particularly well suited to address the composition and correctness issues. Recently, a variety of concrete proposals to formally describe, compose and verify web services have emerged. The majority of these are based on state-action models (e.g. labeled transition systems, timed automata, Petri nets, YAWL, and abstract state machines) or process models (e.g. π-calculus).

Among automata-based approaches, in [16] the authors introduce a framework to verify properties of web service compositions of WS-BPEL processes that communicate via asynchronous XML messages. Their framework first translates the WS-BPEL processes to a particular type of automata, then, these automata are translated into Promela, and is model checked by SPIN [17]. In [5] an abstract executable semantics for WS-BPEL in terms of a distributed ASM [18] are defined. In this work, modeling and integration of compensation behavior and fault handling are not supported. These concepts are added in [19]. This work is continued in [2] in which a complete abstract operational semantics for WS-BPEL is presented by ASM which contains correlation handling, dead path elimination and event handling.

Petri-nets are widely used for formal specification and analysis of web services [20,21,3]. Some of these works can capture exception handling, compensation handling, and timing aspects, and make the variety of petri-net verification tools applicable for automatic analyzing of WS-BPEL processes.

The π-calculus [22] is a process algebra that has inspired modern composition languages including WS-BPEL. In [23] a process algebra called BPE-calculus that contains the main control flow constructs of WS-BPEL is introduced. The main goal was to analyze processes in order to detect possible deadlocks. This work does not cover fault and compensation handling of WS-BPEL. In [4] a two-way mapping is defined between WS-BPEL and the more expressive process algebra LOTOS. An advantage of this translation is that it includes compensations and exception handling.

The work in [24] proposes a method for translating WS-BPEL processes into YAWL workflows which are based on Petri nets. In that mapping, some aspects of WS-BPEL such as correlation sets and partner link types are ignored.

Reo, has also been used for modeling web services and their composition. The work presented in [8] investigates the issues of description, orchestration, and choreography of web services at a unifying abstract level. The authors in [7] and [6] proposed Reo for web service composition, but do not use any specific web service language. In [25], a framework for construction of composite services for distributed computing environments with the aid of Reo is presented. This framework should be integrated with other model checking tools for web service analysis. All of these works on Reo, use Reo in an abstract level for web service specification and composition without considering any specific web service language. But, here, we use WS-BPEL as a standard language for web service specification and composition. This makes our approach more applicable for practitioners working on web services and for analyzing existing WS-BPEL processes.

In comparison to other works that use Petri nets, Process algebra, ASM, and YAWL for modeling web services, our approach benefits from pros of Reo which can be summarized as follows:

- *Inherent fitness of computational models:* Reo is proposed as a coordination language for exogenous management of interactions among concurrent components. Hence, its computational model inherently fits for orchestrating web services as self contained components. Web services, like Reo components, can be composed to build other web services.

- *Visualization and compositionality:* Visual modeling of data flow among components makes the comprehension of component interaction more intuitive. Furthermore, thanks to hide operation and consequently hierarchical composition in Reo, the connectors can be specified in any abstract level and so the modeling can be more comprehensive and better matched with its real configuration. In our work, we benefit from hierarchical composition of Reo in modeling our case study, in which the basic and structured activities are abstracted in components. Similarly, any complex WS-BPEL activities and WS-BPEL processes can be encapsulated in components during modeling web services and their interactions. This makes our model simpler and more manageable. So, another advantage of hierarchical composition is the ability of modeling large scale systems. In YAWL, the high-level view of processes can be expressed by pattern templates while in real modeling, the patterns should be instantiated which may provide complex diagrams. In Reo, the instantiated components can be expressed in any abstract level. The only requirement is knowing their I/O behavior as constraint automata. That is the power of Reo which can be used in conjunction with constraint automata.

7   Conclusion and Future Work

We proposed a mapping from WS-BPEL to Reo which can be used to build the
Reo circuit of a web service compositionally. Our next step is to consider other
notions of BPEL as scope, event handling, fault and compensation handling,
and process instantiation. Furthermore, our approach moves toward using Reo
to reason about dynamic composition of web services.

References

1. Jordan, D., Evdemon, J.: Web services business process execution language version
   2.0. Technical report, OASIS (2006)
2. Fahland, D.: Complete abstract operational semantics for the web service business
   process execution language. Technical Report 190, Humboldt University, Berlin
   (2005)
3. Hinz, S., Schmidt, K., Stahl, C.: Transforming BPEL to Petri Nets. In: van der
   Aalst, W.M.P., Benatallah, B., Casati, F., Curbera, F. (eds.) BPM 2005. LNCS,
   vol. 3649, pp. 220–235. Springer, Heidelberg (2005)
4. Ferrara, A.: Web services: a process algebra approach. In: Proceedings of 2nd International Conference on Service Oriented Computing, pp. 242–251. ACM Press,
   New York (2004)
5. Farahbod, R., Glasser, U., Vajihollahi, M.: Specification and validation of the business process execution language for web services. In: Zimmermann, W., Thalheim,
   B. (eds.) ASM 2004. LNCS, vol. 3052, pp. 78–94. Springer, Heidelberg (2004)
6. Diakov, N., Arbab, F.: Compositional construction of web services using Reo. In:
   WSMAI, pp. 49–58 (2004)
7. Lemniotes, T., Papadopoulos, G.A., Arbab, F.: Coordinating web services using
   channel based communication. In: 28th Annual International Computer Software
   and Applications Conference (COMPSAC 2004), pp. 486–491 (2004)
8. Meng, S., Arbab, F.: Web services choreography and orchestration in Reo and
   constraint automata. In: Proceedings of 22nd Annual ACM Symposium on Applied
   Computing(SAC 2007) (2007)
9. Arbab, F.: Reo: A channel-based coordination model for component composition.
   Mathematical Structures in Computer Science 14(3), 329–366 (2004)
10. Baier, C., Sirjani, M., Arbab, F., Rutten, J.: Modeling component connectors in
    Reo by constraint automata. Science of Computer Programming 61(2), 75–113
    (2006)
11. Arbab, F., Rutten, J.: A coinductive calculus of component connectors. In: Wirsing,
    M., Pattinson, D., Hennicker, R. (eds.) WADT 2003. LNCS, vol. 2755, pp. 35–56.
    Springer, Heidelberg (2003)
12. Mahdikhani, F.: BPEL to Reo tool (2007),
    http://ece.ut.ac.ir/msirjani/B2ReoTool/B2R.jar
13. Klüppelholz, S., Baier, C.: Symbolic model checking for channel-based component
    connectors. In: FOCLASA 2006 (2006)
14. Pourvatan, B., Rouhy, N.: An alternative algorithm for constraint automata prod-
    uct. In: Arbab, F., Sirjani, M. (eds.) FSEN 2007. LNCS, vol. 4767, pp. 409–419.
    Springer, Heidelberg (2007)
15. Clarke, D.: A basic logic for reasoning about connector reconfiguration. Funda-
    menta Informaticae (accepted, 2007)

16. Fu, X., Bultan, T., Su, J.: Analysis of interacting BPEL web services. In: 13th Int. Conf. World Wide Web (WWW 2004), pp. 621–630. ACM Press, New York (2004)
17. Holzmann, G.: The SPIN Model Checker. Addison-Wesley, Reading (2003)
18. Borger, E., Stark, R.: Abstract State Machines: A Method for High-Level System Design and Analysis. Springer, Heidelberg (2003)
19. Fahland, D., Reisig, W.: ASM-based semantics for BPEL: The negative control flow. In: Proceedings of 12th International Workshop on Abstract State Machines, Paris, pp. 78–94. Springer, Heidelberg (2005)
20. Schmidt, K., Stahl, C.: A Petri Net semantic for BPEL4WS - validation and application. In: Proceedings of 11th Workshop on Algorithms and Tools for Petri Nets (2004)
21. Ouyang, C., van der Aalst, W., Breutel, S., Dumas, M., ter Hofstede, A., Verbeek, H.: Formal semantics and analysis of control flow in WS-BPEL. Technical Report BPM-05-15, BPM Center (2005)
22. Milner, R., Parrow, J., Walker, D.: A calculus of mobile processes, parts i and ii. Information and Computation 100(1), 1–77 (1992)
23. Koshkina, M.: Verification of business processes for web services. Master thesis, York University (2003)
24. Brogi, A., Popescu, R.: From BPEL processes to YAWL workflows. In: Bravetti, M., Núñez, M., Zavattaro, G. (eds.) WS-FM 2006. LNCS, vol. 4184, pp. 107–122. Springer, Heidelberg (2006)
25. Diakov, N., Arbab, F.: Software adaptation in integrated tool frameworks for composite services. In: Proceedings of The Third International Workshop on Coordination and Adaptation of Software Entities(WCAT 2006), Nantes, France, pp. 9–14 (2006)

Synthesis of Web Services Orchestrators in a Timed Setting*

Fabio Martinelli[1] and Ilaria Matteucci[1,2]

[1] Istituto di Informatica e Telematica - C.N.R., Pisa, Italy
[2] Dipartimento di Scienze Matematiche ed Informatiche,R. Magari,
Università degli Studi di Siena
{Fabio.Martinelli, Ilaria.Matteucci}@iit.cnr.it

Abstract. In this paper we present a framework based on *partial model checking* technique, *process algebra* and logic for the synthesis of Web Services orchestrators in a timed setting. We suppose to have a network of services and a user's request, expressed as a temporal logic formula by which also time constraints are specified. We define a process algebra operator, called *orchestrating operator* that permits us to manage services in order to satisfy the user's request. In order to isolate the behavior that the orchestrator should have to manage the given services, we extend the definition of the partial model checking function to the orchestrating operator. By using this function we are able to reduce the starting problem to a satisfiability one that we solve by exploiting a satisfiability procedure for temporal logic. In this way we automatically generate an *orchestrator process* as a model of the request.

1 Overview

In the last few years the automated composition of *Web Services* is one of the most promising ideas and, at the same time, one of the main challenges for the taking off of service oriented applications.

In this paper we use formal methods to deal with Web Services. As a matter of fact Web Services can be modeled by process algebras (*e.g.*, see [1,2,3,4,5]). Thus we are able to give an abstract and formal description of the behavior of services. Moreover all known results of process algebras theory can be applied to specify, study and analyze web services.

Services composition can be made on the one hand by a single peer service, which could be involved in different systems at different times, preserving their compositionality (*Orchestration*), and on the other hand, it is fundamental to guarantee overall systems functionalities (*Choreography*).

Here we propose a formal approach based on *CCS process algebra* (see [6]), logic and *partial model checking* (see [7]) in order to synthesize an orchestrator process in a timed setting. Temporal constraints are important in Web Services composition. We deal with time-related properties that are particularly relevant in Web Services scenarios, *i.e.*, they refer to the time required by services to carry out their tasks and take their decisions, and to the assumptions and constraints on these times that guarantee a

---

* Work partially supported by EU-funded project "Software Engineering for Service-Oriented Overlay Computers"(SENSORIA).

M. Dumas and R. Heckel (Eds.): WS-FM 2007, LNCS 4937, pp. 124–138, 2008.
© Springer-Verlag Berlin Heidelberg 2008

successful execution if the distributed business processes. Indeed we expect that a Web Service composition satisfies some global timing constraints, and these constraints can be satisfied only if all the services participating to the composition are committed to respect their own local timing constraints.

Our approach starts from our works on the synthesis of secure systems (see [8,9]), based on the use of partial model checking and process algebras for security analysis (see [10]), to deal with the Web Services composition problem in a timed setting. Moreover, according to the definition given in [11], our method permits to compose services at the *process level*, *i.e.*, the composition takes into account that executing a web service requires interactions that may involve different sequential, conditional, and iterative steps. As a matter of fact we define a process algebra operator ▷ said *orchestrating operator* that, by controlling the behavior of the composed process, permits to synchronize several services in order to satisfy the request.

We follow an approach in which time is discrete, actions are durationless and there is one special action $tick$ to represent the elapsing of time (see [12,13,14,15]). By using this approach we are able to synthesize an orchestrator process in a timed setting that manages a given set of services in order to generate a new process that is the composition of some of previous services and guarantees that this composition satisfies a request made by an external user. A possible request of a user is modeled by an *equational μ-calculus* formula (see [16]), hence, by exploiting a satisfiability procedure for temporal logic, we are able to generate an orchestrator process.

This paper is organized as follows. Section 2 recalls some notions of BPEL (*Business Process Execution Language*, see [17]), process algebras and temporal logic. Section 3 explains our approach by dealing also with a timed setting. Section 4 shows a simple example and Section 5 presents some related works. Section 6 concludes the paper.

2   Background

Here, we give a brief description of the general concepts of so called Web Services, we will show a useful mapping from their description languages to process algebra CCS.

2.1   Web Service Languages: WSDL and BPEL

The *World Wide Web Consortium, $W3C$* for short, defines a *Web Service* as a software system designed to support interoperable *Machine to Machine* interaction over a network. Web Services are frequently just Web $APIs$ that can be accessed over a network, such as the Internet. They are executed on a remote system with respect to the system of the user that invokes that service. Eventually, the user gets the result of such an execution.

This $W3C$ definition encompasses many different systems, but in common usage the term refers to clients and servers that communicate using XML (the *Extensible Markup Language*) messages following the $SOAP$ standard. $SOAP$ is a protocol for exchanging XML-based messages over computer networks.

XML is a general-purpose markup language. It is classified as an extensible language because it allows its users to define their own tags. Its primary purpose is to facilitate the sharing of structured data across different information systems, particularly via the Internet. It is used both to encode documents and serialize data.

WSDL is XML-based language that provides a model for describing Web Services. In particular, the format describes network services as a set of endpoints, or ports, operating on messages containing either document-oriented or procedure-oriented information.

The service is described, at an abstract level, in terms of the messages it sends and receives and, at a concrete level, defines details about protocols and data format specifications implementing operations for that particular service.

The BPEL language [17] has been introduced to describe business processes which manage the interaction of different Web Services, *i.e.*, it describes how Web Services can be composed and can cooperate one each other. Like WSDL, it is an XML-based language. It is layered on top of WSDL and it defines how to coordinate the interactions between services. In this sense, a BPEL process definition provides and/or uses one or more WSDL interfaces, that are lists of message declarations and types, and it provides the description of the behavior and interactions of the services. Indeed, in WSDL no information is given on the sequence of messages sent and received by the service. This is one of the reason because BPEL has been adopted to describe the interactions between services.

In BPEL, specifications are classified as *basic* activities and *structured* activities. Basic activities are sending and reception of a message, *e.g.*, receiving a request from a client, replying to the request, and also assigning data from one container to another, terminating the process, waiting for some period of time and doing nothing.

Structured activities define the control flow of the process. They include basic programming constructs as sequencing, loops and statements of various kind, *e.g.*, :

$$sequencing : \langle\texttt{sequence}\rangle$$
$$activity_1$$
$$activity_2$$
$$\dots$$
$$\langle\texttt{\textbackslash sequence}\rangle$$

$$while\ loops : \langle\texttt{while condition="bool-expr"}\rangle$$
$$activity$$
$$\langle\texttt{\textbackslash while}\rangle$$

$$switch\ statements : \langle\texttt{switch}\rangle$$
$$\langle\texttt{case condition}=\dots\rangle$$
$$\langle\texttt{\textbackslash case}\rangle$$
$$\dots$$
$$\langle\texttt{case condition}=\dots\rangle$$
$$\langle\texttt{\textbackslash case}\rangle$$
$$\langle\texttt{\textbackslash switch}\rangle$$

BPEL also includes a structured activity called `pick`, that allows for nondeterministic selective communication:

$$\langle\texttt{pick}\rangle$$
$$\langle\texttt{onMessage}\dots\rangle$$
$$\langle\texttt{invoke}\dots\texttt{\textbackslash}\rangle\langle\texttt{\textbackslash onMessage}\rangle$$
$$\langle\texttt{onMessage}\dots\rangle$$
$$\langle\texttt{invoke}\dots\texttt{\textbackslash}\rangle\langle\texttt{\textbackslash onMessage}\rangle$$
$$\langle\texttt{\textbackslash pick}\rangle$$

This construct is similar to the nondeterministic choice construct of process algebras.

All the activities in BPEL are modeled as instantaneous, *i.e.*, they take no time. However, there are constructs modeling, *e.g.*, the elapsing of time: the `wait` activity allows a business process to specify a delay for a certain period of time or until a certain deadline is reached.

From BPEL to *timedCCS* process algebra. In the literature, several efforts have been done for relating BPEL with process algebras, see, *e.g.*, [1,2,3]. Indeed, process algebras provide methodologies for the high-level description of interactions, communications, and synchronizations between processes, and this feature may be appealing for specifying interactions between Web Services, or reasoning on the specified system.

CCS is developed by Robin Milner (see [6]). Its actions model indivisible communications between exactly two participants. The notion of communication considered is a synchronous one, *i.e.*, both processes must agree on performing the communication at the same time.

Here we present a variant of CCS that permits to deal also with the elapsing of time, called *timedCCS*. Several languages have been developed in the literature to describe the system in a timed setting (see [12,13,14,15]). We follow a simple approach, where time is discrete, actions are durationless and there is one special *tick* action to represent the elapsing of time (see [12,15]). These are features of the so called *fictitious clock* approach of, *e.g.*, [18,19,20].

A global clock is supposed to be updated whenever all processes of the system agree on it, by globally synchronizing on action *tick*. Hence, between two global synchronizations on action *tick* all processes proceed asynchronously by performing durationless actions.

The set of *timedCCS processes* is denoted with $\mathcal{E}$, ranged over by $E, F, P, Q \ldots$.

Let $\mathcal{L}$ be a set of visible actions and let τ be a special action that models an internal computation, *i.e.*, it is not visible by an external observer. Let $\bar{(\ )} : \mathcal{L} \mapsto \mathcal{L}$ be a *complementation* function such that $\forall l \in \mathcal{L} : \bar{\bar{l}} = l$. Let $Act = \mathcal{L} \cup \{\tau\} \cup \{tick\}$ be the set of actions, ranged over by $\alpha, \beta, \ldots$ and let $\mathcal{L} \cup \{\tau\}$ be ranged over by $a, b, c, \ldots$

The syntax of *timedCCS* is the following:

$$P ::= \mathbf{0} \mid A \mid \alpha.P \mid P_1 + P_2 \mid P_1 \| P_2 \mid P \backslash L \mid i(P)$$

where $\alpha \in Act, L \subseteq \mathcal{L}$.

Informally $\mathbf{0}$ is a process that does nothing, A *(agent)* is a name of a constant process. The name range over a set of processes names. $\alpha.P$ is the *prefix* operator. The result is a process that can perform an α action and then behaves as P. In particular $tick.P$ represents a process willing to let one time unit pass. $P_1 + P_2$, the *choice* operator, represents the nondeterministic choice between the two processes P_1 and P_2; when both are able to perform a *tick* action then $P_1 + P_2$ can perform this action and reach a configuration where both summand derivatives can still be chosen. The *parallel* operator $P_1 \| P_2$ is the parallel composition of processes that can proceed in an asynchronous way but they must synchronize on complementary actions to make a communication, represented by an internal action τ. This is the core operator for time: both components must agree on performing a *tick* action. $P \backslash L$ is the *restriction*. It is the process P when actions in $L \cup \overline{L}$ are prevented and $i(P)$ *(idling)* allows process P to wait indefinitely. At every

Table 1. Operational semantics for timed CCS

Prefixing:

$$\overline{\alpha.P \xrightarrow{\alpha} P}$$

Choice:

$$\frac{P_1 \xrightarrow{\alpha} P_1'}{P_1 + P_2 \xrightarrow{\alpha} P_1'} \qquad \frac{P_2 \xrightarrow{\alpha} P_2'}{P_1 + P_2 \xrightarrow{\alpha} P_2'} \qquad \frac{P_1 \xrightarrow{tick} P_1' \quad P_2 \xrightarrow{tick} P_2'}{P_1 + P_2 \xrightarrow{tick} P_1' + P_2'}$$

Parallel:

$$\frac{P_1 \xrightarrow{a} P_1'}{P_1 \| P_2 \xrightarrow{a} P_1' \| P_2} \qquad \frac{P_2 \xrightarrow{a} P_2'}{P_1 \| P_2 \xrightarrow{a} P_1 \| P_2'} \qquad \frac{P_1 \xrightarrow{l} P_1' \quad P_2 \xrightarrow{\bar{l}} P_2'}{P_1 \| P_2 \xrightarrow{\tau} P_1' \| P_2'}$$

$$\frac{P_1 \xrightarrow{tick} P_1' \quad P_2 \xrightarrow{tick} P_2'}{P_1 \| P_2 \xrightarrow{tick} P_1' \| P_2'}$$

Restriction:

$$\frac{P \xrightarrow{\alpha} P'}{P \backslash L \xrightarrow{\alpha} P' \backslash L}(\alpha \notin L \cup \bar{L})$$

Idling:

$$\frac{P \xrightarrow{tick} \quad P \xrightarrow{\tau}}{i(P) \xrightarrow{tick} i(P)} \qquad \frac{P \xrightarrow{tick} P'}{i(P) \xrightarrow{tick} i(P')} \quad \frac{P \xrightarrow{\alpha} P'}{i(P) \xrightarrow{\alpha} P'}$$

---

instant of time, if process P performs an action α then the whole system proceeds in this state, while dropping the idling operator.

The formal semantics of $timedCCS$ processes is described by *labelled transition system* (*LTS*, for short). A *LTS* over Act is a pair $(\mathcal{E}, \mathcal{T})$ where $\mathcal{T}$ is a ternary relation $\mathcal{T} \subseteq (\mathcal{E} \times Act \times \mathcal{E})$, known as a *transition relation*. It is the least relation between timed CCS processes induced by axioms and inference rules in Table 1. Such a relation is well-defined.

Given a $timedCCS$ process P, $Der(P) = \{P' | P \rightarrow^* P'\}$, is the set of its derivatives, where $\rightarrow^*$ is the transitive and reflexive closure of $\rightarrow$. A $timedCCS$ process P is said *finite state* if $Der(P)$ is finite. $Sort(P)$ (called the *sort of P*) is the set of names of actions that syntactically appear in the process P.

By using this variant of CCS we are able to model time aspect of systems. For instance we can easily model *timeout* constructs. Assume $n_1 \leq n_2$ and define the following process:

$$\text{TIME\_OUT}(n_1, n_2, P, Q) = tick^{n_1}.i(P) + tick^{n_2}.\tau.Q$$

where P and Q are two processes. $\text{TIME\_OUT}(n_1, n_2, P, Q)$ first performs a sequence of n_1 *tick* actions; then, the system may performs $n_2 - n_1$ *tick* actions, unless P resolves the choice by performing an action; instead if P does not do anything, after n_2 time units, via the execution of a τ action, the process is forced to act as Q.

Encoding of BPEL *in* CCS. Referring to [2,3], we recall and adapt here an encoding between BPEL and $timedCCS$. The action notion of $timedCCS$ finds its equivalent

Table 2. Mapping between $timedCCS$ and WSDL/BPEL (extension of [2,3] with time)

BPEL	$timedCCS$
`receive`, `reply`, `invoke`	actions(reply/receive)
`sequence`	sequence ·
`pick` and `switch`	choice +
interacting Web services	parallel composition $\parallel$
interactions and `assign`	restriction \
end of the main `sequence` or `terminate`	termination **0**
new instantiation or `while`	recursive call
(internal) `assign`, (external) interactions	τ-actions
`wait`	idling

in the *Receive*, *Reply* and *Invoke* basic activities of BPEL. As a matter of fact, the *Receive* activity accepts a message through the invocation of a specified operation by a partner. The *Reply* activity sends a message as a response to a request previously accepted through a receive activity. In the end, the *Invoke* basic activities of synchronizes the communication between Web Services. The sequence activity in BPEL matches the prefixing construct of $timedCCS$. The *nondeterministic choice* in $timedCCS$ can be seen as `sequence` and `pick` constructs in BPEL. In case of a deterministic choice described as a `switch` construct, we should use the $timedCCS$ choice operator. An overall activity is completed when the end of its behavior is reached (no explicit construct unlike the termination denoted by **0** in $timedCCS$). Agent *recursion*, corresponding to the repetition of their behavior, could be represented using a `while` activity. To sum up in Table 2 there is the encoding proposed in [2,3]. We stress that some notions that are present in $timedCCS$ do not directly appear in BPEL. This is the case of the τ action and of the restriction operator. Moreover, the behavior of the *idling* operator matches the BPEL `wait` activity. Furthermore, we can imagine that the names needed in the $timedCCS$ restriction set could be easily extracted from the WSDL files.

Table 3. Equational μ-calculus

$$[\![\mathbf{T}]\!]'_\rho = S \quad [\![\mathbf{F}]\!]'_\rho = \emptyset \quad [\![X]\!]'_\rho = \rho(X) \quad [\![\phi_1 \wedge \phi_2]\!]'_\rho = [\![\phi_1]\!]'_\rho \cap [\![\phi_2]\!]'_\rho$$
$$[\![\phi_1 \vee \phi_2]\!]'_\rho = [\![\phi_1]\!]'_\rho \cup [\![\phi_2]\!]'_\rho \quad [\![\langle \alpha \rangle \phi]\!]'_\rho = \{s \mid \exists s' : s \xrightarrow{\alpha} s' \text{ and } s' \in [\![\phi]\!]'_\rho\}$$
$$[\![[\alpha]\phi]\!]'_\rho = \{s \mid \forall s' : s \xrightarrow{\alpha} s' \text{ implies } s' \in [\![\phi]\!]'_\rho\}$$

We use $\sqcup$ to represent union of disjoint environments. Let ρ be the environment (a function from variables to values) and σ be in $\{\mu, \nu\}$, then $\sigma U.f(U)$ represents the σ fixpoint of the function f in one variable U.
$$[\![\epsilon]\!]_\rho = [] \quad [\![X =_\sigma \phi D']\!]_\rho = [\![D']\!]_{(\rho \sqcup [U'/X])} \sqcup [U'/X]$$
where $U' = \sigma U.[\![\phi]\!]'_{(\rho \sqcup [U/X] \sqcup \rho'(U))}$ and $\rho'(U) = [\![D']\!]_{(\rho \sqcup [U/X])}$.
It informally says that *the solution to* $(X =_\sigma \phi)D$ *is the* σ *fixpoint solution* U' *of* $[\![\phi]\!]$ *where the solution to the rest of the lists of equations* D *is used as environment*.

2.2   Equational μ-Calculus and Partial Model Checking in a Timed Setting

Equational μ-calculus is a process logic well suited for specification and verification of systems whose behavior is naturally described using states changes by means of actions. It permits to express a lot of interesting properties like *safety* ("nothing bad happens"). and *liveness* properties ("something good happens"), as well as allows to express equivalence conditions over *LTS*. Even if we are studying system in a timed setting, the properties that we consider are simple hence we can use equational μ-calculus instead of temporal logic, *e.g.*, *TimedCTL* (see [21]).

In order to define recursively properties of a given system, this calculus uses fixpoint equations. Let α be in *Act* and X be a variable ranging over a finite set of variables V. Given the grammar:

$$\phi ::= Z \mid \mathbf{T} \mid \mathbf{F} \mid \phi_1 \wedge \phi_2 \mid \phi_1 \vee \phi_2 \mid \langle \alpha \rangle \phi \mid [\alpha]\phi$$
$$D ::= Z =_\nu \phi D \mid Z =_\mu \phi D \mid \epsilon$$

where the symbol $\mathbf{T}$ means *true* and $\mathbf{F}$ means *false*; $\wedge$ is the symbol for the conjunction of formulas, *i.e.*, $\phi_1 \wedge \phi_2$ holds iff both of the formulas ϕ_1 and ϕ_2 hold, and $\vee$ is the disjunction of formulas and $\phi_1 \vee \phi_2$ holds when at least one of ϕ_1 and ϕ_2 holds. The *possibility operator* $\langle \alpha \rangle \phi$ means that "there exists a transition labeled by α after that ϕ holds". The *necessity operator* $[\alpha]\phi$ means "for all α-actions performed ϕ holds". $Z =_\mu \phi$ is a minimal fixpoint equation, where ϕ is an assertion (*i.e.*, a simple modal formula without recursion operator), and $Z =_\nu \phi$ is a maximal fixpoint equation. Roughly, the semantics $\llbracket D \rrbracket$ of the list of equations D is the solution of the system of equations corresponding to D. Given an LTS $M = \langle S, \rightarrow \rangle$, where S is a set of states and $\rightarrow$ is the transition relation, the semantics of a formula ϕ is a subset $\llbracket \phi \rrbracket_\rho$ of the states of M, defined in Table 3, where ρ is a function (called *environment*) from free variables of ϕ to subsets of the states of M.

Example 1. It is possible to find a formula to express a safety property as a formula that expresses the possibility to open a new file only if the previous one is closed:

$$Z_1 =_\nu [\tau]Z_1 \wedge [\text{open}]Z_2$$
$$Z_2 =_\nu [\tau]Z_2 \wedge [\text{close}]Z_1 \wedge [\text{open}]\mathbf{F}$$

A *liveness property* ("something good happens") like "a state satisfying ϕ can be reached" is expressed by $Z =_\mu \langle \_ \rangle Z \vee \phi$.[1]   □

The following standard result of μ-calculus will be useful in the reminder of the paper.

Theorem 1 ([22]). *Given a formula ϕ it is possible to decide in exponential time in the length of ϕ if there exists a model of ϕ and it is also possible to give an example of such model.*

Partial model checking (*pmc* for short) is a technique that was originally developed for compositional analysis of concurrent systems (see [7]). The intuitive idea underlying the *pmc* is the following: proving that $P\|Q$ satisfies an equational μ-calculus formula

---

[1] In writing properties, here and in the rest of the paper, we use the shortcut notations [_] means [*Act*] and, equivalently, $\langle \_ \rangle$ means $\langle Act \rangle$.

Table 4. Partial evaluation function for parallel operator $P\|(\_)$ of timed CCS

$$Z//t = Z_t$$
$$(Z =_\sigma \phi D)//t = ((Z_s =_\sigma \phi//s)_{s\in Der(E)})(D)//t$$
$$\langle a\rangle \phi//s = \langle a\rangle(\phi//s) \vee \bigvee_{s \xrightarrow{a} s'} \phi//s', \text{ if } a \neq \tau$$
$$\langle \tau\rangle \phi//s = \langle \tau\rangle(\phi//s) \vee \bigvee_{s \xrightarrow{\tau} s'} \phi//s' \vee \bigvee_{s \xrightarrow{\alpha} s'} \langle \overline{\alpha}\rangle(\phi//s')$$
$$\langle tick\rangle \phi//s = \begin{cases} \langle tick\rangle \phi//s' & s \xrightarrow{tick} s' \\ \mathbf{F} & otherwise \end{cases}$$
$$[a]\phi//s = [a](A\!/\!s) \wedge \bigwedge_{s \xrightarrow{a} s'} \phi//s', \text{ if } a \neq \tau$$
$$[\tau]\phi//s = [\tau](\phi\!/\!s) \wedge \bigwedge_{s \xrightarrow{\tau} s'} \phi//s' \wedge \bigwedge_{s \xrightarrow{\alpha} s'} [\overline{\alpha}](\phi//s')$$
$$[tick]\phi//s = \begin{cases} [tick]\phi//s' & s \xrightarrow{tick} s' \\ \mathbf{T} & otherwise \end{cases}$$
$$\phi_1 \wedge \phi_2//s = (\phi_1//s) \wedge (\phi_2//s)$$
$$\phi_1 \vee \phi_2//s = (\phi_1//s) \vee (\phi_2//s)$$
$$\mathbf{T}//s = \mathbf{T}$$
$$\mathbf{F}//s = \mathbf{F}$$

ϕ ($P\|Q \models \phi$) is equivalent to prove that Q satisfies $\phi_{//P}$ ($Q \models \phi_{//P}$), that is a modified specification of ϕ, where $//_P$ is the partial evaluation function for the parallel composition operator. The reduced formula $\phi_{//P}$ depends only on the formula ϕ and on process P. No information is required on the process Q which can represent a possible enemy. A useful result of partial model checking is the following.

Lemma 1 ([7]). *Given a process $P\|Q$ and a formula ϕ we have: $P\|Q \models \phi$ iff $Q \models \phi_{//P}$.*

It is worth noticing that partial model checking function may be automatically derived from the semantics rules used to define a language semantics. Thus, the proposed technique is very flexible.

A lemma similar to Lemma 1 holds for every timed CCS operators (see [7,12,13]). However the most significant operator is the parallel one. For that reason we choose to explain how the partial model checking technique works w.r.t. to parallel operator and we recall the partial evaluation function for that operator in Table 4. In order to explain better how partial model checking function acts on a given equational μ-calculus formula, we show the following example.

Example 2. Let $[\tau]\phi$ be the given formula and let $P\|Q$ a process. We want to evaluate the formula $[\tau]\phi$ w.r.t. the $\|$ operator and the process P. The formula $[\tau]\phi_{//P}$ is satisfied by Q if the following three condition hold at the same time:

– Q performs an action τ going in a state Q' and $P\|Q'$ satisfies ϕ; this is taken into account by the formula $[\tau](\phi_{//P})$.
– P performs an action τ going in a state P' and $P'\|Q$ satisfies ϕ, and this is considered by the conjunction $\wedge_{P \xrightarrow{\tau} P'}\phi_{//P'}$, where every formula $\phi_{//P'}$ takes into account the behavior of F in composition with a τ successor of P.
– the τ action is due to the performing of two complementary actions by the two processes. So for every a successor P' of P there is a formula $[\overline{a}](\phi_{//P'})$. □

3   Synthesis of Orchestration Process in a Timed Setting

The goal of this work is to synthesize an *orchestrator process* in a timed setting, *i.e.*, given a network of services and a user's request, generate a process, said *orchestrator*, that, by managing the given set of services, guarantee the request is satisfied. To do this we apply the same techniques used in [8,9] to guarantee that a system is secure. As a matter of fact we consider an orchestrator process as a monitor that coordinates and composes services in order to satisfy a user request.

Let us consider to have a network of services made up of n endpoints each of them provides a service. According to Section 2.1, we model each BPEL services as a CCS process, *i.e.*, we consider $P_1, \ldots, P_n$ n finite-state processes that model the behavior of n services of the network. Being $P_1, \ldots, P_n$ finite state processes, the satisfiability problem that we are going to solve is decidable.

Moreover we assume that sets of actions of processes P_i are pairwise disjoint. *i.e.*, let L_i and L_j be the sets of actions respectively of P_i and P_j then $L_i \cap L_j = \emptyset$. This assumption guarantees that all possible synchronization between processes are established and coordinated by the orchestrator process.

Let ϕ be an equational μ-calculus formula that expresses a possible request of an user. We want to find a process $\mathcal{O}$, that is the *orchestrator process*, that by managing $P_1, \ldots, P_n$ satisfies the request ϕ.

In order to do this we define a process algebra operator, denoted by $\triangleright$, said *orchestrating operator* whose semantics definition is the following:

$$\frac{\mathcal{O} \xrightarrow{\tau} \mathcal{O}'}{\mathcal{O} \triangleright P \xrightarrow{\tau} \mathcal{O}' \triangleright P} \qquad \frac{P \xrightarrow{\tau} P'}{\mathcal{O} \triangleright P \xrightarrow{\tau} \mathcal{O} \triangleright P'} \qquad \frac{\mathcal{O} \xrightarrow{a} \mathcal{O}' \quad P \xrightarrow{a} P'}{\mathcal{O} \triangleright P \xrightarrow{a} \mathcal{O}' \triangleright P'}$$

$$\frac{\mathcal{O} \xrightarrow{tick} \mathcal{O}' \quad P \xrightarrow{tick} P'}{\mathcal{O} \triangleright P \xrightarrow{tick} \mathcal{O}' \triangleright P'}$$

By the last semantics rule we consider the elapsing of time. As a matter of fact, we consider the possibility that P performs a $tick$ action. In this case the orchestrator process $\mathcal{O}$ permits it.

Hence we can formalize the composition problem as follows:

$$\exists \mathcal{O} \ \mathcal{O} \triangleright P \models \phi \tag{1}$$

where $P = P_1 \| \ldots \| P_n$.

As in [8,9], we reduce the validity problem described in the Formula (1) in a satisfiability problem by exploiting the partial model checking function w.r.t. the orchestrating operator $\triangleright$. The partial model checking function for a given operator is defined according to the operational semantics definition of the chosen operator. The definition of the function is given in Table 5 and the following proposition, similar to Lemma 1 holds.

Proposition 1. *Let P and Q be two finite state processes,*

$$Q \triangleright P \models \phi \text{ iff } Q \models \phi //_{\triangleright P}$$

Proof (Sketch): The proof of this proposition is done by induction of the complexity of the formula we consider. Here we give a sketch of the proof by proving the proposition for conjunction.

Table 5. Partial evaluation function for ▷ operator

$$
\begin{aligned}
Z//_{\triangleright P} &= Z_{\triangleright P}\\
(Z =_\sigma \phi D)//_{\triangleright P} &= ((Z_{\triangleright P} =_\sigma \phi//_{\triangleright P})(D)//_{\triangleright P})\\
[\alpha]\phi//_{\triangleright P} &= \begin{cases} \bigwedge_{P\xrightarrow{\alpha}P'}[\alpha]\phi//_{\triangleright P'} & \text{if } P \xrightarrow{\alpha} P'\\ \mathbf{T} & \text{if } P \not\xrightarrow{\alpha} \end{cases} \quad \alpha \neq \tau\\
[\tau]\phi//_{\triangleright P} &= [\tau](\phi//_{\triangleright P}) \wedge \bigwedge_{P\xrightarrow{\tau}P'} \phi//_{\triangleright P'}\\
\langle\alpha\rangle\phi//_{\triangleright P} &= \begin{cases} \bigvee_{P\xrightarrow{\alpha}P'}\langle a\rangle\phi//_{\triangleright P'} & \text{if } P \xrightarrow{\alpha} P'\\ \mathbf{F} & \text{if } P \not\xrightarrow{\alpha} \end{cases} \quad \alpha \neq \tau\\
\langle\tau\rangle\phi//_{\triangleright P} &= \langle\tau\rangle(\phi//_{\triangleright P'}) \vee \bigvee_{P\xrightarrow{\tau}P'} \phi//_{\triangleright P'}\\
\phi_1 \vee \phi_2//_{\triangleright P} &= (\phi_1//_{\triangleright P}) \vee (\phi_2//_{\triangleright P})\\
\phi_1 \wedge \phi_2//_{\triangleright P} &= (\phi_1//_{\triangleright P}) \wedge (\phi_2//_{\triangleright P})\\
\mathbf{T}//_{\triangleright P} &= \mathbf{T}\\
\mathbf{F}//_{\triangleright P} &= \mathbf{F}
\end{aligned}
$$

Let $\phi = \phi_1 \wedge \phi_2$ be the considered formula. We want to prove that $Q \triangleright P \models \phi$ iff $Q \models \phi//_{\triangleright P}$. $Q \triangleright P \models \phi$ iff $Q \triangleright P \models \phi_1 \wedge \phi_2$ iff $Q \triangleright P \models \phi_1$ and $Q \triangleright P \models \phi_2$. For inductive hypothesis, $Q \triangleright P \models \phi_1$ iff $Q \models \phi_1//_{\triangleright P}$ and $Q \triangleright P \models \phi_2$ iff $Q \models \phi_2//_{\triangleright P}$. Hence $Q \triangleright P \models \phi$ iff $Q \models \phi_1//_{\triangleright P}$ and $Q \models \phi_2//_{\triangleright P}$ iff $Q \models \phi_1//_{\triangleright P} \wedge \phi_2//_{\triangleright P}$. □

By using the partial evaluation function we are able to evaluate the behavior of the composition of services directly into the request of the user. Moreover it permits to underline which is the behavior of the orchestrator in order to guarantee that the request is satisfied according to the semantics definition of the operator ▷.

In order to understand better how partial model checking w.r.t. ▷ operator works, we show a simple application.

Let $\phi = [\alpha]\phi'$ be a given request. We want to evaluate the formula ϕ w.r.t. the ▷ operator and a process P. According to the rule for box formulas in Table 5, the formula $\phi//_{\triangleright P}$ is satisfied by $\mathcal{O}$ if, whenever P performs the action α, $\mathcal{O}$ performs the actions α. This is taken into account by the first case of the formula, *i.e.*, $\bigwedge_{P\xrightarrow{\alpha}P'}[\alpha]\phi//_{\triangleright P'}$. On the other hand, if P does not performs α then the formula becomes always **T**.

Hence the problem described in Formula 1 becomes:

$$\exists \mathcal{O} \quad \mathcal{O} \models \phi'$$

where $\phi' = \phi//_{\triangleright P}$.

Now we are able to synthesize an orchestrator process for a given request in a timed setting by referring to a satisfiability procedure for temporal logic. As a matter of fact, according to Theorem 1, it is possible to find a model for a given equational μ-calculus formula.

The following result holds.

Theorem 2. *The problem described in Formula (1) is decidable.*

The proof of the Theorem 2 is based of satisfiability algorithm already exists in the literature. As a matter of fact, the goal of this paper is not to give a satisfiability algorithm that an interested reader can find in the literature, *e.g.*, [8,9,23,24], but to show how the problem of Web Services orchestrator synthesis can be solved by using results on the synthesis of a model for a logic formula.

4   A Simple Example

Let we suppose there is an user that want to organize a trip. Let us suppose such user makes the following request to a possible network of services:

After booking an hotel I need to receive a confirmation before booking a flight.

We model such request as an equational μ-calculus formula ϕ as follows: Let $Act = \{\texttt{b\_h}, \texttt{b\_f}, \texttt{b\_c}, \texttt{conf}, \tau, tick\}$ be the set of actions, where $\texttt{b\_h}$ permits to book an hotel, $\texttt{conf}$ is the confirmation from the hotel, $\texttt{b\_f}$ is the booking of the flight and $\texttt{b\_c}$ permits to reserve a car. By assuming that a possible confirmation can arrive immediately or after an amount of time, that we model by a *tick* action, the formula that describes the request is the following:

$$\phi = \langle \texttt{b\_h} \rangle (\langle \texttt{conf} \rangle \langle \texttt{b\_f} \rangle \mathbf{T} \vee \langle tick \rangle \langle \texttt{conf} \rangle \langle \texttt{b\_f} \rangle \mathbf{T})$$

This means that after booking the hotel the confirmation arrive immediately and the user books the flight or some time passes before the confirmation arrives and then the user books the flight.

Let we consider two processes P_1 and P_2 such that

$$P_1 = \texttt{b\_h}.tick.\texttt{conf}.\mathbf{0}$$
$$P_2 = \texttt{b\_f}.(\tau.\mathbf{0} + P_2')$$
$$P_2' = \texttt{b\_c}.\mathbf{0}$$

This means that P_1 permits to book an hotel and gives back the confirmation and P_2 permits to book a flight or to book a flight and reserve a car.

After the application of partial model checking to the formula ϕ we obtain $\phi //_{\triangleright P} = \phi'$ as follows

$$\phi' = \langle \texttt{b\_h} \rangle \langle tick \rangle \langle \texttt{conf} \rangle \langle \texttt{b\_f} \rangle \mathbf{T}$$

Hence a possible model for ϕ' is the following:

$$\mathcal{O} = \texttt{b\_h}.tick.\texttt{conf}.\texttt{b\_f}.\mathbf{0}$$

Looking at the semantics definition of $\triangleright$ the execution of $\mathcal{O} \triangleright P$ consists on the following sequence of transitions:

$$\texttt{b\_h}.tick.\texttt{conf}.\texttt{b\_f}.\mathbf{0} \ \triangleright \ (\texttt{b\_h}.tick.\texttt{conf}\mathbf{0} \| \texttt{b\_f}.(\tau.\mathbf{0} + P_2'))$$
$$\downarrow \texttt{b\_h}$$
$$tick.\texttt{conf}.\texttt{b\_f}.\mathbf{0} \ \triangleright \ (tick.\texttt{conf}\mathbf{0} \| \texttt{b\_f}.(\tau.\mathbf{0} + P_2'))$$
$$\downarrow tick$$
$$\texttt{conf}.\texttt{b\_f}.\mathbf{0} \ \triangleright \ \texttt{conf}\mathbf{0} \| \texttt{b\_f}.(\tau.\mathbf{0} + P_2')$$
$$\downarrow \texttt{conf}$$
$$\texttt{b\_f}.\mathbf{0} \ \triangleright \ \mathbf{0} \| \texttt{b\_f}.(\tau.\mathbf{0} + P_2')$$
$$\downarrow \texttt{b\_f}$$
$$\mathbf{0} \ \triangleright \ \mathbf{0} \| (\tau.\mathbf{0} + P_2')$$

At this time the process ends without booking the car. This is exactly what the user required. As a matter of fact the orchestrating operator does not consider additional services that are not required by the user, as the reservation of a car.

5   Related Works

In the literature a lot of works deal with web services composition through formal methods. For instance several works deal with a possible modeling of Web Services by process algebras (see [1,2,3,4,5]) or by automata (see [25]).

In [26,27] the authors have developed a static approach to deal with the composition of web services problem by the usage of *plans*. In particular they use a distributed, enriched λ-calculus for describing networks of services. Both services and their clients can protect themselves, by imposing security constraints on each other's behavior. Then, service interaction results in a call-by-property mechanism (see [28]), that matches the client requests with services.

The planning approach is followed also by Pistore *et al.* (see *e.g.*, [11,29]) in order to generate an orchestrator. As a matter of fact, the authors propose a novel planning framework for the automated composition of Web Services in which, given a set of BPEL abstract specifications of published Web Services, and given a composition requirement, they generate automatically a BPEL concrete process that interacts asynchronously with the published services. Basically they compose all services and then, after building all possible plans, they extract the plan that satisfies the user's request. We start from the problem of the automatic composition of services too but our approach is different. By exploiting the partial model checking technique, we evaluate the behavior of the process directly into the formula generating a new formula and then we synthesize a process that is a model for the formula that represents the request evaluated by the behavior of the composition os services. This approach permits us to treat the problem also in a timed setting, topic that is not addressed in [11,29]. Our approach is general because we can define other process algebra orchestrating operator and, by defining a partial model checking function according to the operational semantics definition of such operators, we can combine services in different ways.

Also Zavattaro *et. al* deal with the problem of composition on services. They have studied choreography more than orchestration. They introduce a formal model for representing choreography which is based on a *declarative part* and on a conversational one. The declarative part of our choreography formal model which is based on the concept of role. A role represents the behavior that a participant has to exhibit in order to fulfill the activity defined by the choreography. Each role can store variables and exhibit operations. In [30] the authors have formalized the concept of orchestrator as a process, associated to an identifier, that can exchange information, represented by variables, with other processes. This model takes inspiration form the abstract non-executable fragment of BPEL and abstracts away from variables values focussing on data-flow. Orchestrators are executed on different locations, thus they can be composed by using only the parallel operator ($\|$). Processes can be composed in parallel, sequence and alternative composition. Communication mechanisms model Web Services *One-Way* and *Request-Response* operations. In our approach the communication between services is managed by the orchestrator process that permits interactions between different services. By partial model checking we evaluate the behavior of the composition in the request formula and the orchestrator process is a monitor that guarantees the composition behaves according the request. In this way we can synthesize the orchestrator process as a model of the resulting formula.

No one of these papers treat the synthesis of orchestrator problem in a timed setting. In the literature there are some works on modelling a timed $BPEL$ with formal method. For instance, in [31] the authors propose the *Web Service Timed Transition System* model, which adopts the formalism of timed automata for capturing the aspects specific to the Web service domain. In this formalism, the fact that the operation takes certain amount of time is represented by time increment in the state, followed by the immediate execution of the operation. Intuitively, WSTTS is a finite-state machined equipped with set of clock variables. The values of these clock variables increase with the passing of time. A Web Services composition thus is represented as a network of several such automata, where all clocks progress synchronously. The semantic of WSTTS is defined as a labeled transition system, where either the time passes or a transition from one state to another immediately takes place. In [32,33] discusses the augmentation of business protocols with specifications of temporal abstractions, focusing in particular on problems related to compatibility and replaceability analysis. In [34] the authors first defines a timed automata semantics for the *Orc* language, introduced in order to support a structured way of orchestrating distributed web services. *Orc* is intuitive because it offers concise constructors to manage concurrent communication, time-outs, priorities, failure of sites or communication and so forth. The semantics of *Orc* is also precisely defined. Timed automata semantics is semantically equivalent to the original operational semantics of *Orc*. In [35] the authors introduce COWS, *calculus for orchestration of Web Services*, as a new foundational languages for service oriented computing, whose design has been influenced by BPEL. It combines in an original way a number of ingredients borrowed from process calculi.

However all these papers deal with the modeling of Web Services in a timed setting but they do not treat the problem of the synthesis of an orchestrator process.

6   Conclusion

In this paper we have proposed an approach to find an orchestrator process in a timed setting given a set of services modeled by CCS. We have applied a similar approach to the one we have developed in [8,9] to guarantee that a system is secure, in a Web Services scenario. As a matter of fact we have exploited our approach in order to synthesize an orchestrator process in a timed setting as a controller program of a controller operator.

Acknowledgement. We thank the anonymous referees of WS-FM07 for valuable comments that helped us to improve this paper.

References

1. Bao, L., Zhang, W., Zhang, X.: Describing and verifying web service using ccs. pdcat 0, 421–426 (2006)
2. Cámara, J., Canal, C., Cubo, J., Vallecillo, A.: Formalizing wsbpel business processes using process algebra. Electr. Notes Theor. Comput. Sci. 154(1), 159–173 (2006)

3. Salaun, G., Bordeaux, L., Schaerf, M.: Describing and reasoning on web services using process algebra. In: ICWS 2004: Proceedings of the IEEE International Conference on Web Services (ICWS 2004), Washington, DC, USA, p. 43. IEEE Computer Society Press, Los Alamitos (2004)

4. Baldoni, M., Baroglio, C., Martelli, A., Patti, V.: Reasoning about interaction protocols for web service composition. Electr. Notes Theor. Comput. Sci. 105, 21–36 (2004)

5. Ferrara, A.: Web services: a process algebra approach. In: Aiello, M., Aoyama, M., Curbera, F., Papazoglou, M.P. (eds.) ICSOC, pp. 242–251. ACM, New York (2004)

6. Milner, R.: Communicating and mobile systems: the π-calculus. Cambridge University Press, Cambridge (1999)

7. Andersen, H.R.: Partial model checking (extended abstract). In: Proceedings of 10th Annual IEEE Symposium on Logic in Computer Science, pp. 398–407. IEEE Computer Society Press, Los Alamitos (1995)

8. Martinelli, F., Matteucci, I.: Through modeling to synthesis of security automata. Electr. Notes Theor. Comput. Sci. 179, 31–46 (2007)

9. Matteucci, I.: Automated synthesis of enforcing mechanisms for security properties in a timed setting. Electr. Notes Theor. Comput. Sci. 186, 101–120 (2007)

10. Martinelli, F.: Partial model checking and theorem proving for ensuring security properties. In: Proceedings of CSFW 1998, pp. 44–52. IEEE press, Los Alamitos (1998)

11. Pistore, M., Roberti, P., Traverso, P.: Process-level composition of executable web services: on-the-fly versus once-for-all composition. In: Gómez-Pérez, A., Euzenat, J. (eds.) ESWC 2005. LNCS, vol. 3532, pp. 62–77. Springer, Heidelberg (2005)

12. Focardi, R., Gorrieri, R., Martinelli, F.: Information flow analysis in a discrete-time process algebra. In: PCSFW: Proceedings of The 13th Computer Security Foundations Workshop, IEEE Computer Society Press, Los Alamitos (2000)

13. Gorrieri, R., Martinelli, F.: A simple framework for real-time cryptographic protocol analysis with compositional proof rules. Sci. Comput. Program. 50(1-3), 23–49 (2004)

14. Asarin, E., Dima, C.: Balanced timed regular expressions. Electr. Notes Theor. Comput. Sci. 68(5) (2002)

15. Gorrieri, R., Lanotte, R., Maggiolo-Schettini, A., Martinelli, F., Tini, S., Tronci, E.: Automated analysis of timed security: a case study on web privacy. Int. J. Inf. Sec. 2(3-4), 168–186 (2004)

16. Andersen, H.: Verification of Temporal Properties of Concurrent Systems. PhD thesis, Department of Computer Science, Aarhus University, Denmark (1993)

17. Andrews, T., Curbera, F., Dholakia, H., Goland, Y., Klein, J., Leymann, K.L.F., Roller, D., Smith, D., Thatte, S., Trickovic, I., Weerawarana, S.: Specification: Business process execution language for web services version 1.1 (2003)

18. Corradini, F., D'Ortenzio, D., Inverardi, P.: On the relationships among four timed process algebras. Fundam. Inform. 38(4), 377–395 (1999)

19. Hennessy, M., Regan, T.: A temporal process algebra. In: FORTE 1990: Proceedings of the IFIP TC6/WG6.1 Third International Conference on Formal Description Techniques for Distributed Systems and Communication Protocols, pp. 33–48. North-Holland, Amsterdam (1991)

20. Ulidowski, I., Yuen, S.: Extending process languages with time. In: Johnson, M. (ed.) AMAST 1997. LNCS, vol. 1349, Springer, Heidelberg (1997)

21. Alur, R., Courcoubetis, C., Dill, D.: Model-checking in dense real-time. Inf. Comput. 104(1), 2–34 (1993)

22. Street, R.S., Emerson, E.A.: An automata theoretic procedure for the propositional μ-calculus. Information and Computation 81(3), 249–264 (1989)

23. Walukiewicz, I.: A Complete Deductive System for the μ-Calculus. PhD thesis, Institute of Informatics, Warsaw University (1993)

24. Matteucci, I.: A tool for the synthesis of controller programs. In: Dimitrakos, T., Martinelli, F., Ryan, P.Y.A., Schneider, S. (eds.) FAST 2006. LNCS, vol. 4691, pp. 112–126. Springer, Heidelberg (2007)
25. Reisig, W.: Modeling- and analysis techniques for web services and business processes. In: Steffen, M., Zavattaro, G. (eds.) FMOODS 2005. LNCS, vol. 3535, Springer, Heidelberg (2005)
26. Bartoletti, M., Degano, P., Ferrari, G.L.: Types and effects for secure service orchestration. In: Proc. 19th Computer Security Foundations Workshop (CSFW) (2006)
27. Bartoletti, M., Degano, P., Ferrari, G.L.: Plans for service composition. In: Workshop on Issues in the Theory of Security (WITS) (2006)
28. Bartoletti, M., Degano, P., Ferrari, G.L.: Security issues in service composition. In: Gorrieri, R., Wehrheim, H. (eds.) FMOODS 2006. LNCS, vol. 4037, Springer, Heidelberg (2006)
29. Pistore, M., Traverso, P., Bertoli, P.: Automated composition of web services by planning in asynchronous domains. In: Biundo, S., Myers, K.L., Rajan, K. (eds.) ICAPS, pp. 2–11. AAAI, Menlo Park (2005)
30. Busi, N., Gorrieri, R., Guidi, C., Lucchi, R., Zavattaro, G.: Choreography and orchestration: A synergic approach for system design. In: Benatallah, B., Casati, F., Traverso, P. (eds.) ICSOC 2005. LNCS, vol. 3826, pp. 228–240. Springer, Heidelberg (2005)
31. Kazhamiakin, R., Pandya, P., Pistore, M.: Timed modelling and analysis inweb service compositions. In: ARES '06: Proceedings of the First International Conference on Availability, Reliability and Security (ARES 2006), Washington, DC, USA, pp. 840–846. IEEE Computer Society Press, Los Alamitos (2006)
32. Benatallah, B., Casati, F., Ponge, J., Toumani, F.: Compatibility and replaceability analysis for timed web service protocols. In: BDA (2005)
33. Benatallah, B., Casati, F., Ponge, J., Toumani, F.: On temporal abstractions of web service protocols. In: Belo, O., Eder, J. (eds.) CAiSE Short Paper Proceedings. CEUR Workshop Proceedings, vol. 161 (2005), CEUR-WS.org
34. Dong, J.S., Liu, Y., Sun, J., Zhang, X.: Verification of computation orchestration via timed automata. In: Liu, Z., He, J. (eds.) ICFEM 2006. LNCS, vol. 4260, pp. 226–245. Springer, Heidelberg (2006)
35. Lapadula, A., Pugliese, R., Tiezzi, F.: A calculus for orchestration of web services. In: De Nicola, R. (ed.) ESOP 2007. LNCS, vol. 4421, Springer, Heidelberg (2007)

From Public Views to Private Views – Correctness-by-Design for Services

Wil M.P. van der Aalst[1], Niels Lohmann[2,*], Peter Massuthe[3],
Christian Stahl[3,**], and Karsten Wolf[2]

[1] Department of Mathematics and Computer Science
Technische Universiteit Eindhoven
P.O. Box 513, 5600 MB Eindhoven, The Netherlands
W.M.P.v.d.Aalst@tue.nl

[2] Universität Rostock, Institut für Informatik
18051 Rostock, Germany
{niels.lohmann,karsten.wolf}@uni-rostock.de

[3] Humboldt-Universität zu Berlin, Institut für Informatik
Unter den Linden 6, 10099 Berlin, Germany
{massuthe,stahl}@informatik.hu-berlin.de

Abstract. Service orientation is a means for integrating across diverse systems. Each resource, whether an application, system, or trading partner, can be accessed as a service. The resulting architecture, often referred to as SOA, has been an important enabler for interorganizational processes. Apart from technological issues that need to be addressed, it is important that all parties involved in such processes agree on the "rules of engagement". Therefore, we propose to use a *contract* that specifies the composition of the *public views* of all participating parties. Each party may then implement its part of the contract such that the implementation (i.e., the *private view*) accords with the contract. In this paper, we define a suitable notion of *accordance* inspired by the asynchronous nature of services. Moreover, we present several *transformation rules* for incrementally building a private view such that accordance with the contract is guaranteed by construction. These rules include adding internal tasks as well as the reordering of messages and are therefore much more powerful than existing correctness-preserving transformation rules.

1 Introduction

Interorganizational cooperation is of increasing importance for enterprises to meet the new challenges of ever faster changing business conditions. Web services and service-oriented architectures (SOA) are rapidly emerging approaches to reduce the complexity of integrating systems within and between organizations. Since SOA enables dynamic binding of services at runtime, it is possible to

---

* Funded by the German Federal Ministry of Education and Research (project Tools4BPEL, project number 01ISE08).

** Funded by the DFG project "Substitutability of Services" (RE 834/16-1).

M. Dumas and R. Heckel (Eds.): WS-FM 2007, LNCS 4937, pp. 139–153, 2008.
© Springer-Verlag Berlin Heidelberg 2008

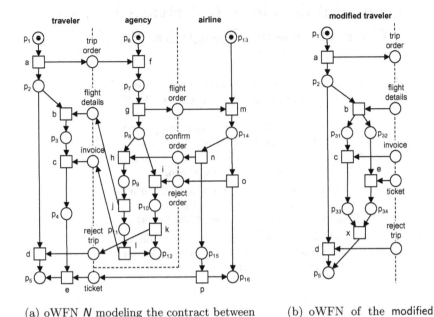

(a) oWFN N modeling the contract between traveler (N_{tr}), agency (N_{ag}), and airline (N_{air}).

(b) oWFN of the modified traveler (N'_{tr}).

Fig. 1. The running example

design a cooperation between parties that do not know each other. However, in practise the parties involved in a cooperation know each other. Therefore, instead of dynamically binding services at runtime, these parties agree on a common *contract*, which is the focus of this paper. This contract has the form of an agreed upon process model, similar to [1,2], and attempts to balance the following two conflicting requirements. On the one hand, there is a strong need for coordination to optimize the flow of work in and between the different organizations. On the other hand, the organizations involved are essentially autonomous and have the freedom to create or modify workflows at any point in time. Therefore, we propose to use a process-oriented contract that defines "rules of engagement" without describing the internal processes executed within each partner.

To illustrate the idea of having a process-oriented contract, we use an example taken from [3], depicted in Fig. 1(a). The example shows a contract expressed in terms of a Petri net [4]. The Petri net is partitioned over three *parties*: traveler, agency, and airline. Each party has a part of the contract which can be seen as a *service*. Different services are connected through *interface places* for asynchronous message passing. Interface places model message buffers and are positioned on dashed lines as shown in Fig. 1(a). As a formalism, we use *open workflow nets* (oWFNs) [5] which extend the well-known concept of *workflow nets* (WFNs) [6] with interface places. However, the presented concepts are not limited to oWFNs and can be translated into other languages using message passing as a communication paradigm.

In our example, the traveler sends a trip order to the agency (transition a). As a result, the agency sends a flight order to the airline (transition g). The airline receives this order and either confirms it (message confirm order) or rejects it (message reject order). In the latter case, the rejection is forwarded to the traveler (transition k). If the flight is confirmed, the agency sends the flight details and an invoice to the traveler, and the airline sends a ticket to the traveler.

Figure 1(a) shows four oWFNs: N, N_{tr}, N_{ag}, and N_{air}. N_{tr}, N_{ag}, and N_{air} specify the *public view* of each of the parties involved. Each of the public views has interface places. For example, N_{tr} has one output place and four input places. Using these places, the public views can be merged together into the *contract*. The whole Petri net shown in Fig. 1(a) can be seen as a single oWFN N by simply ignoring the dashed lines. This oWFN has an empty interface.

After the parties agreed on such a contract, each of them needs to implement its part. A party needs to refine its part of the contract, so the resulting implementation may deviate significantly from the public view. We refer to this as the *private view* of the party. The private view may again be expressed as an oWFN. Figure 1(b) shows an example of a private view of the traveler; that is, oWFN N'_{tr} is the implementation of N_{tr}. In N_{tr}, the traveler first receives the invoice and then the ticket. In N'_{tr}, these two messages are received concurrently. Note that this example is a bit atypical since the implementation tends to have much more internal tasks. Here just transition x and places p_{31} to p_{34} are added while in more realistic scenarios there may dozens of newly added internal tasks. Clearly, N'_{tr} allows for behavior not possible in N_{tr} (even after abstracting from the new transition x). The trace a, b, e, c, x where the ticket is received before the invoice, for instance, is not possible in N_{tr} but in N'_{tr}. In this example it is harmless that N'_{tr} serves as implementation of N_{tr}. However, similar changes could lead to deadlocks and other problems. On this account, a comprehensive set of transformation rules for deriving a private view, which is correct by construction, from a public view would be very helpful for service designers.

In earlier work, we proposed to use *projection inheritance* for WFNs [7,8] for relating the actual realization of a contract to the contract itself [1,2]. It was proven that if private and public view are related by projection inheritance, then a party can execute its private view and no other party is effected by this change. Moreover, we defined *inheritance-preserving transformation rules* that guarantee correctness by construction; that is, the public view is extended into a correct private view by iteratively applying the rules. Unfortunately, N'_{tr} and N_{tr} are *not* related by projection inheritance. This illustrates that the inheritance notion defined is too restrictive, since it excludes private views that obviously do not jeopardize the overall correctness of the interorganizational workflow.

To address the problem, we present a more liberal notion of equivalence: *accordance*. The basic idea is that an oWFN N_2 accords with an oWFN N_1 if there is no interorganizational workflow where the replacement of oWFN N_1 by oWFN N_2 causes a problem. Accordance is weaker than projection inheritance. For example, N'_{tr} accords with N_{tr}.

The core contribution of this paper is a comprehensive set of *accordance preserving transformation rules*. They can be used to incrementally transform the public view of a party into a private view while guaranteeing that the overall process will terminate properly. These new rules are highly relevant because there are many situations where projection inheritance is too strong and accordance is a more suitable notion. In case both public and private view are given, a technique presented in [9] can be used for automatically checking accordance by using operating guidelines [5].

The paper is structured as follows. Section 2 defines oWFNs, contracts, and our accordance criterion. In Sect. 3, we present transformation rules to derive a private view which is correct by construction. A case study in Sect. 4 demonstrates the applicability and the value of these transformation rules.

2   Formalizing Contracts

The notions of a contract, public/private views, the accordance criterion, and transformation rules will be formalized using *open workflow nets* (oWFNs) [5]. Therefore, this section starts by introducing oWFNs. For more details on the formalization of these concepts we refer to a technical report [9].

We use the usual definition of a (place/transition) Petri net $N = (P, T, F)$ with a set of places P, a set of transitions T, and a flow relation $F \subseteq (P \times T) \cup (T \times P)$ representing the arcs (see [4], for instance). We also use the standard notation to denote the preset and postset of places and transitions: $^\bullet x = \{y \mid (y, x) \in F\}$ and $x^\bullet = \{y \mid (x, y) \in F\}$.

Definition 1 (Open workflow net). *An* open workflow net $N = (P, T, F, I, O, m_0, \Omega)$ *consists of a Petri net* (P, T, F) *together with*

- *an* interface *defined as a set* $I \subseteq P$ *of input places such that* $^\bullet p = \emptyset$ *for any* $p \in I$ *and a set* $O \subseteq P$ *of output places such that* $p^\bullet = \emptyset$ *for any* $p \in O$ *and* $I \cap O = \emptyset$,
- *a distinguished* initial marking m_0, *and a set* Ω *of final markings such that no transition of N is enabled in any* $m \in \Omega$. *We further require that* $m \in \Omega \cup \{m_0\}$ *implies* $m(p) = 0$ *for all* $p \in I \cup O$; *that is, in the initial and the final markings, the interface places are not marked.*

We use indices to distinguish the constituents of different oWFNs (e.g., I_j refers to the set of input places of oWFN N_j). In order to assign a reasonable meaning to *final* markings, we restrict our approach to such oWFNs where a marking in Ω does not enable any transition.

As an example, the whole process shown in Fig. 1(a) represents an oWFN with $I = O = \emptyset$, $m_0 = [p_1, p_6, p_{13}]$, and we define $\Omega = \{[p_5, p_{12}, p_{16}]\}$. The part of the traveler, N_{tr}, in Fig. 1(a) is an oWFN with interface: $I = \{$flight details, invoice, reject trip, ticket$\}$ and $O = \{$trip order$\}$.

The behavior of an oWFN is defined using standard Petri net semantics [4]; that is, a transition is enabled if each place of its preset holds at least a token.

An enabled transition t can fire in a marking m by consuming tokens from the preset places and producing tokens for the postset places, yielding a marking m' (denoted $m \xrightarrow{t} m'$).

For composing oWFNs, we assume that all constituents (except the interfaces) are pairwise disjoint. This requirement can be easily achieved by renaming. In contrast, the interfaces often intentionally overlap. For a reasonable concept of composition of oWFNs it is, however, convenient to require that all communication is bilateral; that is, every interface place $p \in I \cup O$ has only one party that sends into p and one party that receives from p. For a third party C, a communication taking place inside the composition of parties A and B is internal matter. These considerations lead to the following definition of composition.

Definition 2 (Composition of oWFNs). *Let* $N_1, \ldots, N_k$ *be oWFNs with pairwise disjoint constituents, except for the interfaces.* $N_1, \ldots, N_k$ *are composable if, for all* $i \in \{1, \ldots, k\}$,

- $p \in I_i$ *implies that there is no* $j \neq i$ *such that* $p \in I_j$ *and there is at most one* j *such that* $p \in O_j$, *and*
- $p \in O_i$ *implies that there is no* $j \neq i$ *such that* $p \in O_j$ *and there is at most one* j *such that* $p \in I_j$.

For markings $m_1 \in N_1, \ldots, m_k \in N_k$ *which do not mark interface places, their composition* $m = m_1 \oplus \cdots \oplus m_k$ *is defined by* $m(p) = m_i(p)$ *if* $p \in P_i$.

If $N_1, \ldots, N_k$ *are composable, the* composition $N = N_1 \oplus \cdots \oplus N_k$ *is the oWFN with the following constituents:* $P = P_1 \cup \cdots \cup P_k$. $T = T_1 \cup \cdots \cup T_k$. $F = F_1 \cup \cdots \cup F_k$. $I = (I_1 \cup \cdots \cup I_k) \setminus (O_1 \cup \cdots \cup O_k)$. $O = (O_1 \cup \cdots \cup O_k) \setminus (I_1 \cup \cdots \cup I_k)$. $m_0 = m_{0_1} \oplus \cdots \oplus m_{0_k}$, $\Omega = \{m_1 \oplus \cdots \oplus m_k \mid m_1 \in \Omega_1, \ldots, m_k \in \Omega_k\}$.

Clearly, the three oWFNs N_{tr}, N_{ag}, and N_{air} in Fig. 1(a) are composable.

Any subset of a set of composable oWFNs is composable as well. Furthermore, we have $N_1 \oplus N_2 \oplus N_3 = (N_1 \oplus N_2) \oplus N_3 = N_1 \oplus (N_2 \oplus N_3)$, and $N_1 \oplus N_2 = N_2 \oplus N_1$; that is, the composition of composable oWFNs is associative and commutative. Thus, composition of a set of oWFNs can be broken into single steps without affecting the final result.

For the oWFN depicted in Fig. 1(a) it is easy to check that the final marking is always reachable. This means that it is always possible to terminate properly. This property is formalized in the following definition.

Definition 3 (Weak termination). *An oWFN* weakly terminates *if, from every marking reachable from the initial marking, a final marking can be reached.*

For composable oWFNs whose composition is weakly terminating, we introduce the term strategy.

Definition 4 (Strategy). *An oWFN* N *is a* strategy *for an oWFN* N' *if* $N \oplus N'$ *is weakly terminating.* Strat(N) *denotes the set of all strategies for* N.

Note that $Strat(N)$ may correspond to a large (in fact infinite) set of oWFNs; that is, it is the set of all potential partners of N. N_{tr} in Fig. 1(a) and N'_{tr} in Fig.1(b) are two examples of strategies for the oWFN $N_{ag} \oplus N_{air}$.

Basically, we see a contract as an oWFN with empty interface where every activity is assigned to one of the involved parties. We impose only one restriction: If a place is accessed by more than one party, it should act as a directed bilateral communication place. In the following, $|X|$ denotes the cardinality of a set X.

Definition 5 (Contract). *Let $\mathcal{A}$ be a set representing the parties involved in a contract. Then, a contract $[N,r]$ consists of an oWFN $N = (P,T,F,I,O,m_0,\Omega)$ with an empty interface ($I = O = \emptyset$) (the overall process) and a mapping $r \in T \to \mathcal{A}$ (the partitioning) such that, for all places $p \in P$, $|\{r(t) \mid t \in {}^\bullet p\}| \leq 1$ and $|\{r(t) \mid t \in p^\bullet\}| \leq 1$. For technical purposes, we further require that N has only one final marking, $\Omega = \{m_f\}$.*

The oWFN shown in Fig. 1(a) is an example of a contract involving $\mathcal{A} = \{\mathsf{traveler}, \mathsf{agency}, \mathsf{airline}\}$. The dashed lines in the figure show the partitioning of transitions over the parties involved in the contract; $r(\mathsf{a}) = \mathsf{traveler}$, $r(\mathsf{f}) = \mathsf{agency}$ and $r(\mathsf{m}) = \mathsf{airline}$, for instance.

A contract can be cut into parts, each representing the agreed share of a single party. In accordance with terminology of service-oriented computing [10], we consider the contribution of a party as a *service*. Correspondingly, the agreed version (specification) of the service is called *public view* while an actual local implementation is called *private view* of the service.

Definition 6 (Public view). *Let $[N,r]$ be a contract with $N = (P,T,F,I,O, m_0,\Omega)$, $\Omega = \{m_f\}$, and $r \in T \to \mathcal{A}$, and let $A \in \mathcal{A}$ be a party. The public view of A's share in the contract is the oWFN N_A where $P_A = \{p \in P \mid \exists t \in {}^\bullet p \cup p^\bullet : r(t) = A\}$, $T_A = \{t \in T \mid r(t) = A\}$, $F_A = F \cap ((P_A \times T_A) \cup (T_A \times P_A))$, $I_A = \{p \in P_A \mid \exists t \in {}^\bullet p : r(t) \neq A\}$, $O_A = \{p \in P_A \mid \exists t \in p^\bullet : r(t) \neq A\}$, $m_{0_A} = m_{0|P_A}$ (i.e., the restriction of m_0 to the places in P_A), and $\Omega_A = \{m_{f|P_A}\}$.*

For a set $\mathcal{A} = \{A_1, \ldots, A_k\}$ of parties and a contract $[N,r]$, it is easy to see that $N_{A_1} \oplus \cdots \oplus N_{A_k} = N$. In this respect, the restriction that Ω contains only one element is indeed crucial, as otherwise $N_{A_1} \oplus \cdots \oplus N_{A_k}$ could have a final marking that results from recombining final markings of different parties but which is not a final marking of N.

Our *accordance* criterion is used to compare a public view and a private view of a party's share of a contract. The goal of the accordance notion is to preserve weak termination (see Def. 3) of the overall process N. Formally, weak termination of N and accordance of each private view N'_{A_i} with the corresponding public view N_{A_i} should imply weak termination of $N'_{A_1} \oplus \cdots \oplus N'_{A_k}$ which obviously models the overall process as actually implemented.

If $[N,r]$ is a contract with $\mathcal{A} = \{A_1, \ldots, A_k\}$ and N is weakly terminating, then $N_{A_1} \oplus \ldots \oplus N_{A_{i-1}} \oplus N_{A_{i+1}} \oplus \ldots \oplus N_{A_k}$ is a strategy for N_{A_i}. For example, $N_{tr} \oplus N_{ag} \oplus N_{air}$ shown in Fig. 1(a) is weakly terminating. Therefore, $N_{tr} \oplus N_{air}$ is a strategy for N_{ag}, and vice versa. These properties of the strategy concept justify the following definition of accordance.

Definition 7 (Accordance). *An oWFN N' (private view) accords with an oWFN N (public view) if it has the same interface ($I' = I$ and $O' = O$) and has at least the strategies that N has; that is, $Strat(N') \supseteq Strat(N)$.*

For example, the private view N'_{tr} accords with its public view N_{tr}. The following theorem shows that N_{tr} can be substituted by N'_{tr} without jeopardizing weak termination.

Theorem 1 (Implementation of a contract). *Let $[N, r]$ be a contract between parties $\{A_1, \dots, A_k\}$ where N is weakly terminating. If, for all $i \in \{1, \dots, k\}$, N'_{A_i} (the private view of A_i) accords with N_{A_i} (the public view of A_i), then $N' = N'_{A_1} \oplus \cdots \oplus N'_{A_k}$ (the actual implementation) is weakly terminating.*

The proof of this theorem can be found in [9]. The result is highly relevant for service composition since it gives each party a criterion (accordance of N'_{A_i} with N_{A_i}) that can be locally verified for asserting a global property (weak termination of the overall process as actually implemented). For example, any combination of arbitrary private views N''_{tr}, N''_{ag}, and N''_{air} according with the corresponding public view (i.e., N''_{tr} accords with N_{tr}, N''_{ag} accords with N_{ag}, and N''_{air} accords with N_{air}) yields a weakly terminating realization of the contract shown in Fig. 1(a).

According to Thm. 1, every party of a contract can implement its public view and finally it has to check accordance between the private and the public view. In the following, we present a different approach: The public view is incrementally transformed into a private view. To this end, fragments of the public view are incrementally replaced by other fragments until the private view is designed. In this approach, a fragment N' of a party is called a *pattern* and will be replaced by another fragment N''. We will prove that if N'' accords with N', then replacing N' by N'' preserves weak termination of the overall contract.

First of all, we formally define an oWFN pattern N' of an oWFN N. Therefore, the set of interface places of N' is divided into two sets: one set contains all places that are interface places of N for communicating with other parties (i.e., subsets of I and O) and the other set, $R \cup S$, contains all places that serve as an interface to the rest of N. R is the set of input places from the other parts of N, and S is the set of output places.

Definition 8 (oWFN pattern). *Let $N = (P, T, F, I, O, m_0, \Omega)$ be an oWFN. An oWFN $N' = (P', T', F', I', O', m'_0, \Omega')$ with $P' \subseteq P$, $T' \subseteq T$ is an oWFN pattern of N iff*

- *$F' = F \cap ((P' \times T') \cup (T' \times P'))$,*
- *$m'_0 = [\,]$,*
- *$I' = I_{|P'} \cup R$ with $R \subseteq P' \setminus I$,*
- *$O' = O_{|P'} \cup S$ with $S \subseteq P' \setminus O$,*
- *$\Omega' = \{[\,]\}$,*
- *for all $p \in P' \setminus R$, there is no $t \in T \setminus T'$, $(t, p) \in F$,*

- *for all $p \in P' \setminus S$, there is no $t \in T \setminus T'$, $(p,t) \in F$, and*
- *for all $t \in T'$, there is no $p \in P \setminus P'$, $(p,t) \in F$ or $(t,p) \in F$.*

The next theorem states that if the public view of a party participating in a contract has an oWFN pattern N' and there is another oWFN pattern N'' with N'' accords with N', then we can replace N' by N'' and the modified contract is still weakly terminating. Such transformations can be applied incrementally and thus we can derive a private view from a public view just by transforming the public view and the resulting private view is correct by construction.

Theorem 2 (Justification of transformation rules). *Let $[N,r]$ be a contract between parties $\{A_1, \ldots, A_k\}$ where $N = N_{A_1} \oplus \cdots \oplus N_{A_k}$ is weakly terminating. Let N'_p be an oWFN pattern of N_{A_i}, $1 \le i \le k$, such that there exists N_{rest} with $N_{A_i} = N'_p \oplus N_{rest}$. Let further N''_p be an arbitrary oWFN. Then, if N''_p accords with N'_p, the modified contract $N' = N_{A_1} \oplus \cdots \oplus N_{A_{i-1}} \oplus (N''_p \oplus N_{rest}) \oplus N_{A_{i+1}} \oplus \cdots \oplus N_{A_k}$ is weakly terminating.*

We omit the proof of this theorem as it is just an application of Thm. 1.

3   Derive a Private View from a Public View

In this section, we show how a party can implement its private view by using *accordance-preserving transformation rules*. This idea is inspired by earlier work on projection inheritance [1,2,7,8]. Accordance is a weaker notion than projection inheritance which was illustrated already using Fig. 1 where N'_{tr} accords with N_{tr} but N'_{tr} and N_{tr} are not related by projection inheritance. However, we will show that projection inheritance implies accordance, and thus, all inheritance-preserving transformation rules presented in [8] also preserve accordance. We will show these rules by reformulating them to fit into the setting of this paper. Afterwards, we will formulate dedicated transformation rules that allow reordering of the sending and receiving of messages still guaranteeing accordance.

3.1   Inheritance-Preserving Transformation Rules

Projection inheritance compares process models by establishing a subclass-superclass relationship. The subclass process is indeed a subclass if it inherits particular dynamic properties of its superclass. Projection inheritance is based on branching bisimulation [11] (to compare the processes) and abstraction (to hide tasks) and was formalized in [8] in terms of workflow nets. The assumption is that the subclass adds tasks to the superclass such that after hiding the additional tasks both are equivalent.

Based on the notion of projection inheritance, three *inheritance-preserving transformation rules* have been defined in [8]. These rules correspond to design patterns for extending a superclass to incorporate new behavior: (1) adding a loops (2) insert a task in-between existing tasks, and (3) put a new task in parallel with existing tasks.

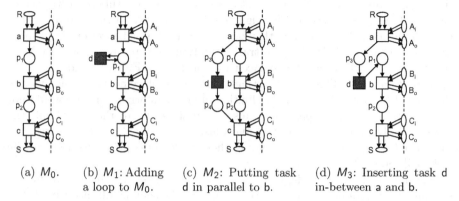

(a) M_0. (b) M_1: Adding a loop to M_0. (c) M_2: Putting task d in parallel to b. (d) M_3: Inserting task d in-between a and b.

Fig. 2. Accordance-preserving transformation rules based on projection inheritance

It is easy to reformulate projection inheritance in terms of the setting of this paper. Instead of redefining these rules formally, we exemplify the rules in Fig. 2. Figure 2(a) represents an oWFN pattern M_0 of an oWFN M. M_0 contains transitions a, b, and c. By Def. 8, there are no other connections of a, b, c, p_1, and p_2 than those shown in Fig. 2(a). $A_i = (^\bullet a) \cap I_M$ is the set of input places of a, $A_o = (a^\bullet) \cap O_M$ is the set of output places of a, etc. A_i, A_o, B_i, B_o, C_i, C_o do not need to be disjoint. $R = (^\bullet a) \setminus I_M$ and $S = (c^\bullet) \setminus O_M$ are (by Def. 8) the places connecting M_0 to the rest of M. Similar remarks hold for the other three oWFN patterns M_1, M_2, and M_3. For example, M_1 is obtained by adding transition d to M_0.

If one ignores the interface places and hides transition d (i.e., all executions of d are mapped onto silent steps), then M_0, M_1, M_2, and M_3 are branching bisimular. Thus, M_0 is a superclass of M_1, M_2, and M_3. It is easy to see that projection inheritance implies accordance.

Theorem 3 (Projection inheritance implies accordance). *Let N' be an oWFN pattern and N'' be an arbitrary oWFN. If N' and N'' are related by projection inheritance, then N'' accords with N' and vice versa.*

Theorem 3 justifies that all inheritance-preserving transformation rules can be used to incrementally build a private view that accords with the public view of a service. As an example, since M_1 accords with M_0, M_2 accords with M_0, M_3 accords with M_0, and vice versa, M_0 in Fig. 2 may be replaced by any of the three other oWFNs M_1, M_2, and M_3 without changing the set of strategies of M. For technical details we refer to the technical report [9].

3.2 Accordance-Preserving Transformation Rules

The inheritance-preserving transformation rules presented in the last section are limited in the sense that they do not allow to change the order of messages. In the following, we present six *accordance-preserving transformation rules*. Five of these rules preserve accordance in both directions and one rule preserves accordance only in one direction. Although these transformation rules are powerful, they are not complete, meaning they do not cover all possible service implementations. Given an oWFN N, each transformation rule specifies a pattern N' of N (see Def. 8) which can be replaced by another oWFN N'' yielding an implementation of N. Theorem 2 justifies that this replacement does not violate the overall contract. As a formal definition of all transformation rules would not add any value to the paper and is also impossible due to the page limit, the rules are only informally described and illustrated by help of some figures. For the formalization of all rules including their correctness proofs we refer to the technical report [9].

The first of the rules is depicted in Fig. 3(a) and specifies that a sequence of sending events can be merged and the events can be sent simultaneously. Rule 1 preserves accordance in both directions. Thus, we can derive that a sequence of sending events can also be reordered or can be sent concurrently. Reordering of sending events and executing sending events concurrently preserve accordance in both directions. The same holds for a sequence of receiving events. The corresponding rule (Rule 2) is, however, not depicted in the paper.

A generalization of the two previous rules is specified by Rule 3 (see Fig. 3(b)). A sequence of receiving events followed by a sequence of sending events can be executed simultaneously while preserving accordance in both directions.

From Rules 1–3 we can derive that every oWFN pattern that has a transition connected to more than one interface place can be transformed into an equivalent oWFN pattern which has only transitions connected to a single interface place. In the following, without loss of generality, we therefore restrict ourselves to patterns where each transition is connected to at most one interface place.

So far, we excluded the possibility that a sending event is followed by a receiving event. Rule 4, depicted in Fig. 4, specifies that first sending and then

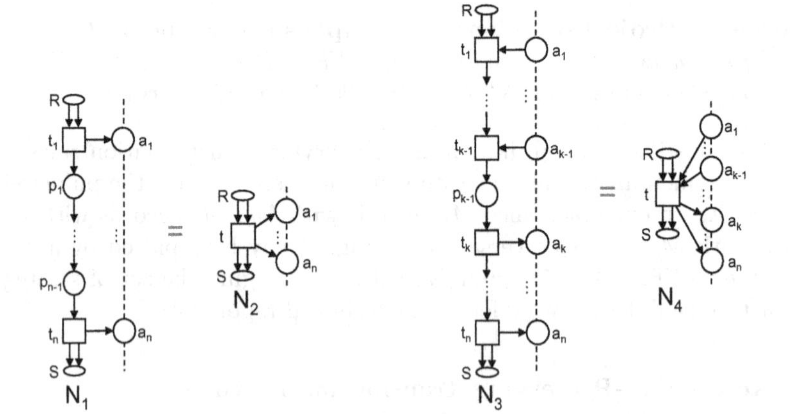

(a) Rule 1: $Strat(N_1) = Strat(N_2)$.   (b) Rule 3: $Strat(N_3) = Strat(N_4)$.

Fig. 3. Rule 1 and Rule 3

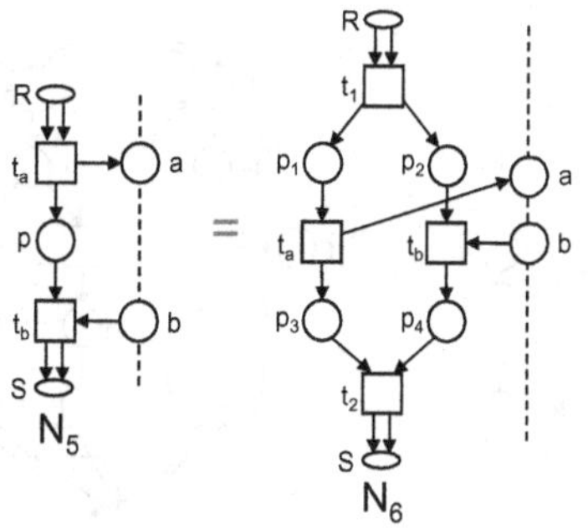

Fig. 4. Rule 4: $Strat(N_5) = Strat(N_6)$

receiving a message can also be executed concurrently and vice versa. Rule 4 preserves accordance in both directions, too.

Figure 5(a) shows that first sending and then receiving cannot be reordered in general: N_7 does not accord with N_5 and N_5 does not accord with N_7. The oWFN depicted in Fig. 5(b) is a strategy for N_5 but no strategy for N_7. The oWFN depicted in Fig. 5(c), in contrast, is a strategy for N_7 but not for N_5.

From this antipattern follows that first sending and then receiving (cf. N_5) cannot be transformed into an oWFN that sends and receives simultaneously, because we could transform the latter net into N_7 by applying Rule 3. Consequently, first sending then receiving does not accord to sending and receiving simultaneously and vice versa.

Rule 5 specifies how an alternative branch can be added to an oWFN pattern N_8 depicted on the left hand side of Fig. 6. The pattern N_8 first receives a and then enters either the left or the right branch. In the left (right) branch, message b (c) is sent, and then message d (e) is received . The pattern N_8 can

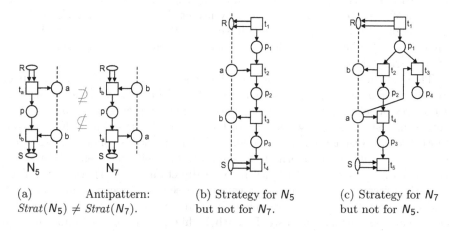

(a)   Antipattern:
$Strat(N_5) \neq Strat(N_7)$.

(b) Strategy for N_5 but not for N_7.

(c) Strategy for N_7 but not for N_5.

Fig. 5. Counterexamples

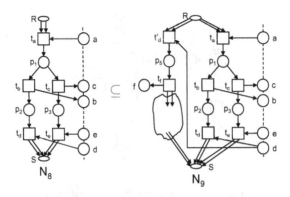

Fig. 6. Rule 5 (adding an alternative branch): $Strat(N_8) \subseteq Strat(N_9)$

be transformed into N_9 by adding an alternative branch. In this branch, d is received, and then a message f is sent. Afterwards, this branch can be arbitrary; that is, there can be any continuation (including direct continuation in S) of this net illustrated by the frame. Rule 5 preserves accordance in one direction only.

The intuition behind the next transformation rule (Rule 6) is the possibility to add (remove) "dead code" to (from) a service. To motivate this transformation rule, consider a party that wants to reuse an existing service in the contract. This service may provide functionality to other parties not involved in the current contract. Technically, in the first step, this party makes internal all interface places of this service that are not used, and in the second step, it looks for transformation rules justifying the service to be a valid private view. Rule 6 is depicted in Fig. 7. N_{10} receives a, then sends b, and then it can behave arbitrarily. The oWFN pattern N_{11} results from adding an alternative branch to N_{10}. This branch can be entered if place c is marked. Afterwards, the branch may behave arbitrarily. In the end, both branches are synchronized in S. However, c is an example of an internal place with empty preset (it is a former interface place). Thus, transition t_c will never be enabled. Rule 6 preserves accordance in both directions, meaning neither adding nor deleting "dead code" will change the set of strategies for N_{10} and N_{11}.

The six transformation rules presented in this section reflect the crucial impact of the order of sending and receiving messages. The first two rules show that sequences of sending events and sequences of receiving events can be executed simultaneously while preserving accordance in both directions. This was our motivation to consider only oWFNs where each transition is connected to at most one interface place. Transforming first-send-then-receive into send-and-receive-concurrently preserves accordance in both directions (Fig. 4). However, first-send-then-receive cannot be transformed into send-and-receive-simultaneously and vice versa. Consider first-receive-then-send next. It can be transformed into receive-and-send-simultaneously (Fig. 3(b)) while preserving accordance in both directions, but it cannot be transformed into receive-and-send-concurrently and vice versa.

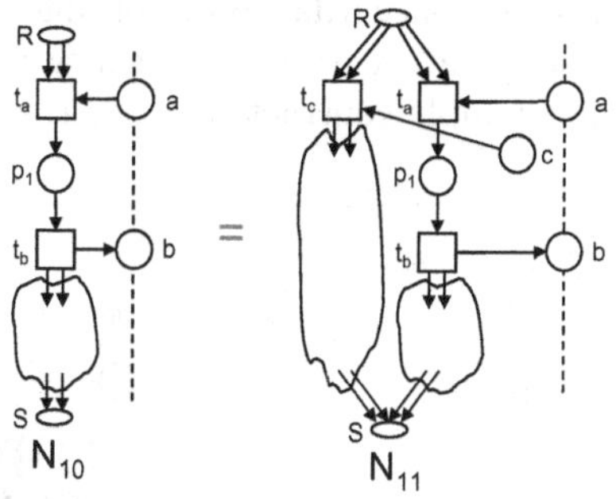

Fig. 7. Rule 6 (adding "dead code"): $Strat(N_{10}) = Strat(N_{11})$

4   Case Study

In this section, we demonstrate how accordance-preserving transformation rules can be applied to derive a private view of the agency from its respective public view, taken from the running example in Fig. 1(a). On first sight, the modified agency depicted in Fig. 8(b) and the (original) agency (depicted again in Fig. 8(a) to ease the comparison) are not very similar. We will now show that the modified agency was derived from the original agency by applying the transformation rules defined in Sect. 3:

- A new transition u (newly-added transitions are depicted in dark gray) is inserted in-between the reception of the trip order and the sending of the flight order. This transition explicitly models the preparation of the flight order from the trip order sent by the traveler. The addition is justified by rule pattern M_3 (cf. Fig. 2(d)) which preserves projection inheritance and thus accordance.
- The rejection message from the airline is instantly routed to the traveler. Rule 3 justifies the merging of transition i and k to the single transition ik (transitions created by merging transitions of the public view are depicted in light gray).
- Messages flight details and invoice can be sent simultaneously to the traveler by transition jl. The merging of transition j and l is justified by Rule 1.
- Finally, a new branch was added to the agency, starting with transition v. Intuitively, this branch models additional behavior that is available when the modified agency service is running in a different environment. When priority order is an input place for messages sent from a (modified) traveler service and priority flight order is an output place for messages sent to a (modified) airline service, the newly-added branch can be triggered by messages. Thus, the modified agency can be reused in a different contract. However, the places priority order and priority flight order are not exposed as interface places, and as the place priority order is not marked, the branch is dead. Therefore, the addition is justified by Rule 6.

As all applied rules are accordance-preserving, the modified agency (cf. Fig. 8(b)) is a correct private view of the agency (cf. Fig. 8(a)), and thus accords with the running example contract (cf. Fig. 1(a)).

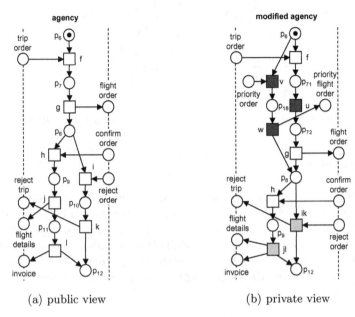

(a) public view   (b) private view

Fig. 8. The public view (a) and a private view (b) of the agency of Fig. 1(a)

5   Conclusion

An interorganizational process couples interacting processes handled by different parties. In this context, a contract serves as an agreement of these parties to a public description of the overall process. Each of the parties implements its part of the contract. These parts correspond to services and are termed "views". Each party has a public view (the part of the process it is responsible for) and the private view (the process actually implemented). The notion of accordance relates these two views and serves as a local correctness criterion. Accordance is particularly suitable for interactions based on asynchronous message passing and the local criterion ensures the correctness of the overall process even if parties do not exactly behave as specified.

In this paper, we presented six *transformation rules* to derive a private view from a public view. As transformation rules preserve accordance between the public and the private view, the private view is correct by construction. Accordance guarantees that the overall process will always terminate properly; that is, the overall process cannot run into a deadlock or livelock. We showed that some of the rules preserve accordance in both directions while other preserve accordance only in one direction. We discussed that the notion of accordance generalizes the notion of projection inheritance [1,2,7,8].

In ongoing work, we look for other correctness criteria than weak termination. Moreover, we want to relate the notion of accordance to other equivalence notions described in literature. Furthermore, an accordance check that returns which rules have to be applied to derive one service from the other one seems to be of practical relevance.

Acknowledgments. The authors would like to thank Arjan J. Mooij for pointing out an error in a preliminary version of this paper.

References

1. van der Aalst, W.: Inheritance of Interorganizational Workflows: How to agree to disagree without loosing control? Information Technology and Management Journal 4(4), 345–389 (2003)
2. van der Aalst, W., Weske, M.: The P2P approach to Interorganizational Workflows. In: Dittrich, K.R., Geppert, A., Norrie, M.C. (eds.) CAiSE 2001. LNCS, vol. 2068, pp. 140–156. Springer, Heidelberg (2001)
3. Decker, G., Kopp, O., Leymann, F., Weske, M.: BPEL4Chor: Extending BPEL for modeling choreographies. In: Proceedings of the IEEE International Conference on Web Services (ICWS 2007), pp. 296–303. IEEE Computer Society, Los Alamitos (2007)
4. Reisig, W.: Petri Nets. EATCS Monographs on Theoretical Computer Science. Springer, Heidelberg (1985)
5. Massuthe, P., Reisig, W., Schmidt, K.: An Operating Guideline Approach to the SOA. Annals of Mathematics, Computing & Teleinformatics 1(3), 35–43 (2005)
6. van der Aalst, W.: The Application of Petri Nets to Workflow Management. The Journal of Circuits, Systems and Computers 8(1), 21–66 (1998)
7. van der Aalst, W., Basten, T.: Inheritance of Workflows: An Approach to Tackling Problems Related to Change. Theor. Comput. Sci. 270(1-2), 125–203 (2002)
8. Basten, T., van der Aalst, W.: Inheritance of Behavior. Journal of Logic and Algebraic Programming 47(2), 47–145 (2001)
9. van der Aalst, W., Massuthe, P., Stahl, C., Wolf, K.: Multiparty Contracts: Agreeing and Implementing Interorganizational Processes. Informatik-Berichte 213, Humboldt-Universität zu Berlin (2007)
10. Papazoglou, M.: Agent-oriented technology in support of e-business. Commun. ACM 44(4), 71–77 (2001)
11. van Glabbeek, R., Weijland, W.: Branching Time and Abstraction in Bisimulation Semantics. Journal of the ACM 43(3), 555–600 (1996)

Event Structure Semantics of Orc[*]

Sidney Rosario[1], David Kitchin[3], Albert Benveniste[1],
William Cook[3], Stefan Haar[4], and Claude Jard[2]

[1] Irisa/Inria, Campus de Beaulieu, 35042 Rennes cedex, France
[2] Irisa/ENS Cachan, Campus de Beaulieu, 35042 Rennes cedex, France
[3] The University of Texas at Austin, Department of Computer Sciences, Austin, USA
[4] Irisa/Inria Rennes and SITE, University of Ottawa, Canada

Abstract. Developing wide-area distributed applications requires
jointly analyzing functional and Quality of Service (QoS) aspects, such
as timing properties. Labelled transition systems and sequential trace
semantics - the common semantic domains - do not facilitate this kind
of analysis because they do not precisely express the causal relationships
between events. *Asymmetric Event Structures* (AES) provide an explicit
representation of the causal dependencies between events in the execution of a system and allow for an elegant coding of preemption. Event
structures are, however, difficult to construct compositionally, because
they cannot easily represent fragments of a computation. The *heaps* we
develop here allow for such a representation, and easily generate AES.
In this paper, we develop a partial-order semantics in terms of heaps, for
Orc, an orchestration language used to describe distributed computations
over the internet. We briefly show how Orc, and this new semantics, are
used for QoS studies of wide area orchestrations.

1 Introduction

Orchestrating Web services consists of a combination of different activities.

A primary concern is to ensure that the expected functionality is indeed correctly implemented. This requires semantic studies for the formalisms used in
specifying the functional aspect of Web service orchestrations. Examples of such
studies include the translation of the industrial standard BPEL into WorkFlow
nets [18] (a special subclass of Petri nets) or the pi-calculus [14], from which
analysis techniques and tools for BPEL [13,2] were developed.

Another important, yet much less addressed task consists in ensuring that the
Web service orchestration offers the due Quality of Service (QoS). QoS parameters are not firmly established, but they typically include response time (latency),
availability, maximum allowed query rate (throughput), and security. The Web
Service Level Agreement (WSLA) framework [11] is a standard proposed by
IBM for QoS parameters in Web Services. When applied to the management
of OEM/supplier cooperations, orchestrations must make precise the duties and

[*] This work was partially funded by the ANR national research program DOTS (ANR-
06-SETI-003), DocFlow (ANR-06-MDCA-005) and the project CREATE ActivDoc.

M. Dumas and R. Heckel (Eds.): WS-FM 2007, LNCS 4937, pp. 154–168, 2008.

responsibilities of the different actors in such chains, via contracts [5]. Having contracts with each subcontractor, the orchestration can establish the overall contract with its customers. This process is called contract composition.

We believe there is a need for semantic studies underpinning the design of Web services orchestrations in all its aspects: functional, QoS, and contracts, including contract composition. Developing such a holistic approach can become quickly cumbersome if rich formalisms for describing Web services orchestrations are considered, such as, e.g., BPEL. The functional semantics of BPEL is in itself complex, due to the large number of features offered. Extending such semantics to encompass QoS aspects can be cumbersome. Orc [12] has been recently proposed as a small and elegant language for wide area computing and Web services orchestrations. While keeping small, it offers the main features required by wide area computing, namely: service call, parallel and sequential composition, preemption, and recursion. Orc has been successfully used to model typical workflow patterns defined by Van der Aalst et al [1,8].

This paper proposes the foundations for an Orc based design of Web services orchestrations, including both functional and QoS aspects, and supporting contract composition. An interleaving semantics, both operational and denotational, was proposed for Orc in [12]. To prepare for a combined functional/QoS use, we propose in this paper a partial order semantics that keeps track of causalities and concurrency. This allows us to address all the aspects of QoS where causality and concurrency relating the different site calls matters. For example, if an orchestration causally depends on a given site call, failure of this site to deliver proper service causes failure of the orchestration. Another example is that of latency: causal dependencies and concurrency between site calls and other events are reflected into the dates of completion of these different events. Companion paper [16] details the use of this semantics for QoS studies and contract composition, and describes the resulting *TOrQuE* tool (**T**ool for **Or**chestration **Qu**ality of Service **E**valuation).

The paper is organized as follows. Section 2 briefly introduces Orc and its operational semantics. Asymmetric event structures and heap semantics of Orc are described in Section 3, where its use in QoS studies is sketched. Related work is given in Section 4.

2   Orc Overview

An Orc program consists of a set of definitions and a *goal* expression which is to be evaluated. Orc assumes that basic services, like sequential computation and data manipulation, are implemented by primitive *sites*. Orc provides constructs to orchestrate the concurrent invocation of sites.

The syntax of Orc is given in the upper portion of figure 1. Orc defines three basic operators. For Orc expressions f, g, "$f \mid g$" executes f and g in parallel. "$f >x> g$" evaluates f first and for *every* value returned by f, a *new* instance of g is launched with variable x assigned to this return value. "f **where** $x :\in g$" executes f and g in parallel. When g returns its *first* value, x is assigned to this value and the computation of g is terminated. All site calls in f having x as a parameter are blocked till x is defined (*i.e*, till g returns its first value).

$$f, g, h \in Expression ::= M(p) \mid E(p) \mid f \mid g \mid f >x> g \mid f \text{ where } x :\in g \mid ?k$$
$$p \in Actual ::= x \mid v$$
$$Definition ::= E(x) \; \Delta \; f$$

$$\frac{k \text{ fresh}}{M(v) \xrightarrow{M_k(v)} ?k} \text{ (SITECALL)} \qquad\qquad \frac{f \xrightarrow{a} f' \quad a \neq !v}{f >x> g \xrightarrow{a} f' >x> g} \text{ (SEQ1N)}$$

$$?k \xrightarrow{k?v} let(v) \quad \text{(SITERET)} \qquad\qquad \frac{f \xrightarrow{!v} f'}{f >x> g \xrightarrow{\tau} (f' >x> g) \mid [v/x].g} \text{ (SEQ1V)}$$

$$let(v) \xrightarrow{!v} 0 \qquad \text{(LET)} \qquad\qquad \frac{f \xrightarrow{a} f'}{f \text{ where } x :\in g \xrightarrow{a} f' \text{ where } x :\in g} \text{ (ASYM1N)}$$

$$\frac{f \xrightarrow{a} f'}{f \mid g \xrightarrow{a} f' \mid g} \quad \text{(SYM1)} \qquad\qquad \frac{g \xrightarrow{!v} g'}{f \text{ where } x :\in g \xrightarrow{\tau} [v/x].f} \text{ (ASYM1V)}$$

$$\frac{g \xrightarrow{a} g'}{f \mid g \xrightarrow{a} f \mid g'} \quad \text{(SYM2)} \qquad\qquad \frac{g \xrightarrow{a} g' \quad a \neq !v}{f \text{ where } x :\in g \xrightarrow{a} f \text{ where } x :\in g'} \text{ (ASYM2)}$$

$$\frac{[\![E(x) \; \Delta \; f]\!] \in D}{E(p) \xrightarrow{\tau} [p/x].f} \text{ (DEF)}$$

Fig. 1. The Syntax (top) Operational Semantics (bottom) of Orc

The operational semantics of Orc is given in Figure 1 [12], using SOS rules. An Orc expression f can perform action a and transform itself into the expression f', which is denoted by the transition $f \xrightarrow{a} f'$. The actions A and values V are described by the following grammar:

$$a \in A ::= M_k(v) \mid k?v \mid !v \mid \tau$$
$$v \in V ::= x \mid \mathbf{v}$$

The actions A are the transition labels of the Orc operational semantics. The x are variable names. They are placeholders for the value which will eventually replace that variable in the expression. The ground values $\mathbf{v}$ are the constant values which are always available.

Observe the following. Due to rule (DEF), recursive definitions are possible in Orc. Also, rule (ASYM1V) exhibits termination of g upon its first publication.

The CarOnLine toy example. CarOnLine is a composite service for buying cars online, together with credit and insurance. A simplified schematic description of the service is given in figure 2. On receiving a car model as an input

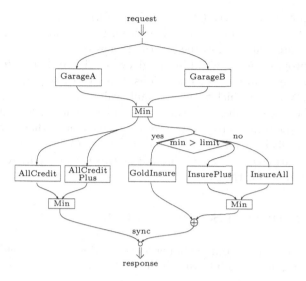

Fig. 2. A simplified view of the CarOnLine orchestration. The calls to GarageA and GarageB are guarded by a timer that returns a "Fault" message at timeout.

$$CarOnline(car) =_{\text{def}} \; CarPrice(car) \; >p> \; let(p, c, r)$$
$$\textbf{where} \;\; c :\in \; GetCredit(p)$$
$$r :\in \; GetInsur(p)$$

$$CarPrice(car) =_{\text{def}} \; \{GuardedMin(p1, p2)$$
$$\textbf{where} \;\; p1 :\in \; GarageA(car) \mid Timer(T)$$
$$p2 :\in \; GarageB(car) \mid Timer(T)\}$$
$$>p> \; \{if(p \neq Fault) \gg let(p)\}$$

$$GetCredit(p) =_{\text{def}} \; Min(r1, r2)$$
$$\textbf{where} \;\; r1 :\in \; AllCredit(p)$$
$$r2 :\in \; AllCreditPlus(p)$$

$$GetInsur(p) =_{\text{def}} \; \{if(p \geq limit) \gg GoldInsure(p)\}$$
$$\mid$$
$$\{if(p \leq limit) \gg Min(ip, ia)$$
$$\textbf{where} \;\; ip :\in \; InsurePlus(p)$$
$$ia :\in \; InsureAll(p)\}$$

Fig. 3. CarOnLine in Orc. *GuardedMin* takes the minimum of the values received before timeout and otherwise returns *Fault*.

query, the CarOnLine service first sends parallel requests to two car dealers (GarageA, GarageB), getting quotations for the car. We guard the calls to each garage by a timer, which kills the waiting when timeout occurs. The best offer (minimum price) is selected and credit and insurances are parallely found for the offer. Two banks (AllCredit, AllCreditPlus) are queried for credit rates and the one offering a lower rate is chosen. For insurance, if the car price of the best offer is greater than a certain limit, any insurance offer by service GoldInsure is accepted. If not, two services (InsurePlus,InsureAll) are parallely called and the one offering the lower insurance rate is chosen. In the end, the (car-price,credit-rate,insurance-rate) tuple is returned to the requestor.

The Orc program for CarOnLine is given in Figure 3. *CarPrice* parallelly calls *GarageA* and *GarageB* for quotations. Calls to these garages are guarded by a timer site *Timer* which returns a fault value T time units after the calls are made. The *let* site simply returns the values of its arguments—sites can only execute when all their parameters are defined and thus can be used to synchronize parallel threads. The value returned by *CarPrice* (here the variable p) is passed as argument to *GetCredit* and *GetInsur* which parallelly find credit and insurance rates for the price.

3   Event Structure Semantics of Orc

In this section we describe our partial order semantics. We first recall asymmetric event structures, and then introduce heaps.

3.1   Asymmetric Event Structures

Following [19,3], an *Asymmetric Event Structure* (AES) is a model of computation consisting of a set of events and two associated binary relations, the *causality* relation $\preceq$ and the *asymmetric conflict* relation $\nearrow$. If for events e and e', $e \preceq e'$ holds, then e must occur before e' can occur. If $e \nearrow e'$ holds, then the occurrence of e' preempts the occurrence of e in the future. Thus if both e and e' occur in an execution, e necessarily happens before e'. In this sense, $\nearrow$ can also be seen as a "weak causality" relation.

Formally, an AES is a tuple $\mathbf{G} = (E, \preceq, \nearrow)$, where E is a set of *events*, and $\preceq$ and $\nearrow$ are the *causality* and *asymmetric conflict* binary relations over E, satisfying the following conditions:

1. $\preceq$ is a partial order, and $\lfloor e \rfloor =_{\text{def}} \{e' \in E \mid e' \preceq e\}$ is finite;
2. $\forall e, e' \in E$:

$$e \prec e' \Rightarrow e \nearrow e' \tag{1}$$

$$\text{the restriction of } \nearrow \text{ to } \lfloor e \rfloor \text{ is acyclic} \tag{2}$$

$$\#^a(\{e, e'\}) \Rightarrow e \nearrow e' \tag{3}$$

where $\#^a$ is the *conflict relation*, recursively defined by:

$$e_0 \nearrow e_1 \nearrow \ldots e_n \nearrow e_0 \Rightarrow \#^a(\{e_0, \ldots, e_n\}) \tag{4}$$

$$[\#^a(A \cup \{e\})] \wedge [e \preceq e'] \Rightarrow \#^a(A \cup \{e'\}) \tag{5}$$

By abuse of notation, we write $e\#^a f$ to mean $\#^a(\{e, f\})$. Condition (5) ensures that a conflict with e is inherited by all the events caused by e. For $\mathbf{G} = (E, \preceq, \nearrow)$ an AES, a configuration of $\mathbf{G}$ is a set $\kappa \subseteq E$ of events such that

1. the restriction of $\nearrow$ to κ is well-founded;
2. $\{e' \in \kappa \mid e' \nearrow e\}$ is finite for every $e \in \kappa$;
3. κ is left-closed with respect to $\preceq$, i.e., $\forall e \in \kappa, e' \in E, e' \preceq e$ implies $e' \in \kappa$.

For our coding of Orc, we will need to label the events. Thus we shall consider *Labeled AES* (LAES), which are tuples of the form $\mathbf{G} = (E, \preceq, \nearrow, \lambda)$, where $\lambda : E \mapsto \Lambda$, ($\Lambda$ is a set of labels) is the labeling (partial) function.

Discussion. Although event structures are a convenient semantic domain for complete programs, they cannot represent fragments thereof, which arise naturally when constructing the behavior of a program from its sub-parts. By offering the additional concept of *place*, Petri nets and their extensions make composition and structural translation easier. Explicit encoding of places allows one fragment to depend upon resources supplied by another fragment. Petri nets with read arcs also allow us to elegantly code the *preemption* behaviour in Orc's **where** operator: the first "publish" event prevents all subsequent events from occuring. To bypass the nontrivial construction of Petri nets supporting recursion, we chose to generate directly a particular representation of unfoldings of nets with read arcs, which we call *heaps*. Heaps can then be easily translated into event structures and allow for easy coding into software.

3.2   Heaps

Heaps are sets of labeled events coded in a particular form, following an original idea of Esparza et al. [10]. A heap event has a label—the Orc action it represents—and is characterized by the conditions that enable its occurrence. These enabling conditions can either be consumed by the event or be read and not consumed. Each condition, in turn, refers to the unique event that created it. Marks are used to distinguish different conditions created by the same event.

More precisely, we are given an underlying set $\mathcal{A}$ of *labels*, an initialization action $\star \in \mathcal{A}$, and a set of initial *marks* $\mathcal{M}_{in}$. Sets $\mathcal{E}$ of all events, $\mathcal{C}$ of all conditions and $\mathcal{M}$ of all marks (which is initialised to $\mathcal{M}_{in}$) are inductively defined as follows:

- $\bot = (\emptyset, \emptyset, \star) \in \mathcal{E}$;
- if $f \in \mathcal{E}$ and $\mu \in \mathcal{M}$, then $c = (f, \mu) \in \mathcal{C}$; μ is the *mark* of c;
- for $\mathbf{c}$ and $\mathbf{c'}$ two subsets of $\mathcal{C}$ such that $\mathbf{c} \cap \mathbf{c'} = \emptyset$ and $\mathbf{c} \cup \mathbf{c'} \neq \emptyset$, then $e = (\mathbf{c}, \mathbf{c'}, a) \in \mathcal{E}$; $a \in \mathcal{A}$ is the *label* of e; $^\bullet e =_{\mathrm{def}} \mathbf{c}$ and $\underline{e} =_{\mathrm{def}} \mathbf{c'}$ are the set of conditions *consumed* and *read* by e, and $^\bullet\underline{e} =_{\mathrm{def}} {}^\bullet e \cup \underline{e}$ is the *preset* of e.
- if $e \in \mathcal{E}$, then $e \in \mathcal{M}$, *i.e* any event can itself be used as a mark.

Definition 1. *A heap is a set of events $E \subset \mathcal{E}$, such that $\bot \notin E$.*

For heap E, we define its set of associated conditions $C_E = \bigcup_{e \in E} {}^\bullet\underline{e}$. The set $S_E = \{f \mid (f, \mu) \in C_E\} \cup E$ is called the *support* of E. For $f \in S_E$, set $f^\bullet =_{\mathrm{def}} \{c \in C_E \mid c = (f, \mu)\}$. Define the set of *minimal conditions* of E to be minConds(E) =$_{\text{def}}$ $\{c \in C_E \mid c = (f, \mu), f \notin E\}$. The support includes *external* events which generate conditions that enable events in E. The initialization event $\perp \in S_E$ but $\perp \notin E$. With this non classical notion of support, heaps can model program fragments (unlike event structures).

Given a heap E we define the following relations between events in E (superscript $*$ denotes transitive closure):

$$\preceq_E = \vartriangleleft^* \text{ where } \vartriangleleft = \{(f,e) \mid f^\bullet \cap {}^\bullet\underline{e} \neq \emptyset\} \cup \{(e,e) \mid e \in E\} \tag{6}$$

$$\nearrow'_E = \prec_E \cup \left\{ (f, e) \,\middle|\, \exists e' \in E, e_1 : \begin{bmatrix} (e',\text{-}) \in \ {}^\bullet\underline{f} \cap {}^\bullet e_1 \\ \wedge \ e_1 \preceq_E e \end{bmatrix} \right\}$$

$$\nearrow_E = \nearrow'_E \cup \{(e,f) \mid e \#^a_E f\} \tag{7}$$

where event variables e, e_1 and f range over E, and the symmetric conflict relation $\#^a_E$ is deduced from $\nearrow'_E$ via (4,5). The reason for the two-step definition of $\nearrow_E$ is that the pair $(\preceq_E, \nearrow'_E)$ satisfies conditions (1) and (2), but not necessarily (3). The latter is enforced by second step in the definition, from $\nearrow'_E$ to $\nearrow_E$. Next, equip E with a labeling map

$$\alpha_E(e) =_{\text{def}} a \tag{8}$$

where event $e = ({}^\bullet e, \underline{e}, a)$. For a heap E, we shall denote by

$$\min(E) = \{e \in E \mid \forall f \in E : f \preceq_E e \Rightarrow f = e\} \tag{9}$$

the events that are minimal for the relation $\preceq_E$. We omit the subscript $_E$ in the sequel. In the SEND heap in Figure 4, $e \preceq f_1$ holds, where e is the event labelled M_{k1} or $k1?v_1$. Also $e \nearrow f_1$ holds for all events e in the heap (except f_1).

Definition 2. *A* configuration *of a heap E is any finite subset κ of E with the following properties:*

1. *the restriction of $\nearrow$ to κ is well-founded;*
2. $\{e' \in \kappa \mid e' \nearrow e\}$ *is finite for every $e \in \kappa$;*
3. κ *is left-closed with respect to $\preceq$, i.e., $\forall e \in \kappa, e' \in E, e' \preceq e$ implies $e' \in \kappa$;*
4. *for each event e belonging to κ, if $f^\bullet \cap {}^\bullet\underline{e} \neq \emptyset$ then $f \in E$.*

Heap configurations represent self-enabled executions. By condition 3, condition 4 is equivalent to $f \in \kappa$. Conditions 1–3 coincide with those involved in the definition of configurations for AES. Condition 4 is new; it amounts to requiring that κ needs no external event from the support, for its enabling. Let **Configs**(E) be the set of all configurations of heap E.

One may expect $(E, \preceq, \nearrow, \alpha)$ to be an LAES. This is not true in general. The reason is that heaps can represent program fragments, whereas LAES don't. In this section we show how to extract from any heap E, an *effective heap* which has a direct correspondence with an LAES.

Definition 3. *Given a heap E, its effective heap $\mathcal{G}[E]$ is defined as:*

$$\mathcal{G}[E] =_{\text{def}} \bigcup_{\kappa \in \mathbf{Configs}(E)} \kappa.$$

Say that heap E is effective *if $\mathcal{G}[E] = E$ holds.*

$\mathcal{G}[E]$ possesses a subset of E as its set of events. Generation of $\mathcal{G}[E]$ from a heap E is by pruning and by Definition 2. This generation is constructive. The introduction of effective heap $\mathcal{G}[E]$ is justified by the following result, where symbols $\preceq, \nearrow$, and α are the restrictions, to $\mathcal{G}[E]$, of the relations and map defined in (6), (7), and (8), respectively.

Theorem 1 ([17]). $\mathcal{A}[E] = (\mathcal{G}[E], \preceq, \nearrow, \alpha)$ *is an LAES. Furthermore, $\mathcal{G}[E]$ is the maximal subset of events of E that induces an LAES.*

Heaps will be used to give the semantics of fragments of Orc programs, i.e., programs requiring a context. This allows for a structural construction of the semantics of Orc. Effective heaps will represent Orc programs that are self-enabled and can be executed.

Generic Operations on Heaps. We list here a few operations on heaps that are useful for wide area computing. From now on, *we specialize marks to being lists*, with the usual operations.

- *Marking:* Marking creates distinct copies of a heap. For a heap E and m a mark, E^m is the heap where symbol m has been appended to the mark $\mu(c)$ of each condition $c \in \text{minConds}(E)$. The recursive definitions of events and conditions in E ensures that this operation creates a new instance of E.
- *Disjoint Union:* for E and F heaps, and *left* and *right* fixed marks:

$$E \uplus F =_{\text{def}} E^{left} \cup F^{right}$$

- *Preemption:* For a heap E and $F \subseteq E$, the preemption of E by F terminates execution of E when any event in F occurs. Formally, $\text{STOP}_F(E)$ is the heap obtained by replacing each event $e = (^\bullet e, \underline{e}, a)$ of E by $\varphi(e)$ as follows:

$$\varphi(e) =_{\text{def}} \begin{cases} (^\bullet e \cup \{(\bot, stop)\}, \underline{e}, a) & \text{if } e \in F. \\ (^\bullet e, \underline{e} \cup \{(\bot, stop)\}, a) & \text{if } e \notin F. \end{cases} \tag{10}$$

- *Copy:* For two heaps E and F, we define $\text{COPY}_l(E, F)$ to be a copy of E with respect to *context heap F*. For a mark l, $\text{COPY}_l(E, F)$ is a fresh heap obtained by changing all minimal conditions $(e, \mu) \in \text{minConds}(E)$ as follows:

$$(e, \mu) = \begin{cases} (e, (\mu, l)) & \text{if } (e, \mu) \notin C_F \\ (e, \mu) & \text{if } (e, \mu) \in C_F \end{cases} \tag{11}$$

where C_F is the set of associated conditions of the context heap F. Intuitively, events in E may share conditions (and thus are related) with events in the context heap F. The copy of E with respect to context F keeps these conditions intact in the copy to preserve the relations between the copied events and those in F.

3.3   The Heap Semantics of Orc

In this section, we construct the heap semantics of Orc in a structural way. Some intermediate steps will require heaps that are not effective. Heaps of well formed Orc expressions will all be effective, however, thus giving rise to an LAES. We introduce an intermediate action τ_v for the construction, which will be removed in a post-processing step after the heap is built.

- *Free Variables:* $E(x)$ is the set of all events in heap E which depend on x.

$$E(x) = \{e \in E \mid \exists e' \in E, e' \preceq_E e, \alpha(e') \in \{M_k(x), !x, \tau_x\}\}$$

Call x a *free variable* of E if $E(x)$ is nonempty. Let $E(\overline{x})$ be the events in E that do not depend on x: $E(\overline{x}) = E - E(x)$.
- *Publication events:* $!E$ is the set of publication events of heap E:

$$!E = \{e \mid \alpha(e) = !v\}$$

- *Preemption:* Stopping E after the first value publication is defined as:

$$\text{STOP}(E) =_{\text{def}} \text{STOP}_{!E}(E)$$

- *Send:* For a publication event $e = (^\bullet e, \underline{e}, !v)$, define the $\tau(e)$ to be the event obtained by changing the label of e as follows:

$$\alpha(e) = \begin{cases} \tau_x \text{ if } \alpha(e) = !x, \text{ for any variable } x \\ \tau \text{ otherwise} \end{cases} \tag{12}$$

The heap $\text{SEND}(E)$ is the heap E where all the publication events e in E are replaced by $\tau(e)$. The publication events are still identifiable by their marks.
- *Link:* For a heap E, a *context heap* C, an event f not belonging to E, and a value v,

$$\text{LINK}(f, v, x, E, C)$$

is a (non effective) heap in which variable x is bound to value v after external event f. The *context* heap C identifies parts of E that are not affected by the variable binding. $\text{LINK}(f, v, x, E, C)$ is the heap obtained as follows:
1. Create $E' = \text{COPY}_f(E, C)$ a new copy of E with respect to context heap C and marked with label f. In making this copy, each event $e \in E$ has a unique corresponding event $e' = \varphi_f(e) \in E'$.
2. Change all $e' = (^\bullet e', \underline{e}', a) \in E'$ as below, where $e = \varphi_f^{-1}(e')$:

$$e' = \begin{cases} (^\bullet e' \cup \{(f, e)\}, \underline{e}', [v/x]a) \text{ if } e' \in \min(E') \\ (^\bullet e', \underline{e}', [v/x]a) \qquad\qquad \text{if } e' \notin \min(E') \end{cases} \tag{13}$$

The substitution $[v/x]a$ replaces the variable x by v in the action a. If the variable x does not occur in a, the substitution leaves a unchanged. The heap constructed here does not contain the event f referred by $e' \in \min(E')$.

- *Receive:* We next construct a (non effective) heap that can receive any value published by another heap. If e is a publication event, $\tau(e)$ is the event e with its action changed according to (12). We define

$$\text{RECV}_x(E, F, C) = \bigcup_{f \in\, !E, \alpha(f) = !v} \text{LINK}(\tau(f), v, x, F, C)$$

Observe that, if $!E$ is empty, this yields $\text{RECV}_x(E, F, C) = \emptyset$.

- *Pipe:* The pipe operator allows G to receive publications from F, subject to a context C that identifies parts of G not affected by the communication.

$$\text{PIPE}_x(F, G, C) = \text{SEND}(F) \,\cup\, \text{RECV}_x(F, G, C)$$

Heaps of Base Expressions. For Orc expression f, $[f]$ is its heap denotation. Symbol *nil* indicates the absence of mark, v_k is the value returned by a site.

$$[0] = \emptyset$$

$$[let(v)] = \{\,(\{c\}, \emptyset, !v)\,\}$$
$$\text{where condition } c = (\bot, nil)$$

$$[?k] = \{\, e = (\{c_1\}, \emptyset, k?v_k), (\{c_2\}, \emptyset, !v_k)\,\}$$
$$\text{where condition } c_1 = (\bot, nil),\ c_2 = (e, nil)$$

$$[M(v)] = \{\, e = (\{c_1\}, \emptyset, M_k(v)), f = (\{c_2\}, \emptyset, k?v_k), (\{c_3\}, \emptyset, !v_k)\,\}$$
$$\text{where condition } c_1 = (\bot, nil),\ c_2 = (e, nil),\ c_3 = (f, nil),$$
$$k \text{ is fresh.}$$

$$[E(v)] = [[v/x]f]$$
$$\text{where } E \text{ is an expression definition and } E(x) \;\underset{=}{\Delta}\; f$$

Heaps for the Combinators

$$[f \mid g] = [f] \uplus [g]$$

$$[f >x> g] = \text{PIPE}_x([f], [g], \emptyset)$$

$$[g \text{ where } x :\in f] = \text{PIPE}_x(\text{STOP}(F), G(x), G(\overline{x})) \cup G(\overline{x})$$
$$\text{where } F = [f]^{right} \text{ and } G = [g]^{left}$$

In a final post-processing step, we rename all the intermediate τ_v actions of the heap to the internal action τ.

Theorem 2 ([17]). *Heaps of base expressions are all effective. If $[f]$ and $[g]$ are effective heaps, then so are their compositions via the above three combinators.*

Recursive Definitions. The treatment of recursive definitions follows that given in [12], except that the denotation of an expression f is the heap $[f]$ instead of the set of traces $\langle f \rangle$. The heap for a recursive Orc definition $f \;\underset{=}{\Delta}\; Exp(f)$ is the limit of a series of increasing approximations $0 \sqsubseteq Exp(0) \sqsubseteq Exp(Exp(0)) \sqsubseteq \ldots$.

To ensure existence of the limit, the least fixpoint of Exp, we show that the Orc combinators are monotonic with respect to $\sqsubseteq$. For F and G two heaps, define

$$F \prec G \text{ if } F \subseteq G \text{ and } C_F \cap C_{G-F} = \emptyset \tag{14}$$

Then for Orc expressions, $f \sqsubseteq g$ if $[f] \prec [g]$. The motivation for having the second condition in (14) is that it is needed in the proof of Lemma 2 below.

Lemma 1 ([17]). *Relation $\prec$ is a partial order on heaps.*

Lemma 2 ([17]). *The Orc combinators are monotonic in both arguments. In particular, given $f \sqsubseteq g$, then*

$$f \mid h \sqsubseteq g \mid h$$
$$f >x> h \sqsubseteq g >x> h$$
$$h >x> f \sqsubseteq h >x> g$$
$$f \text{ where } x :\in h \sqsubseteq g \text{ where } x :\in h$$
$$h \text{ where } x :\in f \sqsubseteq h \text{ where } x :\in g$$

Complete proofs of the theorems and lemmas is given in [17], along with a correctness proof of this semantics, with respect to the semantics of Figure 1.

3.4 Examples

Figure 4 gives the intermediary and the final heap for the Orc expression

$$\{let(1) \gg S(x)\} \text{ where } x :\in \{M \mid N\}.$$

Note the two publications f_1 and f_2, by the parallel composition $M \mid N$. These are made conflicting by the extra (shaded) condition created by the STOP operator. We show in the middle two intermediate steps of the translation. Subexpression $F = M \mid N$ has two emissions, by M and N respectively. By Rule (ASYM1V) of Figure 1, F, when used in the **where** context, must be terminated just after its first publication event f_1 or f_2. This is realized by the SEND(STOP(F)) mechanism; the shaded condition create asymmetric conflict causing the first publication to preempt the other one.

The second heap named RECV$_x$(...) properly puts G in the two conflicting contexts of publication events f_1 or f_2. A dashed arrowhead to a minimal condition of the heap from an event name states that the condition depends on that external event. The external events here are e and f_1, f_2 in heaps $G(\overline{x})$ and SEND(STOP(F)) respectively. When these heaps are combined in the right most heap, these events become internal events, thus showing that the resulting final heap is effective.

The CarOnLine toy example, continued. Figure 5 shows a diagram of the event structure corresponding to the CarOnLine program written in Orc. The event structure is generated by our tool and it collects all the possible executions of CarOnLine, taking into account timers and other interactions between data and control. Each execution has the form of a partial order and can be analysed to derive appropriate QoS parameter composition, for each occurring pattern. Each site call to a service M is translated into three events, the *call* (M), the *call return* (?M) and the *publish action* (!), which lengthens the structure.

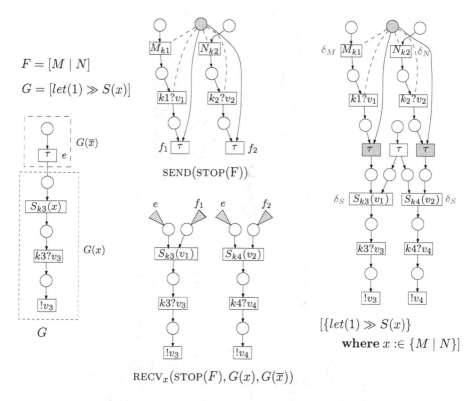

Fig. 4. Heap semantics of the Orc expression $\{let(1) \gg S(x)\}$ **where** $x :\in \{M \mid N\}$. Solid/dashed arcs point back to consumed/read conditions. Dashed arrow heads point back to causes not belonging to the considered heap—this is the way program fragments are captured. The red color refers to QoS aspects, see Section 3.5.

3.5   QoS Studies on Orc

Having the event structure semantics of Orc allows us to address all the aspects of QoS where causality relating the different site calls matters. As an example, we focus on latency, depicted in red in Figure 4. We assign to web service calls M, N and S a latency represented by variables δ_M, δ_N and δ_S respectively. Given outcomes for δ_M, δ_N, and δ_S, we get the overall latency δ_E for the orchestration $E = \{let(1) \gg S(x)\}$ **where** $x :\in \{M \mid N\}$, by using its heap in Figure 4. This heap exhibits two maximal configurations, which correspond to M or N publishing first : these two publish events (the shaded τ events) are in conflict. The resolution of this conflict is driven by the actual value for δ_M and δ_N : for e.g, if $\delta_M < \delta_N$, S_{k3} will occur (but S_{k4} will not). For each configuration, we add the latencies along each causality path, and consider the maximum latency of all the incoming paths at a synchronization event. Here, when $\delta_M < \delta_N$, the overall latency will thus be $\delta_M + \delta_S$. An important fact is that latency and conflict mutually interact: who publishes first has a consequence on which configuration

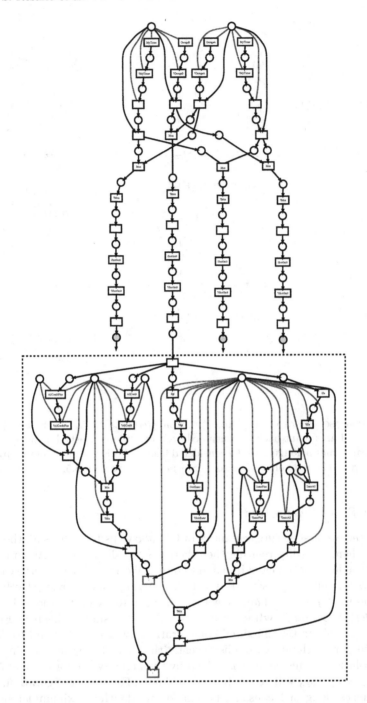

Fig. 5. A labelled event structure collecting all possible executions of CarOnLine, as generated by our tool. The three dangling arcs from the shaded places are followed by copies of the boxed net.

is actually executed, which in turn has a consequence on the overall latency. Note that this analysis also supports the use of timeouts in the orchestration to guard the waiting for answers to site calls.

4 Related Work

Closest to our present study is the work [15], where Orc expressions are translated to colored Petri net systems [4]. Bruni et al. [7] link the Orc language to Petri nets and the join calculus. Together with the event structure semantics for nominal calculi given in Bruni et al. [6], this yields a chain of transformations that yield an event structure semantics for suitable Orc programs. However, [6] focusses on the subclass of persistent grammars, which avoids asymmetric conflicts. We consider asymmetric conflict as central for dealing with orchestration dynamics; in fact, preemption-based constructs such as timeouts, races etc. inevitably lead to asymmetric conflicts not covered by prime event structures, see figure 4. For an approach that focuses on temporal properties without partial orders nor performance evaluation, see [9], where a Timed Automaton semantics of Orc is given and used for verification purposes using the Uppaal tool.

Our work is unique in that it provides a direct coding of a wide area computing language into asymmetric event structures. This is of immediate use in QoS studies, as the latter builds on timed and/or probabilistic enhancements of partial order models [15,16].

5 Conclusion

We have presented a partial order semantics for Orc, a structured orchestration language with support for termination and recursive process instantiation. The semantics uses *heaps* to encode sets of interrelated events because they simplify manipulation of the fragments of program behavior that arise when analyzing the sub-expressions of a program. These fragments are composed to create effective heaps, from which more traditional asymmetric event structures are derived.

The heap semantics provides a model of true concurrency and also directly support analysis of non-functional properties of Orc programs. In [16] some of the authors develop a theory of "soft" contracts in which Service Level Specifications (SLS) are expressed in terms of probability distributions on QoS parameters. Monte-Carlo simulations of the orchestration provide a simple approach to compose these probabilistic contracts. Each simulation is an execution of the orchestration's heap in which latencies of the calls to services are drawn from the corresponding contract's probability distribution. Using the technique given in section 3.5 to compose latencies, the empirical probability distribution for the overall orchestration latency is derived.

References

1. Van Der Aalst, W.M.P., Ter Hofstede, A.H.M., Kiepuszewski, B., Barros, A.P.: Workflow patterns. Distrib. Parallel Databases 14(1), 5–51 (2003)
2. Arias-Fisteus, J., Fernández, L.S., Kloos, C.D.: Applying model checking to BPEL4WS business collaborations. In: SAC, pp. 826–830 (2005)
3. Baldan, P., Corradini, A., Montanari, U.: Contextual Petri nets, Asymmetric Event Structures, and Processes. Inf. Comput. 171(1), 1–49 (2001)
4. Best, E., Devillers, R.R., Koutny, M.: The Box Algebra = Petri Nets + Process Expressions. Inf. Comput. 178(1), 44–100 (2002)
5. Bhoj, P., Singhal, S., Chutani, S.: SLA management in federated environments. Computer Networks 35(1), 5–24 (2001)
6. Bruni, R., Melgratti, H.C., Montanari, U.: Event structure semantics for nominal calculi. In: Baier, C., Hermanns, H. (eds.) CONCUR 2006. LNCS, vol. 4137, pp. 295–309. Springer, Heidelberg (2006)
7. Bruni, R., Melgratti, H.C., Tuosto, E.: Translating Orc Features into Petri Nets and the Join Calculus. In: Bravetti, M., Núñez, M., Zavattaro, G. (eds.) WS-FM 2006. LNCS, vol. 4184, pp. 123–137. Springer, Heidelberg (2006)
8. Cook, W.R., Patwardhan, S., Misra, J.: Workflow patterns in orc. In: Ciancarini, P., Wiklicky, H. (eds.) COORDINATION 2006. LNCS, vol. 4038, pp. 82–96. Springer, Heidelberg (2006)
9. Dong, J.S., Liu, Y., Sun, J., Zhang, X.: Verification of Computation Orchestration via Timed Automata. In: Liu, Z., He, J. (eds.) ICFEM 2006. LNCS, vol. 4260, pp. 226–245. Springer, Heidelberg (2006)
10. Esparza, J., Römer, S., Vogler, W.: An improvement of McMillan's Unfolding Algorithm. Formal Methods in System Design 20(3), 285–310 (2002)
11. Keller, A., Ludwig, H.: The wsla framework: Specifying and monitoring service level agreements for web services. J. Network Syst. Manage 11(1) (2003)
12. Kitchin, D., Cook, W.R., Misra, J.: A language for task orchestration and its semantic properties. In: Baier, C., Hermanns, H. (eds.) CONCUR 2006. LNCS, vol. 4137, pp. 477–491. Springer, Heidelberg (2006)
13. Ouyang, C., Verbeek, E., van der Aalst, W.M.P., Breutel, S.: Formal Semantics and Analysis of Control Flow in WS-BPEL. BPM Center Report BPM-05-15, BPMcenter.org (2005)
14. Puhlmann, F., Weske, M.: Using the pi-Calculus for Formalizing Workflow Patterns. In: Business Process Management, pp. 153–168 (2005)
15. Rosario, S., Benveniste, A., Haar, S., Jard, C.: Foundations for Web Services Orchestrations: functional and QoS aspects. In: Proceedings ISOLA (2006)
16. Rosario, S., Benveniste, A., Haar, S., Jard, C.: Probabilistic QoS and soft contracts for transaction based web services. In: ICWS, pp. 126–133 (2007)
17. Rosario, S., Kitchin, D., Benveniste, A., Cook, W., Haar, S., Jard, C.: Event Structure Semantics of Orc. IRISA Internal Report No 1853 (June 2007), available for download at:
    http://www.irisa.fr/distribcom/benveniste/pub/heaps4Orc2007.pdf
18. van der Aalst, W.M.P., Basten, T.: Life-Cycle Inheritance: A Petri-Net-Based Approach. In: Azéma, P., Balbo, G. (eds.) ICATPN 1997. LNCS, vol. 1248, pp. 62–81. Springer, Heidelberg (1997)
19. Winskel, G.: Event Structures.. In: Advances in Petri Nets, pp. 325–392 (1986)

Author Index

Lecture Notes in Computer Science

Sublibrary 2: Programming and Software Engineering

For information about Vols. 1– 4322
please contact your bookseller or Springer

Vol. 4615: R. de Lemos, C. Gacek, A. Romanovsky (Eds.), Architecting Dependable Systems IV. XIV, 435 pages. 2007.

Vol. 4610: B. Xiao, L.T. Yang, J. Ma, C. Muller-Schloer, Y. Hua (Eds.), Autonomic and Trusted Computing. XVIII, 571 pages. 2007.

Vol. 4609: E. Ernst (Ed.), ECOOP 2007 – Object-Oriented Programming. XIII, 625 pages. 2007.

Vol. 4608: H.W. Schmidt, I. Crnković, G.T. Heineman, J.A. Stafford (Eds.), Component-Based Software Engineering. XII, 283 pages. 2007.

Vol. 4591: J. Davies, J. Gibbons (Eds.), Integrated Formal Methods. IX, 660 pages. 2007.

Vol. 4589: J. Münch, P. Abrahamsson (Eds.), Product-Focused Software Process Improvement. XII, 414 pages. 2007.

Vol. 4574: J. Derrick, J. Vain (Eds.), Formal Techniques for Networked and Distributed Systems – FORTE 2007. XI, 375 pages. 2007.

Vol. 4556: C. Stephanidis (Ed.), Universal Access in Human-Computer Interaction, Part III. XXII, 1020 pages. 2007.

Vol. 4555: C. Stephanidis (Ed.), Universal Access in Human-Computer Interaction, Part II. XXII, 1066 pages. 2007.

Vol. 4554: C. Stephanidis (Ed.), Universal Acess in Human Computer Interaction, Part I. XXII, 1054 pages. 2007.

Vol. 4553: J.A. Jacko (Ed.), Human-Computer Interaction, Part IV. XXIV, 1225 pages. 2007.

Vol. 4552: J.A. Jacko (Ed.), Human-Computer Interaction, Part III. XXI, 1038 pages. 2007.

Vol. 4551: J.A. Jacko (Ed.), Human-Computer Interaction, Part II. XXIII, 1253 pages. 2007.

Vol. 4550: J.A. Jacko (Ed.), Human-Computer Interaction, Part I. XXIII, 1240 pages. 2007.

Vol. 4542: P. Sawyer, B. Paech, P. Heymans (Eds.), Requirements Engineering: Foundation for Software Quality. IX, 384 pages. 2007.

Vol. 4536: G. Concas, E. Damiani, M. Scotto, G. Succi (Eds.), Agile Processes in Software Engineering and Extreme Programming. XV, 276 pages. 2007.

Vol. 4530: D.H. Akehurst, R. Vogel, R.F. Paige (Eds.), Model Driven Architecture - Foundations and Applications. X, 219 pages. 2007.

Vol. 4523: Y.-H. Lee, H.-N. Kim, J. Kim, Y.W. Park, L.T. Yang, S.W. Kim (Eds.), Embedded Software and Systems. XIX, 829 pages. 2007.

Vol. 4498: N. Abdennadher, F. Kordon (Eds.), Reliable Software Technologies - Ada-Europe 2007. XII, 247 pages. 2007.

Vol. 4486: M. Bernardo, J. Hillston (Eds.), Formal Methods for Performance Evaluation. VII, 469 pages. 2007.

Vol. 4470: Q. Wang, D. Pfahl, D.M. Raffo (Eds.), Software Process Dynamics and Agility. XI, 346 pages. 2007.

Vol. 4468: M.M. Bonsangue, E.B. Johnsen (Eds.), Formal Methods for Open Object-Based Distributed Systems. X, 317 pages. 2007.

Vol. 4467: A.L. Murphy, J. Vitek (Eds.), Coordination Models and Languages. X, 325 pages. 2007.

Vol. 4454: Y. Gurevich, B. Meyer (Eds.), Tests and Proofs. IX, 217 pages. 2007.

Vol. 4444: T. Reps, M. Sagiv, J. Bauer (Eds.), Program Analysis and Compilation, Theory and Practice. X, 361 pages. 2007.

Vol. 4440: B. Liblit, Cooperative Bug Isolation. XV, 101 pages. 2007.

Vol. 4408: R. Choren, A. Garcia, H. Giese, H.-f. Leung, C. Lucena, A. Romanovsky (Eds.), Software Engineering for Multi-Agent Systems V. XII, 233 pages. 2007.

Vol. 4406: W. De Meuter (Ed.), Advances in Smalltalk. VII, 157 pages. 2007.

Vol. 4405: L. Padgham, F. Zambonelli (Eds.), Agent-Oriented Software Engineering VII. XII, 225 pages. 2007.

Vol. 4401: N. Guelfi, D. Buchs (Eds.), Rapid Integration of Software Engineering Techniques. IX, 177 pages. 2007.

Vol. 4385: K. Coninx, K. Luyten, K.A. Schneider (Eds.), Task Models and Diagrams for Users Interface Design. XI, 355 pages. 2007.

Vol. 4383: E. Bin, A. Ziv, S. Ur (Eds.), Hardware and Software, Verification and Testing. XII, 235 pages. 2007.

Vol. 4379: M. Südholt, C. Consel (Eds.), Object-Oriented Technology. VIII, 157 pages. 2007.

Vol. 4364: T. Kühne (Ed.), Models in Software Engineering. XI, 332 pages. 2007.

Vol. 4355: J. Julliand, O. Kouchnarenko (Eds.), B 2007: Formal Specification and Development in B. XIII, 293 pages. 2006.

Vol. 4354: M. Hanus (Ed.), Practical Aspects of Declarative Languages. X, 335 pages. 2006.

Vol. 4350: M. Clavel, F. Durán, S. Eker, P. Lincoln, N. Martí-Oliet, J. Meseguer, C. Talcott, All About Maude - A High-Performance Logical Framework. XXII, 797 pages. 2007.

Vol. 4348: S. Tucker Taft, R.A. Duff, R.L. Brukardt, E. Plödereder, P. Leroy, Ada 2005 Reference Manual. XXII, 765 pages. 2006.

Vol. 4346: L. Brim, B.R. Haverkort, M. Leucker, J. van de Pol (Eds.), Formal Methods: Applications and Technology. X, 363 pages. 2007.

Vol. 4344: V. Gruhn, F. Oquendo (Eds.), Software Architecture. X, 245 pages. 2006.

Vol. 4340: R. Prodan, T. Fahringer, Grid Computing. XXIII, 317 pages. 2007.

Vol. 4336: V.R. Basili, H.D. Rombach, K. Schneider, B. Kitchenham, D. Pfahl, R.W. Selby (Eds.), Empirical Software Engineering Issues. XVII, 193 pages. 2007.

Vol. 4326: S. Göbel, R. Malkewitz, I. Iurgel (Eds.), Technologies for Interactive Digital Storytelling and Entertainment. X, 384 pages. 2006.

Vol. 4323: G. Doherty, A. Blandford (Eds.), Interactive Systems. XI, 269 pages. 2007.